Towards a Conservative Left

Towards a Conservative Left

SELECTED WRITINGS OF JEAN-CLAUDE MICHÉA

Edited with an Introduction by Michael C. Behrent

Translated by Michael C. Behrent

VAUBAN
BOOKS

CONTENTS

Why Michéa Matters

PROVINCIAL HIGH SCHOOL teachers with chips on their shoulders are not usually the strongest candidates for capturing the Zeitgeist.[1] Hence the originality of Jean-Claude Michéa. Since the 1990s, Michéa has analyzed the way in which contemporary society has come under the sway of liberalism, in its dual form of free markets and progressive values. He has denounced the left's abandonment of any pretense of being a popular movement focused on economic issues and its transformation into a bastion of cultural liberalism and niche lifestyle causes. He maintains that the ideology pursued by progressive elites—blending hostility to restrictions on personal conduct and an obsession with "social justice"—is less an extension of the left's traditional concern with reducing social inequality than a perfect complement to free-market capitalism. Michéa has sought to rehabilitate older popular political traditions that were deeply skeptical of progress (whether economic or cultural) because of its tendency to undermine the solidarity and "common decency"—as George Orwell famously put it—that shape working-class communities. Yet in the 1990s and early 2000s, when New Democrats and New Labor reigned triumphant, when French socialists boasted about privatizing state companies and liberalizing the labor market, and when it was assumed that "populism" could refer only to the reactionary and xenophobic emotions nourished by the far right, Michéa was a voice crying in

---

1. The editor would like to thank James Graham for his valuable assistance in revising the manuscript.

the wilderness—a noble if somewhat savage malcontent, unable to reconcile himself with the self-evident course of the modern world.

How different things seem in 2025. In the United States, commentators have begun to notice the phenomenon of "class inversion"—the fact that Democrats, once the champion of the working class, have become an elite party, favored by well-educated and high-income voters, while the Republican Party has transformed itself into the new working-class party, attracting a multiracial coalition of lower income voters who are unlikely to have college degrees. Far from being evidence of enlightenment, the "wokeness" embraced by the progressive left has proved, in practice, to be little more than the parochial and self-serving ideology of white professionals—and proof of how out of touch they are with the constituencies they pompously claim to champion. Donald Trump, meanwhile, has managed to blend a defense of the economic interests of working-class populations (notably through his critique of globalization) with an emphasis on conservative cultural values—the mirror image of the positions adopted in recent years by Democrats. The chips that Michéa bore on his shoulder have become some of the most politically salient and hotly debated issues of our time.

While Michéa has become a familiar—if not exactly prominent—figure in France, he is poorly known in the English-speaking world. This volume is the first comprehensive introduction to Michéa's key writings to be translated into English. The timing could not be better. Yet why exactly do the words of this irascible teacher suddenly resonate? Why does Michéa matter?

MICHÉA MATTERS FIRST because of his timeliness. Over the past twenty-five years, he has chronicled the hollowing out of the left and liberalism's seepage into every crevice of modern society. Yet despite his dated and contextual obsessions—his loathing of certain socialist politicians from the 1990s, his constant annoyance at *Libération*, the trendy Parisian newspaper—it is hard not to read Michéa's early writings as prophetic. Just as Israel and Judah's political intrigue and military preoccupations shaped the discourse of the Old Testament prophets even as they articulated a universal message, it is paradoxically Michéa's parochial concerns that make his political insights relevant to the present.

Michéa's outlook was shaped, first, by the fact that he was literally born communist.[2] He was raised, that is to say, in the distinct subculture that flourished around the French Communist Party. His parents met in the French Resistance during the Second World War. Much of the Communist Party's appeal in the postwar years lay in the patriotism it had displayed in fighting German occupation forces. It called itself the "party of the 75,000 executed." Born in 1950, Michéa was raised in a family in which communism mattered. His mother worked for the party press agency, while his father was a sportswriter for *L'Humanité*, the party's daily newspaper. Michéa visited the Soviet Union in his youth and learned Russian. Yet for Michéa, the takeaway of these formative experiences was not lifelong allegiance to communism—he in fact left the party in 1976—but a sincere appreciation of working-class values. Paradoxically, it was in George Orwell—best known to most Americans for his fierce critique of communism—that Michéa found the best description of the values that pervaded the world in which he was raised: "common decency," as the British writer famously defined socialism.

The second factor that determined Michéa's worldview was his career as a teacher. In 1972, Michéa became a *prof de philo*—a high-school philosophy teacher. In France, the modern public-school system was established in the 1880s. It is commonly known as *l'école républicaine*—the republican school—because it was created by politicians who believed that covering the national territory with a tight net of state funded elementary schools was the key to wresting the population from the grips of the Catholic church and ensuring the survival of the Third Republic (1870–1940). A crucial part of the school curriculum was a year-long philosophy course taken in the final year, ensuring that French students who finish high school receive (unlike, say, their American counterparts) a philosophical education. In many ways, Michéa's career was shaped by this Third Republican project. The republican school also sought to spread the benefits of education beyond Paris and major cultural centers. Michéa spent his entire teaching career in Montpellier, a city near the Mediterranean. While it is often taken for granted that intellectuals living in major cities are uniquely positioned to comment on major trends, Michéa's worldview owes much to his experience as a provincial.

---

2.   For the following account of Michéa's career, I have drawn on a previously published article. See Michael C. Behrent, "France's Anti-Liberal Left," *Dissent*, Spring 2019.

One of the first public issues that inspired Michéa to speak out was education reform. In the 1970s and '80s, the French educational system sought to absorb the aftershocks of the student protest movement of May '68 and the far-reaching cultural changes it articulated. Though the Marxist fantasies and utopian slogans of the student movement had little practical impact, May '68 unleashed a thoroughgoing liberalization of French society and a concerted attack on French society's lingering conservatism. Michéa's inner communist recognized that the creation of the public school system was also motivated by capitalist imperatives—the need to eliminate obstacles (such as regional dialects), establish a national market, and instill disciplined work habits. Yet he also believed that public schools remained steeped in values that had little to do with market utilitarianism. The republican school, he observed, was committed to "transmitting . . . knowledge, virtues, and attitudes that were as such perfectly independent of the capitalist order," as seen in their firm commitment to teaching Greek and Latin.[3]

Education reform helped Michéa to formulate his essential claim concerning the dual nature of liberalism—that cultural liberalization (that is, the critique of traditional culture and morality) and the expansion of capitalism are inseparable. After '68, efforts were made to bring the education system in line with new cultural attitudes. The most famous of these reforms, at least symbolically, was the dismantling of the "stages" from which teachers long lectured students, but which were now condemned as authoritarian and archaic. Students, not teachers, were now to be the classroom's focus. A 1972 reform of French language instruction demoted the teaching of literary culture in favor of more pragmatic uses of reading, implicitly endorsing, in Michéa's view, the fashionable radical view that literature was "bourgeois." By the late 1990s, European commissions were encouraging schools to think of students as "clients"—a trend with which American educators are all too familiar—and to see their role as optimizing students' ability to compete in the capitalist marketplace. At a time when the major forces in contemporary society were already undermining the task of transmitting culture and tradition, progressive forces touting the liberalization of values as well as of markets were jumping into the breach and accelerating the trend.

---

3. See chapter 4 of this volume.

A third factor that shaped Michéa's outlook is the course of French politics in recent decades—particularly the evolution of the left. In the postwar years, the two major parties of the left—the communists and a socialist party known as the Section Française de l'Internationale Socialiste, or
SFIO—were either firmly rooted in the working class or closely tied to the
labor movement. In the early 1970s, François Mitterrand transformed the
SFIO into the modern Socialist Party. Mitterrand's election as president in
1981was welcomed by many as a quasi-revolutionary event that would make
good on the longing for social change expressed in the streets in May '68. Yet
while Mitterrand in his first two years in office pursued an ambitious agenda
based on a "rupture with capitalism"—including an aggressive program of
nationalizing major companies—he decided, in 1983, when faced with capital
flight and a potential collapse of the currency, to put socialism on hold.

Socialists—at least those in power—soon lost their appetite for a "rupture with capitalism." To the contrary, they increasingly sought to present
themselves as capitalism's eager pupils. From 1997 to 2002, the socialist
Lionel Jospin served as the prime minister of a coalition known as the "plural left"—the object of a healthy dose of Michéa's ire—consisting of socialists, ecologists, and communists, which oversaw the privatization of large
swathes of the French public sector and the pursuit of European integration
on free-market principles, even as its members professed their progressive
bona fides. Dominique Strauss-Kahn, an economist who served as finance
minister in Jospin's government, went on to become the managing director
of the International Monetary Fund. He was preparing to run for president
as the socialist candidate when, in 2011, he was arrested for assaulting a hotel
maid in New York. François Hollande ran in his place, winning the presidency in 2012. He achieved the rare feat of alienating the business class, who
saw him as too socialist, while also alienating many leftist voters, who saw
him as too willing to accommodate French corporations. In 2015, Hollande
appointed as economics minister a thirty-something investment banker with
no prior political experience named Emmanuel Macron, setting the stage for
his rapid ascent (and betrayal of his benefactor).

While Macron, who won the presidency in 2017, had only loose ties to
socialism (he vaguely described himself as "of the left"), his electoral coalition depended on center-left voters—especially urban progressives—who

opposed the racism and xenophobia they associated with the far right, even as they accepted Macron's moderate free-market policies, which the Socialist Party (before Macron nearly put it out of its misery) had, in practice, pursued for decades. Since 1983, in short, socialism has been seen by many in France as a highly compromised movement, increasingly subservient to the very economic forces that it had historically challenged.

Even more than the left's problematic political direction, it was the demographic and cultural evolution of the left that inspired Michéa's indignation. First and foremost, the left had become *elitist*—in theory as well as practice. The old left sought both to challenge the prerogatives and privileges of economic elites, while also cultivating and validating working-class culture as a way of life. Yet the contemporary left has taken leftist ideology, focused on the critique of social hierarchies, and transformed it into a marker of social status—into a form of conspicuous ideological consumption.

The necessary condition of this shift was the abandonment of the left's traditional anchoring in the working class. In the 1980s, Michéa has argued, Mitterrand deliberately organized the French anti-racist movement to "redirect factions of university and high-school students who might be destabilized by the liberal turn [i.e., the free-market turn of 1983] toward a *substitute struggle* that was sufficiently plausible and honorable." He adds: "A substitute struggle that was 'antiracist,' 'antifascist,' and 'civic'—and had the not insignificant advantage, in the eyes of Mitterrand and his entourage, of gently acclimatizing this youth to the new imaginary of 'no border' neoliberal capitalism."[4] In 2011, Terra Nova, a think tank close to the Socialist Party, released a notorious report recommending that the left sever its ties with the working class and forge a new coalition, composed of the young, the college educated, people of immigrant origin, and women. Justifying this strategy, the report declared: "May '68 drew the political left towards cultural liberalism: sexual freedom, contraception and abortion, a questioning of the traditional family. This evolution on social questions strengthened over time, so that it is now embodied by values such as tolerance, an openness to difference, a favorable view towards immigrants, Islam, and homosexuality, and solidarity with the most vulner-

---

4.   Jean-Claude Michéa, "An Interview with Jean-Claude Michéa," interview with and translated by Michael C. Behrent, *Dissent*, June 7, 2019 (online).

able." Meanwhile, "workers have gone the other way," adopting reactionary attitudes towards immigrants, welfare cheats, and the erosion of moral values.[5]

The trend frankly avowed in the Terra Nova report is precisely what Michéa has been going on about since the 1990s. Michéa maintains, moreover, that the values embraced by this new, professional, and progressive left serve to demean the very classes on which it has turned its back: the left has turned away from them—to view them, as Michéa has put it, as "a sinister and repulsive 'basket of deplorables' who are *naturally* racist, sexist, alcoholic, homophobic, and anti-Semitic."[6]

Michéa's distinctive trajectory—a communist childhood, the French education system, and the twists and turns of French political life since the 1980s—disposed him to arrive at insights that have a curious traction in the present. His experience with old left solidarities—which are not identical to old left ideologies—made him viscerally suspicious of reforming elites bearing antiauthoritarian gifts, that is, the notion that personal fulfillment and the relentless critique of tradition should be regarded as education's highest good. Meanwhile, leftist parties as well as much of the electorate adopted the education reformers' assumptions: a conviction in the inherent superiority of progressive cultural values.

The dominant narrative about recent American politics largely dovetails with Michéa's analysis, even if the specific circumstances in France and the United States differ. Since Trump's unexpected victory in 2016, many analysts have called attention to the phenomenon of "class inversion": the Democratic Party, once a social-democratic party that overtly appealed to the working class (leading it to be dubbed the "party of the people"), has increasingly become the party of educated, high-income, urban professionals—a demographic that is also whiter than the population at large. Meanwhile, the Republican Party, which, despite its occasional embrace of progressive causes, was once a business party that flourished in country clubs and chambers of commerce, has become a magnet for lower-income rural populations lacking college degrees. While in 2016 the focus was on the Republicans' popularity among the white working-class, it has become evident since

---

5. Bruno Jeanbart, Olivier Ferrand, Romain Prudent, *Gauche: quelle majorité électorale pour 2012 ?*, Terra Nova, May 5, 2011.

6. Michéa, "An Interview with Jean-Claude Michéa."

2020 (and especially since the 2024 election) that the party attracts an increasingly multiracial working-class coalition—leading one recent book to provocatively describe the Republicans as the new "party of the people."[7]

Thomas Frank, a leftist deeply skeptical of liberalism's direction, observed in an influential essay (which overlaps significantly with Michéa's analysis) that since George McGovern's 1972 presidential bid, the Democrats have increasingly become the party of the professional class—of the "high born and well graduated," who, while not the upper "one percent" of the income distribution, constitute nonetheless the top Ten Percent.[8] In 2020, according to Patrick Ruffini, the only demographic in which a significant percentage identified as "ideological liberals" were the white college-educated (at 34%), compared to 20% for Asians, 15% for Blacks, and 12% for whites who are not college educated.[9] The white college-educated are also more likely to identify as liberal than other constituencies *within* the Democratic Party—79% compared to 46% of Blacks.[10] This fact illustrates the hegemony that this constituency exercises over the party as a whole, and explains why, for instance, President Joe Biden insisted on using the term "Latinx," even though most Hispanics disregard it. The white college-educated constituency that is so deeply identified with contemporary liberalism consists primarily of people engaged in "knowledge work"—lawyers, tech fields, academia, journalism, and related professions. Their political interests are frequently "postmaterial," in the sense that they are not primarily concerned with economic issues. As Musa al-Gharbi has argued in an important book, the positions that knowledge workers take on cultural issues—related to race and gender, for instance—can often be stakes in a competition for status: the more "woke" one's stance, the more symbolic capital one accumulates.[11]

---

7. Patrick Ruffini, *The Party of the People: Inside the Multiracial Populist Coalition Remaking the GOP* (New York: Simon and Schuster, 2023).

8. Thomas Frank, *Listen, Liberal, or Whatever Happened to the Party of the People?* (New York: Metropolitan Books, 2016), 16, 20.

9. Ruffini, *The Party of the People: Inside the Multiracial Populist Coalition Remaking the GOP*, table 5.2.

10. Ibid., chart 5.4.

11. Musa al-Gharbi, *We Have Never Been Woke: The Cultural Contradictions of a New Elite* (Princeton: Princeton University Press, 2024).

It is perhaps for these reasons—the professional class's identitarian investment in signaling the virtue of its progressive positions and its disdain for groups relegated to the distasteful task of advocating for their economic interests—that today's liberals can only regard the populist instincts of the working and lower-middle classes with contempt. Frank concludes: "Acknowledging that some Trump voters might be desperate and otherwise decent people became a thing unsayable in the small world of America's opinion class. The total depravity of those people was the only acceptable explanation . . . Trump's rise was not about politics, it was about sin, and it was the task of progressives to scold the unrighteous for their iniquity."[12]

"The liberal establishment," Frank adds, "is anti-populist not merely because it dislikes Donald Trump—who is in no way a genuine populist—but because it is populism's opposite in nearly every particular."[13] Liberalism's transformation into an establishment discourse committed to denouncing the interests, preferences, and values of the people—the classes of society that do not constitute the elite—have been Michéa's beat for decades. At a time when these concerns are finally at the forefront of public discourse, the Montpellier schoolteacher's path to these positions is worth contemplating.

THE SECOND REASON WHY MICHÉA MATTERS is because of his critique of intellectuals. As a college professor, I am struck by how often colleagues are inclined to attribute opinions they deem abhorrent to a lack of education. Opinions they view as racist, sexist, nationalistic, or even religious can only be explained, in this mindset, by a failure to be educated properly (which, in a leap of logic, is often equated with stupidity). I do not mean to suggest that education (or lack thereof) has no impact. But what is surprising is that academics are often unwilling or unable to see themselves as ideological—as having a worldview that is tied to the place they occupy in the world and the interests that come with it. This is particularly ironic given the frequency with which, in the humanities at least, current academic paradigms emphasize the "hermeneutics of suspicion," in which unmasking the narrow self-interest lurking in seemingly objective and universalistic discourses becomes

---

12. Thomas Frank, *The People, No. A Brief History of Anti-Populism* (New York: Metropolitan Books, 2020), 238.
13. Ibid., 242.

a kind of intellectual parlor game. Ideology is other people's beliefs—never those of the intellectual class itself.

Michéa shows that to be an intellectual and educated is not identical to possessing the truth. The educated class has its own worldview, interests, and prejudices. This is precisely the point of his interpretation of George Orwell's classic novel *1984*. For Michéa,[14] it is less a critique of communism or even totalitarianism than a merciless examination of the rule of intellectuals: the personal and professional resentments that motivated them, the issues they care about and thus prioritize (like language), and the will to power to which their need for intellectual recognition condemns them.

In *The Road to Wigan Pier*, an essay on the state of the English working class, Orwell reflects on socialism's unpopularity despite the very credible solutions it has to offer. He imagines a skeptic who says: "I don't object to Socialism, but I do object to Socialists."[15] Michéa seeks to explain a related claim: "I don't object to the left, but I do object to leftists"—with the proviso that "leftists" must be understood as intellectuals, knowledge professionals, and the credentialed class. Orwell acknowledges the merits of his imaginary objector's claim. The typical socialist, he observes, is often a "youthful snob-Bolshevik who in five years' time will quite probably have made a wealthy marriage," or "a prim little man with a white-collar job, usually a secret tee-totaler and often with vegetarian leanings . . . and, above all, with a social position which he has no intention of forfeiting."[16] Michéa updates this insight, calling attention to the way the contemporary left has become identified with a range of progressive causes that do little to challenge—and may well reinforce—the social status of the educated elites who espouse them. Given how little socialists seem to be driven by a genuine concern for the laboring classes, Orwell is led to "wonder what the devil [their] motive really *is*." His conclusion is fascinating: "The underlying motive of many Socialists, I believe, is simply a hypertrophied sense of order. The present state of affairs offends them not because it causes misery, still less because it makes freedom impossible, but because it is untidy; what they desire, basically, is to reduce

---

14. See chapter 2 of this volume.
15. Orwell, *The Road to Wigan Pier* (New York: Berkley Medallion Books, 1961 [1937]), 146.
16. Ibid., 146–147.

the world to something resembling a chess-board."[17] This insight, too, resonates with our present. The progressivism of the educated class is obsessed with rules and nomenclature far more than it is with intuitive notions of fairness. Indeed, as Michéa repeatedly stresses, the intellectual class seems committed as a class to promoting values that are *counter-intuitive*, in the sense that they seek to challenge or shame the spontaneous moral beliefs of ordinary people, which Orwell—as Michéa constantly reminds us—called "common decency."

Michéa's misgivings about the educated class's domination of the left also explains why he is drawn to the American historian and cultural critic Christopher Lasch. Besides Orwell, no other writer has influenced Michéa as much. Lasch was a Marxist and a Freudian who was interested in how the rise of intellectuals as a distinct social group in early twentieth-century American society drove the emergence of a "new radicalism," notably progressivism. For these "new radicals"—philosophers and education theorists like John Dewey, social reformers like Jane Addams, political strategists like Colonel Edward House, and journalists like Lincoln Steffens—"the end of social and political reform . . . [was] the improvement of the quality of American culture as a whole, rather than simply . . . equalizing the opportunities for economic self-advancement." For Lasch, this was the whole problem with intellectuals' incursion into politics: "It is precisely this confusion of politics and culture, so essential to the new radicalism, that seems to me to betray its origins in the rise of the intellectual class; for such a program, with its suggestion that men of learning occupy or ought to occupy the strategic loci of social control, has an obvious appeal to intellectuals, and particularly to intellectuals newly conscious of their own common ties and common interests."[18]

In the wake of the sixties, the cultural radicalism pioneered by the progressives had become, Lasch believed, the dominant idiom of American public life. It manifested itself in the liberatory ethos of the 1970s—in pop psychology and the "awareness" movement, the reduction of sports to entertainment, education's abandonment of any notion of a common cultural

---

17. Ibid., 150–151.

18. Christopher Lasch, *The New Radicalism in America, 1889–1963: The Intellectual as Social Type* (New York: Vintage Books, 1965), xiv.

inheritance, the sexual revolution, and New Age spirituality. So much effort devoted to revolutionizing culture went hand in hand, in Lasch's view, with shockingly complacent political attitudes. In his blistering 1979 essay, *The Culture of Narcissism*, Lasch wrote: "Cultural radicalism has become so fashionable, and so pernicious in the support it unwittingly provides for the status quo, that any criticism of contemporary society that hopes to get beneath the surface has to criticize, at the same time, much of what currently goes under the name of radicalism."[19] Wokeness, identity politics, and the relentless psychologization of political issues are the contemporary avatars of the phenomena Lasch described. The dead-ends to which they lead are evidence, for Michéa, of the need to rehabilitate dispositions that are frowned upon by intellectuals but far more familiar to the working classes: common decency, respect for authority and tradition, and humility.

The insights that drive Michéa's thought have also begun to surface in American political discourse, particularly among those rare segments of the left that are prepared to draw hard lessons from Trump's 2024 victory. Writing for the Substack site "The Liberal Patriot" (one of the more "Michéaist" outlets on the American left), Ruy Teixeira argues that if the Democrats ever want to regain the voters they have lost to the Republicans, they should submit every policy proposal to a simple test: "What would the working class say (WWWCS)?" The whole problem with the Democratic Party, according to Teixeira (as he argues at length in the excellent book he co-wrote with John Judis, *Where Have All the Democrats Gone?*),[20] is that it is now dominated by a "liberal college-educated bubble," as a result of which it is completely out of touch with working-class Americans. Before adopting a position, Teixeira argues, liberals should subject themselves to the WWCS test: "Talk to actual working-class people—there are lots of them! Listen to your intuitions about how working-class people would likely react to policies and rhetoric currently associated with the Democrats—*not* how you think they should react. . . . Try to get inside their heads. They are less ideological, more focused on material concerns, more likely to be struggling economi-

---

19. Lasch, *The Culture of Narcissism: American Life in an Age of Diminishing Expectations* (New York: W. W. Norton, 1976), 21–22.

20. Ruy Teixeira and John B. Judis, *Where Have All the Democrats Gone?: The Soul of the Party in the Age of Extremes* (New York: Henry Holt, 2023).

cally, less interested in cutting edge social issues, more patriotic and generally more culturally conservative."[21] These intuitions overlap considerably with the analysis Michéa has proposed of the French left for decades.

It goes without saying—and it is crucial to acknowledge—that Michéa's entire project is, in a sense, brazenly self-contradictory. He is an intellectual who is profoundly suspicious of intellectuals, a talented writer who disdains much of the reading public, a professional philosopher who wonders just how much ideas can help us. Like Socrates, Michéa is a philosopher who sees himself as a kind of midwife: his writing helps his readers, if not to be reborn, at least to rethink who they are and reconsider their assumptions about the world, even if he does not claim that he can absolve them of their inconsistencies. He appeals to the *hypocrite lecteur*—intellectuals who are uneasy with the outlook and assumptions of their milieu, academics who doubt that the Truth was providentially bestowed upon them, knowledge workers who fear that there is much about the social world that they do not understand. To be clear, Michéa's work is not anti-intellectual. In the vein of Pierre-Joseph Proudhon, the nineteenth-century anarchist theorist and master printer who taught himself to read Latin (which he also hoped would improve the quality of his printing), working-class cultures often have great respect for genuine learning. What Michéa disdains is modish concepts and new-fangled ideas that intellectuals use to build their social capital and compete for status. If anything, these pursuits are more likely to result in anti-intellectualism (in the pursuit of intellectual prestige) than common decency and populism. His project is less philosophical than moral. He asks us not to be more critical or insightful, but wiser. Michéa's work, one might say, is an introduction to the humble intellectual life.

THE THIRD REASON Michéa matters concerns political affiliation—and specifically, what it means, at present, to situate oneself on the left-right spectrum. In recent years, waning consensus around globalization and neoliberal free-market policies have resulted in extensive political disruption and ideological flux. In France, two very different political movements have

---

21. Ruy Teixeira, "One Simple Question for Democrats," *The Liberal Patriot*, February 20, 2025, https://www.liberalpatriot.com/p/one-simple-question-for-democrats.

declared themselves to be "neither right nor left." On the one hand, the movement led by Emmanuel Macron (who was elected president in 2017) blends a range of progressive cultural values that are typically associated with the left—support for European integration, carbon taxes, abortion rights, a critical attitude towards France's colonial history—with free-market policies that are often connected to the right, such as the abolition of the wealth tax and raising the retirement age. On the other hand, the National Rally (formerly the National Front), led by Marine Le Pen, combines themes that have long been right-wing territory—opposition to immigration, reserving state benefits for citizens, skepticism towards the European Union—with a left-leaning economic agenda, including measures to support the purchasing power of low-income populations, hostility to trade deals, financial aid for students, and even, at times, support for progressive cultural values (such as secularism and same-sex marriage). While Macron mixes a right-wing economic agenda with left-wing cultural policies, Le Pen combines an often left-wing economic agenda with an ideology that borrows freely from the repertoire of conservative nationalism.

Similar topsy-turviness has also been in evidence in the United States. Since the rise of Bill Clinton with the support of the Democratic Leadership Council in the 1990s, the Democrats have become a neoliberal party, committed to the free market, globalization, and relatively low taxes—even if Barack Obama and Joe Biden occasionally bucked this trend. Indeed, it was the free-market consensus (particularly relating to global trade deals) prevailing between mainstream Democrats and Republicans that, to a considerable degree, explains the populist upsurge of 2016, when Bernie Sanders, from the left, and Donald Trump, from the right, sought to shake up the reigning orthodoxy. Trump's denunciation of the "American carnage" inflicted on the working class due to globalization, his defense of entitlement programs, and, more recently, his overtures to organized labor have moved the Republicans into ideological territory once claimed by Democrats, even as his aggressive nationalism and unapologetic American exceptionalism arguably push the Republicans well to the right of traditional conservatism (though it should not be forgotten that some of his anti-immigration policies once aligned with the Democratic mainstream). Meanwhile, the Democrats, once champions of civil liberties, have become a party of ideological orthodoxies and the regulation of speech. Rather than being the party of rational skepticism—in contrast to the Republicans' embrace of hierarchy and blind faith—the Democrats have, in the Trump era, adopted an unquestioning trust in science and their reverence for professionalism has even turned them into champions of the military and the intelligence community. Even if both parties still snap back to their default settings, ideological instability has become the new normal.

Well before the ideological spectrum became as blurred as it now is, Michéa intuited the fragility of our vocabulary for talking about political conflict. He realized that the categories of left and right were losing their descriptive value. One of his most important contributions as a thinker is to wean us off our need to view the world through the left-right dichotomy. From his earliest writings, he admired Orwell for his paradoxical political stance: that of a "Tory anarchist," who combined an appreciation for tradition and skepticism towards progress with a critical attitude towards established authority. Michéa has argued, moreover, that all radical movements have their "conservative moment," when they realize that their values commit them to preserving a way of life threatened by allegedly "progressive" forces. Michéa's work also offers a critical history of the left—focused on France, but with broader implications—that challenges the conflation of the workers' movement and political parties (including socialist ones) identified with the left. Most importantly, Michéa argues that despite the seeming difference between cultural liberalism—which is generally associated with the left—and economic liberalism—which is typically associated with the right—liberalism is, in its origins, a "unitary" ideology, rooted in the emergence of a "value neutral" political philosophy in the aftermath of the Wars of Religion. Michéa shows that some of the political differences that we take for granted (like the left's cultural liberalism and the right's economic liberalism) are misleading, as are some similarities (such as between the left and the workers' movement).

An important upshot of Michéa's analysis of the confusing nature of contemporary political language is the insight that just as liberalism can be elitist, so the left can be conservative. This does not mean, of course, that the left is *simply* conservative. After all, Michéa's writing shows an impressive familiarity with Marx's *Capital*; he speaks of "the bourgeoisie" with the disdain of a nineteenth-century socialist; and he remains deeply attached to the revolutionary tradition. Yet he also thinks that the left's ideological embrace of the idea of progress (which is not the same as endorsing every policy that purports to be progressive) is a fool's bargain—one in which liberalism has played the middleman's role. Michéa's thought is an intriguing blend of working-class sensibilities and what the British philosopher Michael Oakeshott called the "conservative disposition" (which he distinguished from political conservatism). For Oakeshott, the conservative disposition is characteristic of "a man who is acutely aware of having something to lose which he has learned to care for."[22] This is the sentiment that animates so many of Michéa's jeremiads against modern society: the workers' movement, and indeed, working-class culture, along with its distinctive practices, language, and traditions are things that he *cares for* and whose loss pains him. Anyone who has been employed in the past decade or two will be familiar with the trite paeans to change that are so common in the discourse of employers ("change is the only constant," "change is the new normal") and which admonish us not to be "afraid of change." Yet the conservative disposition is premised on the belief that fear of change is perfectly reasonable. A man of conservative disposition, according to Oakeshott, dislikes changes "not because what he has lost in them was intrinsically better than any alternative might have been or was incapable of improvement, nor because what takes its places is inherently incapable of being enjoyed, but because what he has lost was something he actually enjoyed and had learned how to enjoy and what takes its place is something to which he has acquired no attachment."[23] There is a personal and even intimate dimension to Michéa's reflection that captures this sense of attachment to things that the engine of progress whisks away: the stages from which French high-school teachers used to teach; the Malet and Isaac history textbooks of his childhood; his Moscow-published copy of Lenin's *Materialism and Empirio-Criticism*; and the cafés and shops that have disappeared from the small village in which he now lives. It is precisely our all-too-human attachment to such things (we all have our equivalents) that serves as a reminder, especially for those on the

---

22. Michael Oakeshott, "On Being Conservative," in *Rationalism in Politics and Other Essays* (London/New York: Meuthen & Co./Barnes & Noble, 1974), 168–196, at 169.
23. Ibid., 170.

left, that progress and change cannot be the be-all and end-all of politics. The left is not opposed to conservation; it simply wishes to conserve different things than conservatives. Though he never uses the term, Michéa helps us intuit the possibility of a conservative left.

A major goal of Michéa's thought is to challenge the habits of thought that make such connections seem self-evident. He does not ask us to rally to the left or switch over to the right. He asks us to disrupt our assumptions about what these terms mean—and to question the work we let such language do for us.

THIS VOLUME IS AN INTRODUCTION to Michéa's writings—with an eye to the way in which the present moment has made his work peculiarly relevant. Included in this collection are selections from books that Michéa published between 1995 and 2014. Though he is unquestionably a political thinker, Michéa is also a cultural critic. The selection of texts reflects the wide range of topics that have come under his critical scrutiny. These include Michéa's interpretations of Orwell and Lasch, two authors who proved instrumental in forging his philosophical perspective; considerations on the French education system and liberal "reform"; reflections on his upbringing and personal trajectory; an historical and philosophical analysis of liberalism's fundamental unity, in opposition to those who would distinguish between economic and political (or cultural) liberalism; speculations on the psychological tendencies that shape modern society, particularly the will to power pervasive among intellectual and political elites; a theory of common decency's anthropological foundations; an application of Orwell's concept of "doublethink" to an explanation of contemporary liberalism; an exploration of how common decency could become the basis of a reinvigorated form of socialist politics; and a foray into the history of the left, emphasizing that the working-class' place in this history is more tenuous than is commonly recognized. The collection concludes with an interview with Michéa conducted in February 2025 for this volume.

The wager of this collection is that Michéa is a vital thinker whose work might play an important role in understanding as well as changing our world. Though his outlook was forged in a particular context—France in the late twentieth and early twenty-first centuries—this selection seeks to "de-provincialize" Michéa's thought by identifying passages that have traction in settings outside of those in which it developed. This goal has shaped how the texts are presented. First, the volume has minimized the presence of some of Michéa's stylistic idiosyncrasies. Though he is a skilled essayist, he often thinks of his writings as anti-hierarchical texts that veer off freely into multiple tangents. He does this through lengthy footnotes (which this collection has generally preserved) as well as through what he calls "scholia." Borrowing the term and idea from Baruch Spinoza, the seventeenth-century philosopher, Michéa's scholia (*scolie* in French) are an author's running commentary on his own work (usually he will insert a capital letter, which refers to a commentary, usually at the end of the chapter, to some aspect of his argument that he could not pursue in the text itself without deviating from its main thrust). While often fascinating, the scholia break the flow of essays that may already have a style that is unfamiliar to English-language readers. Consequently, they have been left out of the volume's selections (Michéa is aware of this fact). Furthermore, while this volume's premise is that Michéa's thought transcends its context, it is hard to deny that Michéa is a thinker who is immersed in his context. He rails against particular politicians (many of whom have long left the political stage), bemoans certain newspapers, and lampoons canned phrases. Editing out these allusions to Michéa's own world would not only be impossible, but it would also be counterproductive, as his insights are often perceptive reactions to this world (even if their significance extends beyond it). Without detracting from Michéa's polemical verve, this volume seeks to explain these contextual references and asides through short introductions to each chapter and through brief explanatory endnotes—though the footnotes are in most instances Michéa's own.

It is the aspiration of this volume not only to introduce Michéa to an English-speaking audience, but also to encourage readers to gauge their own political identifications and assessments in light of the texts' included in the collection. For decades, Michéa has been decomposing the taken-for-granted premises and associations on which Western politics is based. Like many angry people, he is not a cynic. While he believes that the political forces that now govern the world have been disastrous for ordinary people and are grossly disingenuous, he also suggests that we may be living in a time when politics can be recomposed. The left is not fated to emphasize progress, any more than liberalism should be automatically assumed to imply emancipation. By stirring up our assumptions, Michéa has created the space for a kind of agency—intellectual agency, for sure, and perhaps political agency, as well.

It is a good time, in short, to be a provincial teacher with a chip on your shoulder.

Michael C. Behrent
April 2025

CHAPTER 1
Orwell: Tory Anarchist

A major goal of Michéa's early work was to rehabilitate George Orwell. This might sound unnecessary: Orwell is, after all, one of the twentieth century's better-known authors. Yet, as Michéa has argued, Orwell is primarily known for two novels he wrote late in life—*Animal Farm* and *1984*—that became popular during the Cold War largely because they were seen as critiques of Soviet totalitarianism. This aspect of Orwell's work, Michéa believes, obscures his earlier writing, particularly his political essays, in which the British author simultaneously attacked the capitalist system in the name of "common decency"—which Orwell considered to be the cornerstone of socialist values—and denounced the way in which socialist movements were veering away from working-class principles and losing ground to fascism (Orwell explored these ideas most notably in his 1937 essay *The Road to Wigan Pier*). By the early 1980s, the European left, in Michéa's view, was in a situation similar to that of the socialists in the 1930s, as its politics became increasingly detached from working-class concerns. It was in this spirit that, in 1983, Michéa wrote an article on Orwell exploring these ideas, which he struggled to get published. It was rejected by the prominent French journal *Critique*, and even Michéa's friend Jorge Semprún, the Spanish writer and politician, was unable to find a journal that would print it. In the early 1990s, an editor at *Climats*, an imprint of the Flammarion publishing house based near Montpellier, where Michéa lived, came across his 1983 article and encouraged him to expand it.

The result was Michéa's first book, *Orwell, anarchiste Tory*, published in 1995.

THE TENDENCY OF INTELLECTUALS to believe that the only legitimate states are those that bring their own ideas to power—totalitarianism ultimately being a power that seeks to embody an idea in all its implications—is as old as Plato's fantasy of the philosopher-king. What is new, however, is the development of the modern intelligentsia as a force that is historically active and sociologically ambiguous. It represents what George Orwell called the "least useful section of the middle class."[1] Twentieth-century intellectuals are thus, in the first place, *déclassés*. The growing impossibility, which they experience first-hand, of finding positions consistent with their former prestige is obviously tied to the evolution of a society that knows of no value worthy of greater respect than exchange value. Corporations are not inclined to offer people who live for ideas the same rewards—real or symbolic—that the latter once received from royal courts, salons, and academies. Consequently, intellectuals tend to have a negative experience of a system that by virtue of its very structure humiliates them. This is why, Orwell maintains, since "about 1930 everyone who might be described as an 'intellectual' has lived in a state of chronic discontent with the existing order."[2] Clearly, their revolt is not driven by the "common decency" of the proletariat. The intellectuals' hatred of the existing order feeds primarily off the contradiction between their consciousness of their abilities and capitalist society's practical indifference to them. In short, the intellectual's attitude of rejection is underpinned by a will to power—one that is nothing more than the humiliated consciousness' desire for recognition. According to Orwell, Julien Sorel, the socially ambitious priest who is the protagonist of *The Red and the Black*, Stendahl's novel about postrevolutionary French society, is "the type of the revolutionary."[3]

---

1. George Orwell, *The Lion and the Unicorn: Socialism and the English Genius* (Harmondsworth & New York: Penguin Books, 1982 [1941]), 99.
2. Ibid., 62–63.
3. Orwell, Review, *Stendahl* by F. C. Green, in *Collected Essays, Journalism and Letters*, vol. 1, *An Age Like This, 1920–40*, ed. Sonia Orwell and Ian Angus (New York: Harcourt Brace Jovanovich, 1968), 398–401, at 400.

To satisfy this secret ambition, only two possibilities are still available to the modern intellectual: "literary reviews and the left-wing political parties."[4] Activism is thus the shortest path (since literary glory implies other qualities) by which the intellectual can achieve, within the hierarchical apparatus of "parties," the power that fascinates him and of which the bourgeoisie has dispossessed him. From this perspective, the history of the socialist movement becomes the story of how intellectuals, after baptizing themselves "professional revolutionaries," gradually took over a movement that had been the spontaneous initiative of the working class and which had stood up to the industrial order not by invoking the imperatives of "science" but in the name of justice at its most elemental.[5]

Of course, this expropriation of working-class socialism, which aspires to justice, by intellectual socialism, which aspires to power, was not achieved with the lucid consciousness of Big Brother's men. On the contrary, party intellectuals make it a point of honor to hide from themselves the true cause of their political engagement. Ideology's task is to make this subterfuge possible. As Orwell recognizes, the content of ideology can vary considerably. "Monday's truth" can always become "Tuesday's heresy." What matters is that, to achieve its purpose, it must be *delirious*—that is, it must operate in complete indifference to lived experience and objective reality (that is, to "2 + 2 = 4"). To accept reality as it is would mean reintroducing its moral conditions and making room for "common decency"—an attitude that the Party must deny if it is to preserve its leading role. Once reality has been bracketed, ideology has no difficulty "not only tell[ing] you which horse to back, but also provid[ing] the reason why the horse didn't win."[6]

Yet this ability to say anything and its opposite, which is essential to ideology, is also fragile. Delirium can always be cured. Consequently, it is imperative that partisans be protected from the risk, however unlikely, that reality will return. This can be achieved through orthodoxy, which takes the

---

4. Orwell, *The Lion and the Unicorn*, 63.
5. This idea of the "Party" as an historical form allowing intellectuals to accumulate power by using the working class as a springboard bears some resemblance to the analysis developed by Jan Wacław Machajski in *Le socialisme des intellectuels* (Paris: Seuil, 1979).
6. Orwell, Review, *The Freedom of the Streets* by Jack Common, in *Collected Essays, Journalism and Letters*, vol. 1, *An Age Like This, 1920–40*, 335–336, at 335.

form of ideological cant,[7] whose codified rigidity makes it possible to cast off once and for all the moorings that anchored the organization in reality.

Once intellectuals who are more or less consciously motivated by the desire for power have built a partisan apparatus that seeks to transform society based on an ideology that is indifferent to reality and that manifests itself as cant, we can then say, with Orwell, that the conditions necessary for totalitarianism exist.[8]

"[T]HE CONNECTION BETWEEN totalitarian habits of thought and the corruption of language is an important subject which has not been sufficiently studied."[9] If cant is partisan ideology's security mechanism and if contemporary discourse increasingly tends towards cant,[i] it is no surprise that "the connection between clarity of language and truth" was one of Orwell's "great concerns."[10] Clarifying this connection is crucial, because although the perversion of language ultimately has "political and economic causes,"[11] its efficacy is relatively autonomous. One "ought to recognize that the present political chaos is connected with the decay of language, and that one can probably bring about some improvement by starting at the verbal end. If you simplify your English, you are freed from the worst follies of orthodoxy.... Political language—and with variations this is true of all political parties, from Conservatives to Anarchists—is designed to make lies sound truthful and murder respectable, and to give an appearance of solidity to pure wind.

---

7.   [Trans. The term Michéa uses is *langue de bois*. It literally means "wooden language," and is commonly used to refer to the tendency of officials, particularly politicians, to speak in meaningless stock phrases. While far from a literal translation, "ideological cant" captures some of the French term's spirit.]

8.   It goes without saying that this analysis, founded on the examples of Nazism and Communism, is perfectly transposable on cases of religious totalitarianism ("fundamentalism") in which ideological cant becomes a monotonous drone.

9.   Orwell, "Editorial to *Polemic*," in *Collected Essays, Journalism and Letters*, vol. 4, *In Front of Your Nose, 1945–1950*, ed. Sonia Orwell and Ian Angus (New York: Harcourt Brace Jovanovich, 1968), 153–156, at 160.

10. Bernard Crick, *George Orwell: A Life* (London: Secker & Warburg, 1980), 235.

11. Orwell, "Politics and the English Language," in *Collected Essays, Journalism and Letters*, vol. 4, *In Front of Your Nose, 1945–1950*, 127–140, at 127.

One cannot change this all in a moment, but one can at least change one's own habits . . ."[12]

The analysis of language gradually became the center of gravity of Orwell's reflection on totalitarianism. This recentering of his problematic was not due to a sudden overvaluation of the power of criticism. It was the necessary counterpart to a theory that emphasizes the role of ideas in the emergence of totalitarian power. If ever something "started in our heads," it is our fascination with these societies. Considering what happens in them is not a speculative luxury.

Yet the problem of language does not only define the main content of Orwell's mature work. In a sense, it also dictates its form and is the reason why literature became his preferred method of critical investigation. The role played by writers, from Yevgeny Zamyatin to Aleksandr Solzhenitsyn, in exposing the totalitarian world has often been noted. "New Words," an essay written by Orwell in 1940 (but which he decided not to publish) contains a possible explanation of this singular fact.

The premise of this essay, which is one of his strangest, is that present-day language is incapable of articulating "anything that goes on inside the brain."[13] Orwell is referring to our entire inner sensibility, "all likes and dislikes, all aesthetic feeling, all notions of right and wrong"—in short, "the reasons for [our] actions."[14] If the proletarian project consisted initially in spreading a feeling,[15] it becomes clear why communicating this feeling ran into difficulty. For pre-reflective experience to express itself, there are only two possible strategies. One, following the example of Esperanto, consists in deliberately fabricating the words we are missing. This could be done by "several thousands of gifted but normal people who would give themselves to word-invention as seriously

---

12. Ibid., 140.

13. Orwell, "New Words," in *Collected Essays, Journalism and Letters*, vol. 2, *My Country Right or Left, 1940–1943*, ed. Sonia Orwell and Ian Angus (New York: Harcourt Brace Jovanovich, 1968), 3–12, at 3.

14. Ibid, 4.

15. Orwell defined the "common decency" of Dickens and the proletariat as "an emotional perception that something is wrong." "Charles Dickens," 1939, in *Collected Essays, Journalism and Letters*, vol. 1, *An Age Like This, 1920–40*, 413–460, at 458.

as people now give themselves to Shakespearean research."[16] Orwell wrote "New Words" to prove that such an effort is achievable. Another strategy is less perfect but more "normal": literary writing. Orwell writes: "Nearly all literature is an attempt to escape from this isolation by roundabout means—the direct means (words in their primary meanings) being almost useless." If we give up on artificially expanding our existing language, there exists no other means for expressing sensibility than the never-ending language game that is literature. Writing of this kind, which is intended to express everything that is not "coldly 'intellectual,'" means adopting in relation to language a strategy that could be described as a "flank-attack upon positions that are impregnable from the front."[17] This is what Orwell calls the "roundabout method": the hard work of articulation thanks to which literature, exploiting the obscurity and multiple meanings of words, attempts to translate, as much as possible, the world of sensation. Literature, in other words, is the only kind of discourse that escapes the constraints of ordinary intellectual activity. If simple people express themselves primarily through feelings, literature must be the most suitable form for presenting their viewpoint. Hence Orwell's idea, which at first blush is surprising, that "[l]anguage ought to be the joint creation of poets and manual laborers."[18] This is not leftwing romanticism. If the intellectualization of socialism is indeed one of the sources of totalitarian perversion, literature remains one of the few options for the people to bear witness coherently to their experiences.[19]

Admittedly, written literature is not "general literature," if such an abstraction has any meaning. Its program is very specific. From the moment that it articulates the worldview of the powerless, its essence can only be political.[20] In the 1940s, Orwell renounced once and for all "art for art's sake" and the for-

---

16. Orwell, "New Words," 9.

17. Ibid., 5.

18. Orwell, "The English People," 1944, in *Collected Essays, Journalism and Letters*, vol. 3, *As I Please, 1943–1945* ed. Sonia Orwell and Ian Angus (New York: Harcourt Brace Jovanovich, 1968), 24–29, at 29.

19. To be exact, it is worth noting that Orwell mentions in "New Words" a third way of expressing what existing words cannot say: film. But he believed that the latter, "if only from commercial necessity," had proved unable to develop its own specific language, except occasionally, as with *The Cabinet of Dr. Caligari*.

20. Orwell, "The Frontier Art of Propaganda," 1941, in *Collected Essays, Journalism and Letters*, vol. 2, *My Country Right or Left, 1940–1943*, 149–153.

mal aestheticism that had always tempted him. In *Coming Up for Air* (1938), he used no semicolons, which he saw as a ridiculous symptom of the "artistic" mythology from which he had yet to detach himself. By deliberately anchoring themselves in history, literary works of the future would find their true purpose. Orwell would later sum up this position: "What I have most wanted to do throughout the past ten years is to make political writing into an art."[21]

THUS IT IS NO ACCIDENT that one of the most lucid texts ever written about totalitarian society is a work of fiction. And the space that *1984* devotes to the construction of Newspeak only reflects Orwell's previous analyses of language's role in ideological societies. Newspeak represents ideological cant taken to the extreme.

Admittedly, other factors contributed to this idea. For instance, Orwell's description of Newspeak derives from his interest in constructed languages, which led him to take a close look at Lancelot Hogben's Interglossia (1943).[ii] It is likely that Orwell's basic ideas about simplifying natural grammar were inspired by Esperanto. The handful of examples that constantly recur in his essays on language—the permutability of nouns, verbs, adjectives, and adverbs, the role of prefixes and suffixes, and syntactic regularity—are borrowed directly from L. L. Zamenhof's idiom, the basic contours of which were presumably familiar to him (as evidenced by his allusion to Esperanto in "New Words").

Yet beyond these formal influences, it is important to see that that the logic of Newspeak is no different from that which already governs modern ideological discourse. This is made evident in the two major essays Orwell devoted to the problem of language: "The English Language" (1944) and "Politics and the English Language" (1946). The main thesis of these two studies anticipates *1984*'s appendix on Newspeak. The English language, according to Orwell, possesses a distinct advantage. Like Asian languages, its grammar is minimal, and this property makes it one of the simplest existing languages. But this simplicity has a flip side: "The great weakness of English is its capacity for debasement. Just because it is so easy to use, it is easy to use *badly*."[22] This is why the English people will never be linguists, as they

---

21. Orwell, "Why I Write," *Collected Essays, Journalism and Letters*, vol. 1, *An Age Like This, 1920–40*, 1–7, at 6.

22. Orwell, "The English Language," in *Collected Essays, Journalism and Letters*, vol. 3, *As I Please, 1943–1945*, 42.

are often "quite unable to grasp what is meant by gender, person, and case." This vulnerability resulting from its excessive simplicity explains the ease with which the jargons of the official proprietors of speech spread among the public. Hence "the deadliest enemy of good English is what is called 'standard English.' This dreary dialect [is] the language of leading articles, White Papers, political speeches, and BBC news bulletins. . . ."[23] Its most characteristic trait is the generalization of ready-made expressions, "which may once have been fresh and vivid, but have now become mere thought-saving devices, having the same relation to living English as a crutch has to a leg. Anyone preparing a broadcast or writing to *The Times* adopts this kind of language almost instinctively, and it infects the spoken tongue as well."[24]

The *lignification* of language—its tendency to become "wooden"—thus appears well before totalitarianism, even if the latter completes the process. But the origins of these processes are analogous. "The people likeliest to use simple, concrete language, and to think of metaphors that really call up a visual image, are those who are in contact with physical reality," namely, workers. Consequently, the "temporary decadence of the English language is due, like so much else, to our anachronistic class system. 'Educated' English has grown anemic because for long past it has not been reinvigorated from below."[25]

The inability to speak one's native tongue in a lively way thus comes from above. In this sense, it can be said that ideological cant is implicit in the way the powerful express themselves, be they politicians, businesspeople, or journalists. If "Marxist English"[26] has become the unrivaled template of ideological cant, it is because it is the language of those with the greatest will to power. The official discourse of communist regimes is the most perfect fruition of a rhetoric from which thought has been completely purged. In orthodoxy's coded drudgery, ideology becomes "duckspeak" and strives patiently to eliminate its human character: "The appropriate noises are coming out of his larynx, but his brain is not involved as it would be if he were choosing his words for himself." This sentence sounds like it comes from *1984*. Yet

---

23. Ibid.
24. Ibid., 43.
25. Ibid.
26. Orwell, "As I Please," in *Collected Essays, Journalism and Letters*, vol. 3, *As I Please, 1943–1945*, 108–111, at 109.

it appeared earlier, in "Politics and the English Language."[27] Newspeak, in short, is the truth of our times.

YET THE CONCEPT OF NEWSPEAK contains another element. It presupposes that lignification can be pursued to such a degree that language no longer allows for any thought independent of official truth. The power of Newspeak's syntactic structures and mini-vocabularies is so great that it becomes possible to imagine that self-mastery would no longer be needed to avoid "thought-crimes": "In the end we shall make thoughtcrime literally impossible, because there will be no words in which to express it."[28]

The idea that language alone might determine what is thinkable is often seen as Orwellian philosophy's major claim. Marina Yaguello even sees it as reflecting the "linguistic currents that dominated much of the twentieth century," citing the Sapir-Whorf hypothesis.[29] Yet while the Newspeak project (the idea of the "Eleventh Edition")[iii] can indeed by seen as consistent with the Sapir-Whorf hypothesis, this does not mean that Orwell, even for a moment, believed that such an undertaking could succeed. When analyzing Newspeak, it is important to distinguish Syme's presentation of it, which is undeniably based on linguistic determinism,[30] and the far more nuanced account given by the narrator in the appendix (which is full of qualifiers: "almost," "so far as possible," "so far as thought is dependent on words"). Such a distinction is hardly surprising for an author who, as he made clear in "New Words," maintained that one could always improve on the poverty of existing language. Orwell was a genuine linguistic voluntarist, who resisted the common assumption that language cannot be changed "by conscious action."[31] Not only was he constantly encouraging people to oppose "Standard English's" grip on his language, but his essays also contain detailed plans for the defense of popular English. In 1946, he even proposed six rules[32] which, if methodically adopted

---

27. Orwell, "Politics and the English Language," 136.
28. Orwell, *1984* (New York: Alfred A. Knopf/Everyman's Library, 1992 [1949]), 55.
29. Marina Yaguello, *Les fous du langage: Des langues imaginaires et de leurs inventeurs* (Paris: Seuil, 1984), 80.
30. Orwell, *1984*, chapter 5.
31. Orwell, "Politics and the English Language," 127.
32. Ibid., 139.

by committed individuals, could thwart the formulaic use of language. The decadence of language, Orwell contends, is "probably curable."[33]

If, despite textual evidence to the contrary, we continue to attribute to Orwell a pessimistic conception of Newspeak's power, it is because, consistent with the dominant interpretation, we read *1984* as a pessimistic work. Yet there are good reasons for believing that this interpretation gets the book exactly wrong.

First, pessimism is not an Orwellian attitude. Part of his work is devoted precisely to denouncing pessimism's contemporary resurgence. "Perhaps its best-known living exponent is Marshal Pétain. But the new pessimism has queerer affiliations than that. It links up not only with Catholicism, Conservatism, and Fascism, but also with Pacifism (California brand especially) and Anarchism."[34] After such a list, it is hardly surprising that "neo-pessimism" is one of the terms that Orwell uses most freely in his essays. If there was one individual who personified pessimism, it was, without question, James Burnham.

"James Burnham and the Managerial Revolution" is one of Orwell's most important essays. It is, in any case, the essay in which his final position on the left and socialism is presented most lucidly. The text first appeared in *Polemic* in May 1946[35] but was later published as a stand-alone piece. Three months later, Orwell began writing *1984*. The similarities between the two texts are astonishing. This is how Burnham's ideas are presented: "The new 'managerial' societies will not consist of a patchwork of small, independent states, but of great super-states grouped round the main industrial centers in Europe, Asia, and America. These super-states will fight among themselves for possession of the remaining uncaptured portions of the earth, but will probably be unable to conquer one another completely. Internally, each society will be hierarchical, with an aristocracy of talent at the top and a mass of semi-slaves at the bottom."[36]

---

33. Ibid., 137.

34. Orwell, "Review. Collected Poems of W. H. Davies," 1944, in *Collected Essays, Journalism and Letters*, vol. 3, *As I Please, 1943–1945*, 61–65, at 63.

35. Orwell, "James Burnham and the Managerial Revolution," in *Collected Essays, Journalism and Letters*, vol. 4, *In Front of Your Nose, 1945–1950*, 160–181.

36. Ibid., 160–161.

The political context of *1984* is immediately recognizable. If we now turn to the description of the new ruling class in Goldstein's book,[iv] we can see that it follows Burnham's account of the new "managerial" class word for word: "The new aristocracy was made up for the most part of bureaucrats, scientists, technicians, trade-union organizers, publicity experts, sociologists, teachers, journalists, and professional politicians."[37] It is thus quite clear that if Oceanian society[v] borrows much of its décor from 1948, the idea of the future it embodies comes from none other than Burnham.

Orwell's criticism of this idea is thus particularly interesting. His main complaint is that Burnham's position is simply "a projection of the past into the future," rooted in a deterministic conception of human nature. For Burnham, human beings are condemned to a perpetual struggle for power. Consequently, history can never be anything more than variations on what has always existed. Burnham argues that "because a society of free and equal human beings has never existed, it never can exist. By the same argument one could have demonstrated the impossibility of airplanes in 1900, or of motor cars in 1850."[38] This deterministic vision naturally entails a form of radical pessimism: "All historical changes finally boil down to the replacement of one ruling class by another. All talk about democracy, liberty, equality, fraternity, all revolutionary movements, all visions of Utopia, or 'the classless society,' or 'the Kingdom of Heaven on earth,' are humbug (not necessarily conscious humbug) covering the ambitions of some new class which is elbowing its way into power."[39] Following a classic chain of reasoning, this deterministic-pessimistic framework results in an apology of political realism (which Burnham defended explicitly in *The Machiavellians*).[vi] Since the advent of "managerialism" is inevitable,

---

37. Orwell, *1984*, 213.

38. Orwell, "James Burnham and the Managerial Revolution," 178.

39. This contemporary relevance does not only concern totalitarian countries. If Big Brother has Stalin's moustache, the inability to escape background noise coming from a machine has more liberal origins: "In very many English homes the radio is literally never turned off . . . This is done with a definite purpose. The music prevents the conversation from becoming serious or even coherent . . ." Orwell, "Pleasure Spots," in *Collected Essays, Journalism and Letters*, vol. 4, *In Front of Your Nose, 1945–1950*, 78–81, at 80.

political wisdom consists in finding a place within the system, while trying to moderate its excesses from within.

If Orwell rejects this vision as "apocalyptic" and "melodramatic,"[40] it is, first, because he sees it as partaking in the same scientism that he always denounced in the ideology of the traditional left. For Orwell, socialism was, from its outset, an opportunity for working-class action and not an historical necessity entrusted to theoretical experts. Burnham's deterministic metaphysics (which resembles the Wagnerian constructs of Toynbee and Spengler)[vii] clashed with Orwell's most basic convictions. The second target of Orwell's critique, which follows directly from the previous one, is Burnham's tendency to overestimate the power of totalitarian oligarchies: "The huge, invincible, everlasting slave empire of which Burnham appears to dream will not be established, or, if established, will not endure, because slavery is no longer a stable basis for human society."[41] In other words, if Burnham is wrong, it is because, according to Orwell, he shares the illusions concerning the omnipotence of the governing organization that, in *1984*, are embraced by O'Brien.[viii]

Yet up to this point, Orwell's critique has only addressed the most obvious features of Burnham's system. A truly radical critique, however, must identify the causes of which this system is the effect. This means investigating the origins of this conception of human nature as the pure desire for power, which underpins the entire architecture of "neo-pessimism." For Orwell, the answer is clear: "Burnham's theory is only a variant—an American variant, and interesting because of its comprehensiveness—of the power worship now so prevalent among intellectuals. A more normal variant, at any rate in England, is Communism. If one examines the people who, having some idea of what the Russian regime is like, are strongly Russophile, one finds that, on the whole, they belong to the 'managerial' class of which Burnham writes. That is, they are not managers in the narrow sense, but scientists, technicians, teachers, journalists, broadcasters, bureaucrats, professional politicians: in general, middling people who feel themselves cramped by a system that is still partly aristocratic, and are hungry for more power and more prestige."[42]

---

40. Orwell, "James Burnham and the Managerial Revolution," 174.
41. Ibid., 180.
42. Ibid., 178.

Burnham is thus led to imagine a *1984*-like future because he is an intellectual and this future is simply the truth of his own will to power. If his ideas deserve particular attention, it is because he is an American intellectual.

The American perspective has, according to Orwell, a privileged philosophical standpoint: it represents the point of view of the spectator. A cold and sympathetic description of totalitarian society assumes that one has not experienced communism or fascism first-hand: "If totalitarianism triumphs and the dreams of the geopoliticians come true, Britain will disappear as a world power and the whole of western Europe will be swallowed by some single great state . . . Whatever happens, the United States will survive as a great power, and from the American point of view it does not make much difference whether Europe is dominated by Russia or by Germany."[43] Burnham's unique perspective on totalitarianism is due to his distance from the battlefield. This is why he can afford to be lucid and cynical in a way that his European peers could not. With Burnham, for the first time, the modern intelligentsia becomes conscious of itself. It understands that, as far as it is concerned, "power has no other goal than power" and begins its program of world domination: "Burnham, although the English Russophile intelligentsia would repudiate him, is really voicing their secret wish: the wish to destroy the old, equalitarian version of Socialism and usher in a hierarchical society where the intellectual can at last get his hands on the whip."[44] A few lines later, he adds that no particularly great intellectual effort is required to not admire Hitler and Stalin. But it does require "a moral effort."[45] Burnham has no more common decency than his peers. But because he is an American, he is more intelligent and thus more dangerous—in a way that closely resembles O'Brien.

FROM ALL THAT HAS BEEN SAID, it follows that one cannot reasonably attribute *1984*'s pessimism to Orwell himself. The future the book describes is not that of the world to be (*1984* is not a prophecy) but the world of which every partisan intellectual dreams (as Orwell said repeatedly, *1984* is a "satire"). History is written from the O'Brien-Burnham perspective, and

---

43. Ibid., 175.
44. Ibid., 179.
45. Ibid., 181.

Winston Smith's failure is not Orwell's. If we are not careful, of course, such a world might come about: "I believe also that totalitarian ideas have taken root in the minds of intellectuals everywhere, and I have tried [in *1984*] to draw these ideas out to their logical consequences. The scene of the book is laid in Britain in order to emphasize that the English-speaking races are not innately better than anyone else and that totalitarianism, if not fought against, could triumph anywhere."[46]

But there is a way to defeat this world, and it lies before our very eyes. Is it Orwell's fault that Winston Smith could not see it? On multiple occasions Winston writes or tells himself: "If there is hope . . . it lies in the proles." But while the phrase may leave his lips, he never thinks it, except when it is too late. And to defeat the ruling Party, he dreams only of a clandestine double.[47] This is why his fate is sealed, which he is intelligent enough to sense, even at the beginning of the novel.

Could he really understand that the working class and *its* socialism was the free world's only hope? This point was lost even on *1984*'s first readers, forcing Orwell to make a clarification that is often taken too lightly: "My recent novel is NOT intended as an attack on Socialism or on the British Labour Party."[48] The contrary is in fact true: keeping in mind the special meaning these words had for Orwell, *1984* could only be written and only had meaning from the standpoint of the "working class" and "democratic socialism."

---

46. Orwell, "Letter to Francis A. Henson (extract)," *Collected Essays, Journalism and Letters*, vol. 4, *In Front of Your Nose, 1945–1950*, 502.

47. Evelyn Waugh was perceptive when he wrote to Orwell: "Winston's rebellion was false. His 'Brotherhood' was simply another gang like the Party." Letter of July 17, 1949, cited in Simon Leys, *Orwell ou l'horreur de la politique* (Paris: Herman, 1984).

48. Orwell, "Letter to Francis A. Henson (extract)," 502.

.

CHAPTER 2

On *1984*

The following text was a talk delivered by Michéa to Montpellier's Anarchist Federation (*Fédération anarchiste*) in 1995. It was included in later editions of Michéa's *Orwell, anarchiste Tory*. In his talk, Michéa presents what he sees as the political lessons of Orwell's novel *1984*. He uses Orwell to make the case that any genuine revolutionary movement must have a sense of the past, and thus a conservative element.

If you had asked me why I had joined the militia I should have answered: 'To fight against Fascism,' and if you had asked me what I was fighting for, I should have answered: 'Common decency.'

GEORGE ORWELL, *HOMAGE TO CATALONIA*

MANY ASPECTS OF GEORGE ORWELL'S philosophy come very close to an anarchist sensibility. In *Homage to Catalonia*,[i] he explicitly admitted as much: "As far as my purely personal preferences went, I would have liked to join the Anarchists." The defense of imprisoned anarchists was, moreover, one of the main concerns of the Freedom Defense Committee, which, with Herbert Read, he helped organize towards the end of the Second World War[ii] (Orwell served as its vice president). Even so, the author of *1984* obviously cannot be considered an anarchist in the doctrinal and activist sense of the term. At no point in his essays does he claim that it is possible, let alone desirable, for a modern society to exist without a state. Orwell was, in fact, simply a radical democrat who favored a state based on the rule of law that could perform its duties with a "maximum efficiency and a minimum of interference."[1]

The fact that Orwell on several occasions described himself as an "anarchist Tory" is thus a reflection of the complexity of his political thought. It is also worth remembering that, for Orwell, "anarchist Tory" was a quip, not a theoretical concept. The term nevertheless remains, as Simon Leys[iii] notes, the "best definition of his political temperament."[2] This quip can serve as a springboard for teasing out several overlooked and under-estimated aspects of *1984*.

FIRST AND FOREMOST, *1984* is the story of the revolt of one individual, Winston Smith, against the absolute power of Oceania's rulers. By the novel's end, his revolt has been crushed. It has, however, been often overlooked that, if Winston's revolt failed, it was not because challenging Big Brother was impossible, but because his rebellion was ill conceived. On the one hand, it failed to rely on the proletariat (even though its massive and silent presence haunts the book). On the other hand, when Winston finally decides to take action and organize, he does so by joining the mysterious Brotherhood and

---

1. Orwell articulated this goal in the manifesto he wrote for "The League of the Dignity of the Rights of Man." See Bernard Crick, *George Orwell: A Life* (London: Secker & Warburg, 1980), 344–345.

2. This comment by Simone Leys (in *George Orwell ou l'horreur de la politique*) is also the analysis of George Woodcock, the anarchist activist and Orwell's friend, notably in chapter 3 ("Orwell: Radical or Tory?") of his book *Orwell's Message: 1984 and the Present* (Madeira Park, Canada: Harbour Publishing, 1984). It is worth noting right away that Orwell's main criticism of contemporary anarchism relates less to the idea of a society without a state than its fascination with modernity: "Read is too kind a critic. The range of his sympathies . . . is very wide, perhaps too wide. The only thing he acutely dislikes is conservatism . . . He is always on the side of the young against the old. . . . [H]e is in favor of Anarchism because the political Conservatives, including the official Left, don't like that. The contradiction into which this leads him remains unresolved." Orwell, Review, *A Coat of Many Colours: Occasional Essays* by Herbert Read, in *Collected Essays, Journalism and Letters*, vol. 4, *In Front of Your Nose, 1945–1950*, ed. Sonia Orwell and Ian Angus (New York: Harcourt Brace Jovanovich, 1968), 48–52, at 51.

the equally mysterious Goldstein. Yet this organization ultimately proves to be contrived, as it is set up and manipulated by the Party itself. This is the book's first political lesson: while an individual's revolt against tyrannical power is always understandable from a psychological standpoint, nothing guarantees that the results will be legitimate or effective. *There is such a thing as alienated revolt*—that is, a form of revolt that is perfectly in sync with the system it claims to be fighting, and which usually ends up strengthening it. According to Orwell, this occurs when a rebellion does not arise from the "generous anger" that informed, for example, Dickens' novels (a generous anger, as we shall see, that is inseparable from common decency), but from envy, hatred, and resentment. No authentic revolt can find its raison d'être in so poisoned a source.[3] Of course, people consumed with hatred can certainly imagine that they embody the most radical negation of an existing despotism. Yet they can only be its negative, in the photographic sense of the term. One need only read the famous scene in which Winston joins the Brotherhood to discover that this strange organization was, as Evelyn Waugh put it, just "another gang like the Party":

> [O'Brien] began asking his questions in a low, expression-
> less voice, as though this were a routine, a sort of catechism,
> most of whose answers were known to him already.
> "You are prepared to give your lives?"
> "Yes."
> "You are prepared to commit murder?"
> "Yes."
> "To commit acts of sabotage which may cause the death
> of hundreds of innocent people?"

---

3. Carlyle represents a good example of false revolt. Not only was "personal unhappiness [. . .] the symptom of [his] egoism," but his "occasional championship of the poor came more from a desire to thump society than from benevolence. Spleen, of course, is the exact word for Carlyle's peculiar temper; the spleen of the *unconscious* egoist, the denouncer of this and that, the discoverer of new sins." Orwell, Review, *The Two Carlyles*, by Osbert Burdett, in *Collected Essays, Journalism and Letters*, vol. 1, *An Age Like This, 1920–40*, ed. Sonia Orwell and Ian Angus (New York: Harcourt Brace Jovanovich, 1968), 33–36, at 35.

"Yes."

"To betray your country to foreign powers?"

"Yes."

"You are prepared to cheat, to forge, to blackmail, to corrupt the minds of children, to distribute habit-forming drugs, to encourage prostitution, to disseminate venereal diseases—to do anything which is likely to cause demoralization and weaken the power of the Party?"

"Yes."

"If, for example, it would somehow serve our interests to throw sulfuric acid in a child's face—are you prepared to do that?"

"Yes."

"You are prepared to lose your identity and live out the rest of your life as a waiter or a dockworker?"

"Yes."

"You are prepared to commit suicide, if and when we order you to do so?"

"Yes."

(1984)

These lines are unambiguous. Winston does not symbolize the "ordinary man" that Orwell's work otherwise celebrates. He is, above all, a replica of the thousands of intellectuals and Party members who, due to some residual humanity (or a minimum of critical intelligence), throw themselves, for reasons that are always unique, against a machine that will destroy them but which they had hitherto served with exemplary loyalty.[4]

---

4.   In Amélie Audiberti's first French translation of *1984* (Paris: Gallimard, 1950), there is a curious slip that later editions have not always corrected. In Oceania, the proletariat (all those who do not belong to the inner or outer Party) represent 15% of the population (Folio edition, 296). Needless to say, the original edition says that it is 85% of the population (Penguin edition, 179). Winston Smith thus does not represent the people, but the lower strata of the elite (the outer Party). It is worth noting, at this juncture, that Smith is neither particularly warm nor especially sympathetic. Throughout his childhood, the narrator explains, he was afflicted by a terrible inability to give or share. His revolt is only humanized by his love for Julia and his love of nature and old things.

AS WE KNOW FROM EVERYDAY LIFE, power mostly fascinates those who see it as a radical means for avenging themselves against the humiliation—real or imagined—they have experienced. This is why the will to power cannot easily be separated from resentment. This crucial truth, already firmly established by Dostoyevsky, takes us to the heart of Orwellian anarchism. *1984*'s second lesson is that the love of power is usually the main obstacle to achieving a just society—that is, in Sonia Orwell's striking formulation,[iv] a "free, equal, and decent society." Insofar as the modern intellectual's revolt against the established order is motivated by resentment—and not, as with workers and society's humblest members, by a spontaneous rejection of injustices they have directly suffered or witnessed—it is only natural, for Orwell, that classes that define contemporary society's intellectual framework embody the will to power. This is why, in Oceania,

> [T]he new aristocracy was made up for the most part of bureaucrats, scientists, technicians, trade-union organizers, publicity experts, sociologists, teachers, journalists, and professional politicians. These people, whose origins lay in the salaried middle class and the upper grades of the working class, had been shaped and brought together by the barren world of monopoly industry and centralized government. As compared with their opposite numbers in past ages, they were less avaricious, less tempted by luxury, hungrier for pure power, and, above all, more conscious of what they were doing and more intent on crushing opposition.

This hunger "for pure power"—that is, the psychological need to have others be at one's mercy—obviously exists in various degrees, the simplest of which is already apparent in everyday relationships: for example, the maniacal pleasure some people find in constantly controlling what those close to them say and do, in arranging their schedules and organizing their lives; at a more developed stage, the strange taste for giving orders, "disciplining and punishing," bullying and humiliating. But the highest stage of the love for power is the pathological desire to have a permanent and violent hold on others, be it physical or psychological. It is precisely at this level that totalitarian politics occurs. The best explanation is found in O'Brien's speech:

"How does one man assert his power over another, Winston?"

Winston thought. "By making him suffer," he said. "Exactly. By making him suffer. Obedience is not enough. Unless he is suffering, how can you be sure that he is obeying your will and not his own? Power is in inflicting pain and humiliation. Power is in tearing human minds to pieces and putting them together again in new shapes of your own choosing. Do you begin to see, then, what kind of world we are creating? It is the exact opposite of the stupid hedonistic Utopias that the old reformers imagined. A world of fear and treachery and torment, a world of trampling and being trampled upon, a world which will grow not less but MORE merciless as it refines itself. Progress in our world will be progress towards more pain. The old civilizations claimed that they were founded on love or justice. Ours is founded upon hatred. In our world there will be no emotions except fear, rage, triumph, and self-abasement. Everything else we shall destroy—everything. Already we are breaking down the habits of thought which have survived from before the Revolution. We have cut the links between child and parent, and between man and man, and between man and woman. No one dares trust a wife or a child or a friend any longer. But in the future, there will be no wives and no friends. Children will be taken from their mothers at birth, as one takes eggs from a hen. The sex instinct will be eradicated. Procreation will be an annual formality like the renewal of a ration card. We shall abolish the orgasm. Our neurologists are at work upon it now. There will be no loyalty, except loyalty towards the Party. There will be no love, except the love of Big Brother. There will be no laughter, except the laugh of triumph over a defeated enemy. There will be no art, no literature, no science. When we are omnipotent, we shall have no more need of science. There will be no distinction between beauty and ugliness. There will be no curiosity, no enjoyment of the process of life. All competing pleasures will be destroyed. But always—do not forget this, Winston—always there will be the intoxication of power, constantly increasing and constantly growing subtler. Always, at every moment, there will be the thrill of victory, the sensation of trampling on an enemy who is helpless. If you want a picture of the future, imagine a boot stamping on a human face—forever.[5]

This pitiless manifesto not only lays bare the psychological structure of the man of power in general and the intellectual in particular. It also and by way of contrast describes the mentality of what Orwell calls "the common man" or "ordinary people"—that is, those *who are indifferent to power* and have no need to dominate their peers to feel that they exist. "Ordinary human feelings" boil down to a capacity for "love, . . . friendship, . . . joy of living, . . . laughter, . . . curiosity, . . . courage, [and] integrity," which men of power generally lack. Taken together, these dispositions define common decency, that is, the everyday practice of civility, mutual aid, and benevolent reciprocity, which may be innate.[6] These tendencies are, in any case, the necessary foundation for a good life and any revolt that claims to be just. It should be noted that, defined in this way, common decency cannot be reduced to the qualities that Orwell finds in Dickens. It is not a literary ideal, but a daily disposition—at least among the working classes—to give, receive, and give back that, when elaborated and universalized, constitutes socialism's psychological foundation. It was Orwell's report on the workers at Wigan Pier and especially his experience in Spain[v] that finally convinced him that the traditional civility of ordinary people was the only guarantee

5. Orwell, *1984* (New York: Alfred A. Knopf/Everyman's Library, 1992 [1949]), 279–280. This image recurs frequently in Orwell's essays. Perhaps it shows the influence of Jack London's *The Iron Heel*.

6. It is, in any case, a virtue that does "not really belong to the twentieth century" (Orwell, *Homage to Catalonia*, New York: Harcourt, 1980 [1952], chapter 8). In the same book, Orwell describes Spanish common decency several times: "The Spaniards, who, with their innate decency and their ever-present Anarchist tinge, would make even the opening stages of Socialism tolerable if they had the chance" (chapter 7).

that socialism might, one day, be something other than a utopian dream or a really existing nightmare: "There is a sense in which it would be true to say that one was experiencing a foretaste of Socialism, by which I mean that the prevailing mental atmosphere was that of Socialism," that is, a society in which "[h]uman beings [are] trying to behave as human beings and not as cogs in the capitalist machine" (*Homage to Catalonia*).

This celebration of common decency and the necessarily connected critique of resentment and the will to power are the hallmark of Orwell's brand of socialism. In his eyes, the true revolutionary is not a puritan driven by what Spinoza calls the "sad passions" (whatever positive mask ideological rhetoric invariably manages to place on them). His "innate" decency, natural benevolence, and sense of humor are the very antithesis of the "hate-world [and] slogan-world"[7] that, from Nechayev to Che Guevera, make up the natural element of totalitarian intellectuals.[8]

THE LATTER EXPRESSION allows us to introduce *1984*'s third political theme, as the affinity between the world of hate and that of slogans is indeed structural. This intuitive understanding of the relationship between "totalitarian habits of thought and the corruption of language"[9] clearly accounts for Orwell's longstanding aversion to stereotypical uses of language. Yet, while ideological cant is the best example of thought that dispenses with the need for a brain, Orwell also grasped that this decomposition of critical intelligence was fully underway in liberal society. And, to judge by the kinds

---

7.   This term is found in Orwell's *Coming Up for Air* (Harmondsworth and New York: Penguin Books, 1962 [1939])—one of Orwell's most interesting and least known books.

8.   Nechayev: "Tyrannical toward himself, he must be tyrannical toward others. All the gentle and enervating sentiments of kinship, love, friendship, gratitude, and even honor, must be suppressed in him and give place to the cold and single-minded passion for revolution." *The Revolutionary Catechism* (1869), https://www.marxists.org/subject /anarchism/nechayev/catechism.htm. Che Guevera: "Hate as a factor in the struggle, intransigent hatred for the enemy that takes one beyond the natural limitations of a human being and converts one into an effective, violent, selective, cold, killing machine. Our soldiers must be like that . . ." "Create Two, Three, Many Vietnams," *The Militant*, October 14, 1996, https://www.themilitant.com/1996/6036/6036_33.html.

9.   Orwell, "Editorial to *Polemic*," in *Collected Essays, Journalism and Letters*, vol. 4, *In Front of Your Nose, 1945–1950*, 153–156, at 160.

of jargon that now saturate media, business, and government, the passage of time has done nothing to disprove his diagnosis. When "hip" journalists, "energetic" executives, "competent" experts, and "shrewd" managers become incapable of expressing themselves except according to the rules of their respective Newspeaks, this is not, from an Orwellian perspective, an innocuous development. Rather, it is a measure of the growing hold these powers have over our lives.

This is why Orwell's repeated criticisms and warnings about the accelerated decadence of modern language, his appeals to preserve a living and colloquial form of English, and his choice of literature as his preferred form of political writing must not be seen as evidence of a fanatical and elitist purism. In fact, the opposite is true: the clear impoverishment of contemporary language (particularly among young people, market society's main target) and the gradual disappearance of colloquial ingenuity and poetic sensibility testify to the ability of modern elites to recreate the world entirely in their own image.[10]

IT IS THIS DESIRE TO PROTECT civility and traditional language from the effects of class domination that very likely accounts for the need, which appears so often in Orwell, to rehabilitate a degree of "conservatism." For no decent society can exist or even be imagined if we persist, in the apostolic tradition begun by John and Saint Augustine, in celebrating the advent of the "new man" and preaching the permanent need to "make a clean slate of the past." In fact, there is no hope of "changing life" without drawing upon our vast anthropological, moral, and linguistic legacy, the forgetting or rejection of which has always led "revolutionary" intellectuals to build the most perverse and stifling political systems imaginable. This is just another way of saying that no society worthy of humanity's contemporary potential has the slightest chance of being born if radical movements cannot embrace conservative principles. This is *1984*'s final—and most important—lesson: the sense of the past, which necessarily entails a nostalgic disposition, is an

---

10. On Newspeak, see the crucial essay by Jacques Dewitte, "Le pouvoir du langage et la liberté de l'esprit: Réflexions sur l'utopie linguistique de George Orwell," *Les temps modernes*, 538 (1991): 43–75.

essential condition for any revolutionary undertaking that seeks to be something other than a variation on existing errors and crimes.

> "What shall it be this time?" he said, still with the same faint suggestion of irony. "To the confusion of the Thought Police? To the death of Big Brother? To humanity? To the future?"
>
> "To the past," said Winston.
>
> "The past is more important," agreed O'Brien gravely.

If Winson Smith, a competent and efficient official in the Ministry of Truth, retains a bit of humanity (this being the one respect in which he resembles the working class), it is first and foremost to be found in his fascination with the past in all its forms. This fascination will admittedly be his downfall, since Mr. Charrington, who runs the antique store, turns out to belong to the Thought Police. Even so, this fascination with the past remains, throughout the novel, the psychological key to his revolt against the Party, even before his romantic relationship with Julia places his desire for resistance on a more fruitful foundation. Conversely, the methodical effort to destroy everything about the past is the cornerstone of Ingsoc's policy.[vi] This means that Smith's revolt, alienated though it might be,[11] is thus primarily and essentially a conservative revolt, and that when it fails to draw deliberately on positive aspects of the past, the struggle against modern servitude is condemned to radical and definitive failure.

There is a real problem here: in modern Newspeak—that is, in a way of speaking designed to render "politically incorrect" thought impossible—

---

11. This revolt is buttressed by love and a sense of the other—key elements of common decency—only belatedly and imperfectly: "'You are prepared, the two of you, to separate and never see one another again?' 'No!' broke in Julia. It appeared to Winston that a long time passed before he answered. For a moment he seemed even to have been deprived of the power of speech. His tongue worked soundlessly, forming the opening syllables first of one word, then of the other, over and over again. Until he had said it, he did not know which word he was going to say. 'No,' he said finally. 'You did well to tell me,' said O'Brien. 'It is necessary for us to know everything.'" Orwell, *1984*, 180. This passage clearly shows that Winston Smith's psychological universe is not that of Dickens: his anger is not generous, or is only barely so.

"conservativism" is the "blanket word"[12] for referring to thoughtcrimes, a word that makes us complicit with every form of political evil, be it "archaicism," the "right," the "established order," or "social intolerance and exclusion." As this incredible mystification lies at the very heart of modern capitalism (and constitutes its principal line of defense), it is absolutely necessary to briefly consider its main postulates, if only to gauge the intellectual courage that Orwell needed to rehabilitate, however playfully, a word that the *bien pensant* left had so powerfully demonized.[13]

STARTING IN THE SEVENTEENTH CENTURY, the Whig-Tory distinction became pervasive in seventeenth-century England as a way of distinguishing between the "party of movement" and the "party of conservation." At the time, these terms referred, on the one hand, to the party of liberal capitalism, which favored the development of market society, calculating individualism, and corresponding moral reforms, and, on the other, to the partisans of an old regime that was both communitarian and rigidly hierarchical. The philosophical trap into which the "left" would inevitably fall is obvious: as soon as it began equating conservatism with the "right," the left was at risk of acquiescing to the foundational myths of Whig progressivism. However, if by "socialism" we mean the project, first formulated in the nineteenth century, of overcoming the internal contradictions of liberal capitalism, it becomes apparent that the effort to render socialism consistent with the progressive left (which, in France, occurred with the Dreyfus Affair)[14] would

---

12. In Newspeak, "compound words" are words whose meaning has been extended "until they contained within themselves whole batteries of words which, as they were sufficiently covered by a single comprehensive term, could now be scrapped and forgotten." Orwell, *1984*, 318.

13. To my knowledge, the only radical critic to have demonstrated comparable originality is the American anarchist Paul Goodman (1911–1972). See his *New Reformation: Notes of a Neolithic Conservative* (New York: Random House, 1970).

14. In its original form, socialism (like Marx) did not situate itself in relation to the left-right framework, but in relation to the opposition between the proletariat and bourgeois political economy (the idea of "the people of the left" is thus a theoretical monstrosity). Even references to the French Revolution are not essential to this project, as can be seen with Charles Fourier. On this point, see Jonathan Beecher, *Charles Fourier: The Visionary and His World* (Berkeley: University of California Press, 1986).

not be easy. For in practice, this almost necessarily meant describing the supposedly coherent forces of modernization that, since the beginning of the nineteenth century, were undermining the established order as "socialist" or "progressive." As Arno Mayer has convincingly shown,[15] this means overlooking the fact that until 1914, the social and economic basis of this order was largely agricultural and aristocratic. In such circumstances, the left's call for innovation on all fronts and for a radical break with every hint of the "archaic" or "conservative" mindset made it increasingly difficult for the left to differentiate itself from capitalism's other cultural requirements. Capitalism has little in common, after all, with the tyranny of the Church, the nobility, or the military. In fact, capitalism represents a type of society that is anything but conservative, as Marx, Joseph Schumpeter, and Daniel Bell have all made perfectly clear:

> The bourgeoisie cannot exist without constantly revolutionizing the instruments of production, and thereby the relations of production, and with them the whole relations of society. Conservation of the old modes of production in unaltered form was, on the contrary, the first condition of existence for all earlier industrial classes. Constant revolutionizing of production, uninterrupted disturbance of all social conditions, everlasting uncertainty and agitation distinguish the bourgeois epoch from all earlier ones. All fixed, fast-frozen relations, with their train of ancient and venerable prejudices and opinions, are swept away, all new-formed ones become antiquated before they can ossify. All that is solid melts into air, all that is holy is profaned . . .
>
> MARX AND ENGELS, *MANIFESTO OF THE COMMUNIST PARTY*

In other words, capitalism is by definition a self-contesting social system. The permanent dissolution of all existing conditions is capitalism's categorical imperative. By continuing to define itself purely and simply as

---

15. Arno Mayer, *The Persistence of the Old Regime: Europe to the Great War* (New York: Pantheon, 1981).

the "party of change" and the "forces of progress," the modern left, which could no longer use the excuse that it was fighting the old regime (whose last vestiges had been mostly eliminated by the two world wars), found itself condemned to close the historical trap that had ensnared workers and ordinary people. In this sad but very modern tale, "socialism" became just another word for the endless development of the new industrial order and for the uncritical endorsement of unchecked modernization (globalization, financialization, out-of-control urbanization, the permanent revolution in technologies of over-communication, and so on).[16] One should not be surprised that the pathetic fear of appearing "outdated"—a fear that now takes the place of thought for most left intellectuals—can only realize itself in the utopian vision of the cyberworld as a glorious future and its inevitable spiritual counterpart, the "liberal-libertarian"[vii] spirit

---

16. As early as his Wigan Pier study (1936), Orwell was able to describe this process with remarkable precision: "What I am concerned with is the fact that Socialism is losing ground exactly where it ought to be gaining it. With so much in its favor—for every empty belly is an argument for Socialism—the *idea* of Socialism is less widely accepted than it was ten years ago. The average thinking person nowadays is not merely not a Socialist, he is actively hostile to Socialism. This must be due chiefly to mistaken methods of propaganda. It means that Socialism, in the form in which it is now presented to us, has about it something inherently distasteful . . .The kind of person who most readily accepts Socialism is also the kind of person who views mechanical progress, as such, with enthusiasm. And this is so much the case that Socialists are often unable to grasp that the opposite opinion exists. As a rule, the most persuasive argument they can think of is to tell you that the present mechanization of the world is as nothing to what we shall see when Socialism is established. Where there is one airplane now, in those days there will be fifty! All the work that is now done by hand will then be done by machinery: everything that is now made of leather, wood, or stone will be made of rubber, glass, or steel; there will be no disorder, no loose ends, no wildernesses, no wild animals, no weeds, no disease, no poverty, no pain—and so on and so forth. The Socialist world is to be above all things an *ordered* world, an *efficient* world. But it is precisely from that vision of the future as a sort of glittering Wells-world that sensitive minds recoil. Please notice that this essentially fat-bellied version of 'progress' is not an integral part of Socialist doctrine; but it has come to be thought of as one, with the result that the temperamental conservatism which is latent in all kinds of people is easily mobilized against Socialism." Orwell, *The Road to Wigan Pier* (New York: Berkley Medallion Books, 1961 [1937]), 144–145, 158–159.

that reigns supreme in the mendacious world of the media and the entertainment industry.

OURS IS A CURIOUS AGE, in which simple truisms are taken for paradoxes. Yet if, over the course of the last century, the left's (and especially the far left's) historic ambitions have been so easily turned against the people, and "progressivism" and "modernization" increasingly look like capitalism's idealized truth, what better proof is there that *cultural conservatism* has become a necessary foundation for any radical critique of capitalist modernity and the synthetic forms of life it imposes on us? That, in any case, was Orwell's message. It is up to us to give his idea of "Tory anarchism" the philosophical status it deserves in the new Resistance.

CHAPTER 3

Preface to Christopher Lasch,
The Culture of Narcissism

The American historian and social critic Christopher Lasch is, along with George Orwell, one of the most important influences on Michéa's thinking. Lasch's work is a profound examination of the intellectual and political influence of the American progressive political tradition (as conceived by John Dewey and his disciples). Lasch interrogated the expert-driven social reform movement and its antagonism towards the instincts and values of common people. In *The Culture of Narcissism: American Life in an Age of Diminishing Expectations*, published in 1979, Lasch examined how the emancipation from social norms initiated by the counterculture of the 1960s was rapidly changing American society in ways that harmonized with elite progressivism and the demands of consumerist capitalism. In 2000, Michéa wrote the following preface for a French translation of Lasch's essay. Lasch's work allows Michéa to ponder the intimate connection between the modern left and the idea of progress. This idea was particularly relevant to Michéa in 2000, given that the French left, as exemplified by then Prime Minister Lionel Jospin's "Plural Left" government (1997–2002), was the embodiment of a progressive ideology disconnected from working-class concerns.

AT THE BEGINNING of his wonderful little book on George Orwell, Simon Leys observes that Orwell is an author who "continues to speak to us with more vigor and clarity than the prose of most politicians and commentators we read in the morning papers."[1] This observation applies perfectly to the work of Christopher Lasch and particularly *The Culture of Narcissism*, which is unquestionably his masterpiece. This book was published over twenty years ago,[2] yet it feels far more contemporary than most essays published since then that seek to explain our world.

The book's astonishing relevance is due, first, to its topic. By choosing to study, through the prime example of America, the cultural and psychological transformations resulting from capitalism's modernization, Lasch anticipated developments that years later—and with fewer excuses—would become the ordinary fate of Western societies.[3] Yet it would be a mistake to reduce *The Culture of Narcissism* to this aspect alone. If it has retained its critical power over the years, it is because Lasch's philosophical viewpoint manages to avoid the difficulties and contradictions that usually befall those who denounce capitalism while situating their criticisms within the ideological divisions the system imposes.

Lasch's early intellectual training (in Western Marxism and, specifically, the Frankfurt School), inoculated him against the cult of "progress" (or, as we now call it, "modernization"), which has become the residual cate-

---

1.   Simon Leys, *Orwell ou l'horreur de la politique* (Paris: Herman, 1984).

2.   *The Culture of Narcissism* was published in the United States in 1979. A French translation was published in 1981 by Robert Laffont in the Libertés 2000 series edited by Georges Liébart and Emmanuel Todd, under the title *Complexe de Narcisse*. It is this translation, which quickly became unavailable (and which, incidentally, is excellent) that we are republishing, with an afterward by the author.

3.   Consider Marx's warning at the beginning of *Capital:* "In this work, I have to examine the capitalist mode of production, and the conditions of production and exchange corresponding to that mode. Up to the present time, their classic ground is England. That is the reason why England is used as the chief illustration in the development of my theoretical ideas. If, however, the German reader shrugs his shoulders at the condition of the English industrial and agricultural laborers or in optimist fashion comforts himself with the thought that in Germany things are not nearly so bad; I must plainly tell him, *De te fabula narratur!*" (The Latin quote is from Horace, and translates as: "It is of you that the story is told").

chism of the left's electorate and one of the main psychological reasons it remains within the fold of that strange church despite its obvious historic failures. When discussing the logic of his philosophical trajectory, Lasch observed that his starting point had always been a "deceptively simple question. How does it happen that serious people continue to believe in progress in the face of massive evidence that should have led them to abandon the idea once and for all?"[4] Not only does the simple fact of asking this question make it possible to reconnect with several forgotten aspects of early socialism,[5] it also allows one to abandon several theoretical taboos which, as they solidified over time, have made a radical critique of capitalism inconceivable. Lasch's question allows one to critically reexamine the conventional equation (made possible by the "ruse of reason") between society's supposedly inevitable subjugation to the reign of the economy and individual and collective emancipation. Put differently, if one brings progressivism before the court of reason and no longer accepts as self-evident the idea that every attempt to modernize any aspect of human life necessarily benefits the human race, then there is no longer a *theological guarantee* that capitalism, due to the magical effect of "the development of the forces of production," is destined, with "the inexorability of natural transformations" (as Marx put it), to prepare the "material basis for socialism"—that is, technical and moral conditions for capitalism's "dialectical transcendence." This means, in short—to consider only capitalism's better-known problems— that the development of genetically modified agriculture, the methodical destruction of cities and corresponding forms of urban life, and the general dumbing-down of society promoted by the media and online culture

---

4. Christopher Lasch, *The True and Only Heaven: Progress and its Critics* (New York and London: W. W. Norton, 1991), 13.

5. If, in the historiography of popular revolts against capitalist industrialization, there is an episode that is always censored or profoundly distorted—indeed, demonized—it is the struggle of the English Luddites, at the beginning of the nineteenth century, against the fanatics of industrial progress and its "murderous idolatry of the future, which now kills species, languages, cultures, and possibly the entire natural world" (John Zerzan, *Elements of Refusal* [Seattle: Left Bank Books, 1988]). If one wants to rediscover the rational kernel of this foundational rebellion, one must read Kirkpatrick Sale's remarkable study, *Rebels Against the Future: The Luddites and Their War on the Industrial Revolution: Lessons for the Computer Age* (Cambridge, Mass: Perseus, 1996).

cannot be seriously considered as necessary historical preconditions or even contributing factors to a "free, equal, and decent society."[6] To the contrary, such trends are clear obstacles to human emancipation. The more these obstacles develop and expand (for instance, some of the probably irreversible harm that has been inflicted on the environment), the more difficult it will become to recreate the ecological and cultural conditions that are necessary for a truly human society. In other words, capitalism being what it is, *time is now essentially working against individuals and societies*. The longer they content themselves with *waiting* for a better world, the more the world they inherit will be unsuitable for their aspirations, even the most modest ones. Yet this idea represents the very negation of the progressive dogma, which posits that reason must always prevail and that the twenty-first century will be wonderful and the future glorious. This is why the critique of *progressive alienation* is a prerequisite of social critique. Regrettably, this critique has barely taken its first steps.[7]

The secret to Lasch's admirable clairvoyance is not hard to discern. It can be found in the basic commitments that have always underpinned his work. First, an absolute impermeability to modernist mythologies. Second, an unwavering loyalty to the perspectives of workers and ordinary people—those who, due to their circumstances, are used to interpreting society from the only appropriate standpoint, *the bottom up*. The most tangible benefit of such a position, which is both political and epistemological, is that it immediately lays bare the illusions that sustain the modern left (and its ridiculous "pluralism"),[i] whose incoherence gives it the semblance of autonomy it needs to ensure its electoral survival.

The left's illusion—a transcendental illusion, as it were—is the well-known belief that capitalism is *inherently* conservative, authoritarian, and patriarchal, as it is founded on the permanent repression of desire mandated by labor discipline, with the family, the church, and the military as

---

6.   On this phrase, see Sonia Orwell's introduction to George Orwell's *Collected Essays, Journalism and Letters*, vol. 1, *An Age Like This, 1920–40*, ed. Sonia Orwell and Ian Angus (Penguin, 1993).

7.   On the historical and philosophical conditions for the formation of the progressive paradigm between 1680 and 1730, see Frédéric Rouvillois' excellent study, *L'invention du progrès* (Paris: Kimé, 1996).

its privileged agents. For the modern mindset, this belief is very soothing. Yet it asks us to forget that, in 1848, Marx preemptively condemned this theory as absurd and implausible. "The bourgeoisie," he wrote, "cannot exist without constantly revolutionizing the instruments of production, and thereby the relations of production, and with them the whole relations of society. Conservation of the old modes of production in unaltered form, was, on the contrary, the first condition of existence for all earlier industrial classes." This is why, he adds, that as the capitalist system progresses, "[a]ll fixed, fast-frozen relations, with their train of ancient and venerable prejudices and opinions, are swept away, all new-formed ones become antiquated before they can ossify. All that is solid melts into air, all that is holy is profaned . . ." One of Lasch's greatest theoretical merits is that he always took Marx's thesis seriously and demonstrated its illuminating power at every level of American society. Naturally, when one recognizes that capitalism holds within itself, like clouds containing a storm, the need to constantly disrupt existing conditions, several unappealing and heretical consequences follow. In one of *The Culture of Narcissism*'s most disturbing passages, Lasch shows that it was the peculiar genius of the Marquis de Sade—one of the left intelligentsia's sacred cows—to have "uncannily" anticipated, in the late eighteenth century, *all* the moral and cultural implications of the capitalist hypothesis first formulated by Adam Smith, albeit in a very different vein. Lasch writes: "Sade imagined a sexual utopia in which everyone has the right to everyone else, where human beings, reduced to their sexual organs, become absolutely anonymous and interchangeable. His ideal society thus reaffirmed the capitalist principle that human beings are ultimately reducible to interchangeable objects. It also incorporated and carried to a surprising new conclusion Hobbes's discovery that the destruction of paternalism and the subordination of all social relations to the market had stripped away the remaining restraints and mitigating illusions from *the war of all against all*. In the resulting state of organized anarchy, as Sade was the first to realize, pleasure becomes life's only business—pleasure, however, that is indistinguishable from rape, murder, unbridled aggression. In a society that has reduced reason to mere calculation, reason can impose no limits on the pursuit of pleasure—on the immediate gratification of every desire no matter how perverse, insane, criminal, or merely immoral. For the standards that would condemn crime or cruelty derive from religion, compassion, or the kind of reason that rejects purely instrumental applications; and none of these outmoded forms of thought or feeling has any logical place in a society based on commodity production."[8]

If we accept this analysis, it becomes easier to grasp the metaphysical connections that, from the beginning, unite however unconsciously the two theoretical moments of the capitalist ideal: first, the "libertarian" appeal to emancipate individuals from the historical and cultural "taboos" that allegedly impede their ability to function as "desiring machines";[ii] and second, the liberal project of a homogenous society in which the self-regulating market is the necessary and sufficient condition for ordering the Brownian motion of "rational" individuals—that is, individuals who have been liberated of all philosophical concerns other than enlightened self-interest. Lasch's "modern narcissistic individual," who is immature and afraid of growing old (and of which the middle-class American is a caricatural prefiguration), is simply a psychological and cultural expression of the liberal-libertarian compromise that has become a historical reality. Lasch's skill lies in his rigorous demonstration of how this connection, which seems so shocking, became possible thanks to the metamorphoses of contemporary capitalism. When consumption is celebrated as a full-fledged cultural form, with its own conventions and symbolic universe, nothing prevents the two metaphysically complementary facets of the liberal paradigm (which had until now previously developed independently and even in opposition to one another) from converging and even fusing, united in a coherent modern sensibility. It is hardly surprising that Lasch's analysis shocked progressivism's good conscience, in the United States as well as Europe. It forced progressives to recognize that capitalism's ingenious hypothesis of a "commercial society," which Adam Smith had imagined as the solution to the political problems of his day, did not borrow its principles (individuality, reason, liberty) from ancient barbarians or the "dark Middle Ages," but from the axioms of the Enlightenment. Capitalism bor-

---

8. Lasch, *The Culture of Narcissism: American Life in an Age of Diminishing Expectations* (New York: W. W. Norton, 1979), 131–132.

rowed its principles, in other words, from the same cultural matrix that gave birth to the left.[9]

There is no need to emphasize the great political interest of Lasch's thesis. It shines a particularly cruel light on the fate of a period that has witnessed, without irony, the torch of revolt being passed from Rosa Luxembourg to Ségolène Royal.[iii]

The traditional left, despite its simplistic faith in the bourgeois myth of progress, always managed to keep one foot in the blue-collar world—thanks to union bureaucracies and working-class involvement in local government—allowing it to understand popular culture and sensibilities. This is why its political program, and, at times, its struggles preserved an anti-capitalist flavor—a tangible legacy of the historic compromise between the left and working-class socialism.

Starting in the Sixties, however, the convergence—which, in retrospect,

---

9. The modern distinction between "left" and "right" (which is a French transposition of the English antonym of Whig and Tory) corresponded, throughout the nineteenth century, to the conflict between the defenders of the old regime—that is, of an agricultural and theological-military society—and the partisans of "progress," for whom the industrial and scientific revolutions (that is, the practical form of reason's triumph) would result, through their own internal logic, in humanity's reconciliation with itself. Socialism, in its original form, existed in complete independence from this split. It consisted primarily as a philosophical counterpart to the first popular protests (the English Luddites and Chartists, the *canuts* of Lyon, the Silesian weavers, and so on) against the disastrous human and ecological effects of liberal industrialization. One will not find, in Karl Marx or Charles Fourier, stirring calls to unite some mysterious-sounding "people of the left" against all the forces that are supposedly "opposed to change." Throughout most of the nineteenth century, the most radical socialists were particularly careful not to compromise the workers' political autonomy when forming ephemeral alliances, sometimes against the old regime, sometimes against liberal industrialists. Only after the Dreyfus Affair—and not without passionate debate—does one see, *for better or for worse*, mass adherence of the socialist movement to the left, defined as "the forces of progress." To validate this historical undertaking, which was fruitful yet ambiguous, it was necessary to place a different emphasis on the genealogy of the socialist project (in this respect, Émile Durkheim played an important role). It would be seen less as the product of workers' creativity than as a "scientific" development of Enlightenment thought, made possible by the work of Auguste Comte and Saint-Simon, and subsequently imported into working-class culture "from outside."

was perfectly logical—between various modernization processes (that, at the time, could appear independent from one another) quickly dissolved what little remained of the anti-capitalist spirit that still pervaded the old left's leadership. First, the rapid decline of the seductive appeal of the Soviet empire, due to its sad "state imitation" of capitalist progress. Next, and far more decisively, Western Europe's entry into the era of consumer capitalism and the emergence of a "youth culture" tasked with legitimating capitalism's imagination and ensuring the endless circulation, in countless, ever-new packages, of enjoyable junk. Finally and most importantly, the *destruction of the working class itself*: not the actual disappearance of actual workers (which is in part a statistical artifice), but of *the class consciousness that united them*. The latter was achieved, on the one hand, by the methodical liquidation of working-class neighborhoods and, on the other, through new forms of labor organization in modern companies and the "anti-authoritarian" management techniques that made it possible to impose them.[10] What became known as the New Left was no more than the political counterpart to these processes. This diverse current was simply the political expression to the growing power of the *new middle classes* that Georges Perec described so accurately.[iv] Because they are predisposed to the technical, managerial, and "cultural"[11] administration of capitalism's most modern forms, the middle classes base their self-image (which they often hold in low esteem) on their ability to embrace the latest technical innovation. This pathetic "flexibility" makes them the ideal prey for therapists and perfect electoral fodder for the progressive left. It is due to this distinct cultural configuration that the most ambitious representatives of the new liberal-libertarian sensibility were finally able to seize the only tools of struggle and influence still available to the working class and make them their sole possession.

---

10. On the programmed destruction of the working class, see Stéphane Beaud and Michel Pialoux, *Retour sur la condition ouvrière* (Paris: Fayard, 1999). This detailed study begins with a common-sense question (meaning that, at present, it is very subversive): "How are we to explain that workers, at present, are the largest social group in French society and that their existence is more and more unnoticed?"

11. As the imaginary of consumption plays an ever more important role in contemporary capitalism, the diffusion and celebration of this imaginary has been a major economic priority. In the age of mass communication, this necessarily means that *media lies, manipulation through advertising*, and *stupefaction through spectacles* (achieved by showbiz and *citizen* artists) are becoming *actual* productive forces.

In one putsch after another (including the famous Épinay Congress),[v] workers and their unfashionable penchant for class struggle were gradually put back in their place, to no one's surprise, as they were replaced by more glamorous social and political elites. These elites, for their part, were aware that, at the dawn of the twenty-first century, the decisive political cleavages were those pitting the incorrigible archaism of the working classes (now described as "rubes," "trailer trash," and "rednecks"[vi]) against the insolent intellectual youthfulness of the planet's new masters, which newspapers like *Libération* and *Le Monde*[vii] promote with admirable dedication.[12]

If *The Culture of Narcissism* seems so prophetic, it is because it uses the empirical data already available in Lasch's time to study the forms of individualization necessitated by consumer capitalism ("the psychological man of our times [who is] the final product of bourgeois individualism").[13] Well ahead of his time,[14] Lasch also defined the narrow psychological and intellectual contours that determined the kinds of discussion available to the modern left and, more generally, the new middle classes, whose false consciousness has become the spirit of the age. Thus we see the curious and

---

12. Interested readers will find a good description of analogous changes on the British left in Keith Dixon, *Un digne héritier: Blair et the thatchérisme* (Paris: Raisons d'agir/Seuil, 1999).

13. Lasch, *The Culture of Narcissism*, 22.

14. At the time, Lasch could not, of course, take into consideration the new political, economic, and technological constraints (implemented as "globalization") that capital would soon impose on the entire planet to counteract, by brutally expanding the scope and forms of economic war, the declining rate of profit, which had become apparent in the early 1970s. Yet from a philosophical standpoint, these changes were ultimately secondary. "New technologies" cannot unleash their primary effects on human relationships except in a world that is culturally prepared to accept them. The principle of the steam engine, for instance, was perfectly known in second-century Alexandria. But given the period's cultural conditions, no industrial revolution could have resulted. The mobile telephone could only extend its forms of uncivility in a world in which autistic individualism and the elimination of the boundaries surrounding private life ("everything is political") had already developed, for reasons having nothing to do with modern technology, even if the latter, of course, amplifies all the effects that preceded it. Readers interested in an analysis that fleshes out Lasch's insights will find a treasure trove of useful information and intelligent perspectives in the important book by Luc Boltanski and Ève Chiappello, *Le nouvel esprit du capitalisme* (Paris: Gallimard, 1999) (translated by Gregory Elliott as *The New Spirit of Capitalism*, New York: Verso, 2007).

only superficially paradoxical fate of the Western left which, in one country after another, has modernized itself only to "renounce social emancipation, content to organize a field hospital for those wounded on the economic battlefield"[15]—that is, when it does not assume a leading role in this war, with the enthusiasm of the neophyte and the zeal of the *parvenu*. For their part, because they allowed themselves to be dispossessed of their remaining political autonomy by these benevolent and open-minded tutors (most of whom, it goes without saying, were trained on the right side of the barricades), the defeated parties of the modern world—that is, workers and ordinary people—have wound up, for analogous reasons, in the same impotent situation as nineteenth-century workers before they created independent political organizations. "At this stage," wrote Marx (who did not imagine that, in theorizing the past, he was also theorizing the future), "the laborers still form an incoherent mass scattered over the whole country, broken up by their mutual competition. If anywhere they unite to form more compact bodies, this is not yet the consequence of their own active union, but of the union of the bourgeoisie, which class, in order attain its own political ends, is compelled to set the whole proletariat in motion, and is moreover, for a time, still able to do so. At this stage, therefore, the proletarians do not fight their enemies, but the enemies of their enemies, the remnants of absolute monarchy, the landowners, the non-industrial bourgeois, the petty bourgeois. Thus, the whole historical movement is concentrated in the hands of the bourgeoisie; *every victory so obtained is a victory for the bourgeoisie.*" This is the main historical reason why, for the past twenty years, every victory of the left necessarily amounts to a defeat for socialism.

---

15. Philippe Cohen, *Protéger ou disparaître* (Paris: Gallimard, 1999). The distance traveled by the modern left can be measured by considering the paradigmatic case of the city of Montpellier, whose mayor, Georges Frêche—a visionary man of the left, of the sort only the present age can invent—took it upon himself to completely modernize his city through several five-year plans. This is how his brilliant deputy, who is responsible for local urban planning, describes the philosophical foundations of Frêche's grandiose project known as "Odysseum," the culmination of an exalting crusade and a radiant utopia worthy of the twenty-first century—that is, young, technological, and civic. "Teens like to walk in malls. We're moving towards the pleasure of buying, the need for conviviality, in a secure environment. Odysseum is a new neighborhood for meeting up, young people, and modern consumption." *Gazette de Montpellier*, November 26, 1999.

By this point, it should be clear that the kind of intellectual revolution encouraged by Lasch's work can only be poorly received by "enlightened" opinion, which believes that, by divine right, it is on the side of goodness and truth. For readers primarily concerned with the political correctness of their ideas, which they see less as tools for understanding the world than as means for calming their doubts, there can be no question as to the meaning of the present age: it consists in a titanic confrontation between the meagre forces assembled by modernity's heroic guerillas and the swarming, well-organized hordes seeking a return to a much-despised past. According to this admittedly touching view of history, anyone who stubbornly maintains that the globalized ruling classes are still in charge and that their primary interest is to create a new humanity that aligns with their selfish interests must have a predisposition to paranoia. As for fighting these powers by relying on the dignity and virtue of the working classes, this belief testifies at best to a misplaced nostalgia for a world that has disappeared and, at worst, to a blameworthy fascination with "populism," which, as journalists never miss a chance to remind us, could still give birth to a repulsive beast that we know all too well. By taking the risk of republishing *The Culture of Narcissism*, it was not our intention—nor was it within our abilities—to disturb the intellectual tranquility of this sector of the public. Yet even some of the latter may recognize that Lasch's book at least has the virtue of disrupting intellectual habits (which for most moderns is a good thing) and triggering, thanks to its provocative character, the refutation it deserves. Such readers should also have the courage to ask the logical follow-up: how could such a stimulating work, a worldwide success by the time it was published in France in 1981, have gone so quickly out of print here, after circulating by word of mouth alone, since not one of our official critics or loquacious state sociologists felt compelled to analyze it in a manner worthy of the questions it raises? This way of operating has, for some time, become the trademark of the French intellectual scene. Any book that would truly disrupt the established order and its "civic" good conscience is typically met with deathly silence or a deluge of slander. But this is yet another reason why we must interrogate this strange state of affairs and clarify its implications. Does it mean, for example, that even as they have "modernized" themselves, official and media-based intellectuals have returned to the morals of an earlier era when, as Marx said, it was "no longer a question, whether this theorem or that was true, but whether it was useful to capital or harmful, expedient or inexpedient, politically dangerous or not" and in which, consequently, in "place of disinterested inquirers, there were hired prize fighters; in place of genuine scientific research, the bad conscience and the evil intent of apologetics" (Afterword to the Second German Edition of *Capital*.) If this were indeed the case, the situation would, of course, be grounds for profound despair. Unless, by contrast, one interpreted it precisely as Hegel once did—as an irrefutable sign that "everything continues" and, consequently, that no one is yet in any position to claim that the *old mole* is digging its tunnels in vain.[viii] Choosing the right interpretation may, after all, be only a matter of temperament. But it is clear that Lasch was among those who helped this endearing animal pursue its thankless task. And in these strange and difficult times, I know of no better way to recommend a book.

CHAPTER 4

Teaching Ignorance

For much of his life, Michéa worked as a high school philosophy teacher in Montpellier. His 1999 essay, *L'enseignement de l'ignorance et ses conditions modernes* (Teaching Ignorance and Its Modern Conditions), presents his reflections on education in liberal society and the meaning of educational "reform." In particular, Michéa considers the case of the so-called *école républicaine*, or "republican school," which in France refers to the network of public schools created in the 1880s, during the Third Republic, by Prime Minister Jules Ferry, who made education "free, secular, and mandatory." In addition to being a significant "site of memory," the republican school is also seen as a key component of France's distinctive (i.e., republican) form of democracy. In "Teaching Ignorance," Michéa defends the education and moral values provided by the republican school system, despite its ties to capitalism. He also examines the educational reform movements that had been launched periodically in France since the late 1960s as embodying the cultural liberalism that flourished in the student movement of May '68 and the mindset of the progressive intellectuals analyzed by Orwell and Lasch. Michéa is particularly contemptuous of Claude Allègre, a scientist who served as education minister from 1997 to 2000 in the government of Lionel Jospin. Allègre was notorious for his criticism of French teachers, whom he regarded as lazy, selfish, and recalcitrant to change.

AS IT DISAPPEARS FROM OUR LIVES—as it soon will from our memories—we are beginning to better understand the nature of the modern world (as it existed until recently). Its complexity, over and above the ritualistic simplifications of ideology, lay in the permanent contradiction between the universal rules of the capitalist system and the native civilities of the societies in which these rules were implemented.

It was a world in which the "capitalist mode of production" was far from achieving mastery.[1] There coexisted with capitalism a vast array of ecological, anthropological, and moral conditions, in which the bad existed alongside the good. While these conditions allowed capitalism to develop, they did so (as has become evident in retrospect) only to the extent that, in various ways, they *limited* and *blunted* capitalism's most devastating effects. It is this historical framework that, more than anything, renders intelligible the inherent ambiguity of most institutions of our time, notably the republican school.

A key function of the republican school was, of course, to subject young people to the constraints of the New Order—that is, to the emerging reign of commercial universalism and the technical and scientific conditions on which it depended. This is evident in the obstinate struggle that secular schools waged against *patois* or local languages and various local and popular traditions which, from a capitalist standpoint, were seen as archaic and irrational. Schools were also spaces—due to the institution's ancient historical origins—that all too frequently exercised authoritarian forms of discipline, surveillance, and control that were at odds with modern conceptions of personal dignity. Yet at the

---

1. The main error of Marx and his successors (with the possible exception of Antonio Gramsci) was to have always overestimated the degree to which capitalist relations had actually penetrated the societies they studied. This overestimation, as we shall see, is one of the reasons for the left's constant inability to understand capitalism's essence and fight it intelligently. One gets a (naturally quite vague) sense of capitalism's scale by considering the work of Ahmet Insel. Through a series of ingenious comparisons, Insel shows that the non-commercial circulation of goods and services still represents "in contemporary French society something on the order of three quarters of GDP." See Insel, "La part du don," *Revue de MAUSS* 1 (1993): 221–234). On this topic, see, too, Albert Caillé, "Comment on écrit l'histoire du marché," in *Splendeurs et misères des sciences sociales* (Paris: Droz, 1986); Serge Latouche, *L'autre Afrique. Entre don et marché,* (Paris: Albin Michel, 1998); and Arno Mayer, *The Persistence of the Old Regime: Europe to the Great War* (New York: Pantheon, 1981).

same time, the republican school was genuinely and sincerely concerned with passing on knowledge, virtues, and attitudes that were completely independent of the capitalist order. It would be very difficult, for example, to explain the decision to teach Latin, Greek, literature, and philosophy as consequences of the laws of capitalist accumulation. A mastery of classical culture, one that is nourished, for instance, by the example of ancient courage and masterpieces of critical intelligence, is at least as likely to forge minds like those of Marc Bloch or Jean Cavaillès[i] as it is to produce spectators lacking intellectual curiosity and consumers susceptible to every iteration of the seductive reign of commodities.[2]

This was the fragile historical compromise upon which modern society in its various forms was for better or worse based, one that was gradually destroyed over the course of the unforgettable 1960s.[3]

* * *

Run faster, comrade, the old world is behind you!

MODERN PROVERB[ii]

---

2. Yet it was enough to reduce this humanistic learning to mere *symbolic capital*, a necessary sign of bourgeois distinction (a task that was confined, in the sixties, to Pierre Bourdieu in all his naiveté), to provide capital with the necessary ideological pretext for abolishing it once the related imperatives of profitability and political calculation made it indispensable to do so. This was the first effect—or first function—of the overestimation mentioned previously. First, it was proclaimed that schools are *already* nothing more than a tool that allows capital to reproduce itself. Then, inspired by this apparent radicalism, one could demand, in the name of anti-capitalism, that an end be put to everything that is an obstacle to extending the reign of commodification. This procedure is repeatedly used by capitalism's Red Guards.

3. How is one to explain the inimitable magic of Hollywood musical comedies, John Ford and Howard Hawks' Westerns, and Ernst Lubitsch and Frank Capra's movies? Or the jazz of Duke Ellington and Count Basie? Quite simply because all these works marvelously captured a unique moment of balance, experienced by all modern societies—though in circumstances that were unique to each—between the madness of freedom and the not-yet-abandoned respect for common decency. This historical moment was obviously not an *ideal society* but—and this is not completely unrelated—a society that was *capable of idealizing itself* because freedom had not yet been given the opportunity to show its *dark side*. This is why popular culture from this period has for us the "eternal charm" of an historical stage that is "never to return" (to quote Marx).

IN FRANCE, THE EVENTS of May '68[iii] represent the received wisdom of "the Sixties," a privileged and emblematic moment when modern society was brought up to date. May '68 was the "great cultural liberal-libertarian revolution" (to use Serge July's[iv] excellent description, which he intended as a compliment), the effect of which was to delegitimize, in one fell swoop, pre-capitalist sociability in its various forms. These earlier forms of sociability were, in fact, very different in nature and of unequal importance, making them an historical and cultural ensemble that it is difficult to simplify. By declaring them *equally archaic*, one gives oneself the intellectual weapons to demand their immediate disappearance. Through the kind of ruses that are so common to commercial logic, the abolition of all cultural obstacles to the unimpeded reign of economic relations was paradoxically presented as the first goal of anti-capitalist revolution. A joyful bonfire was lit, in which everyone was encouraged to throw away the legacies of a burdensome past. For some participants, there were very real psychological benefits. By piously submitting to the most sacred commandment inscribed on the tablets of received wisdom—"it is forbidden to forbid"[v]—the youth of the new middle classes, finding themselves at the forefront of society (and who, even as they have aged, have never left it), discovered a form of freedom that seemed tailor-made for their needs: one that entailed a radical break (at least to the degree that it was conscious)[4] with all the obligations associated with family, group membership, and linguistic, moral, and cultural heritage. It also came with an intoxicating feeling that always accompanies radical breaks (at least at first)—one that many would try endlessly to relive.

It is in these radically new conditions, and on the basis of a corresponding metaphysics of desire and happiness, that *consumption*, which had hitherto only been one human activity among others, finally became what it now is everywhere: a *full-fledged way of life*—the obsessive and pathetic pursuit of the always deferred pleasure of an elusive object—that is demanded in practice and

---

4. Most of the time, this consciousness, of course, is perfectly illusory. When a culture's explicit prohibitions are simply *denied* and their open transgression becomes the main way in which they are accepted (no one at present, G.K. Chesterton observes, blasphemes Thor or Odin), what becomes inevitable is not the wonderful Arcadia prophesized by Wilhelm Reich's disciples, but, to the contrary, the *tyranny of the unconscious*, which turns many a human into a slave.

celebrated in fantasy as an emancipatory counter-culture. "I want everything and I want it now!" "Take your desires for realities!" "Experience pleasure without obstacles!" "Live with no down time!"[vi] Along with other Oedipal foolishness, these slogans quickly became the stuff of marketing companies.

Were one less familiar with alienation's astounding powers, one might ask—after so much icy water has passed under the bridge—how some people have managed to remain, until the bitter end, impervious to the magnificently blank slate that the Sixties cleared.[5] It was an ideal foundation upon which the great predators of industry, media, and finance—with the complicity of international institutions (the World Bank, the IMF, the OECD, the G7, the WTO) and the more or less enthusiastic support of the entire Western political class—would construct, in complete intellectual tranquility, a comprehensive cybersociety whose sole commandment was Gournay's old motto: *Laissez faire, laissez passer.*[vii]

THE MOVEMENT THAT, over the last thirty years, has sought to transform schools according to a common pattern can now be grasped in its sad historical reality. Through two justifications—"democratizing education" (a total lie)[6] and the "need to adapt to the modern world" (a half-truth)—these equally bad reforms seek to establish schools for total capitalism, that is, transform them, once they have been reshaped, into logistical bases upon which the great multinational corporations can efficiently wage the economic world war of the twenty-first century.

If one has any doubt about this claim or believes it to be exaggerated, one need only, as Machiavelli advised, consider the perspective of one's enemy and ask what their aims are, given who they are. The task of verification is made simple by the fact that the warlords of the global economy's belligerent

---

5. This tabula rasa became even cleaner several years later with the collapse of the main Leninist empire. This empire, in fact, was never anything more than an *imitation by the state*—and thus crueler and clumsier—of the most harmful effects of capitalist modernity, most notably the destruction of civility.

6. Even Antoine Prost has finally admitted that "reforms seeking to guarantee equal opportunity have had the contrary result." (*L'enseignement s'est-il démocratisé?*, Paris: Presses universitaires de France, 1992). For example, "the percentage of students from working-class backgrounds at the ENA, the ENS, and X has gone from 15.4% in 1966–1970 to 7% in 1989–1993."

kingdoms, with their armies of lawyers and literati, must constantly coordinate their rival strategies and ensure that they never jeopardize what they call the world's governability. Hence the need for reports, documents, communications, notes, memoranda, and testimonials that, while usually unknown to the public, remain, at least for now, partly accessible to curious minds and obstinate investigators.[7]

Under the aegis of the Gorbachev Foundation, "five hundred high-level politicians [and] economic and scientific leaders"[8] who considered themselves to be the world's elite met at San Francisco's Fairmont Hotel in 1994 to share notes on our civilization's fate. Given its aims, the forum was obviously committed to the most ruthless efficiency: "Strict rules required all participants to dispense with rhetoric. Speakers were given no more than five minutes to introduce topics. During discussions, no comments could last more than two minutes."[9] Once these working principles were laid down, the gathering began by acknowledging—as a self-evident truth meriting no discussion—that, "in the coming century, two-tenths of the working population will be sufficient to keep the global economy going." Once it has been stated so frankly, the main political problem that the capitalist system would face in coming decades could be rigorously formulated: how could the global elite ensure the governability of a superfluous humanity, whose obsolescence had been planned by liberal rationality?

---

7.   Following the revelations by several non-governmental organizations of the secret negotiations relating to the AMI (*appel à manifestation d'intérêt*), some warlords complained about this accessibility and promised measures for dealing with it. In the media world, it is the function of the journalist Alain Duhamel (I use this name generically, the way one uses "Tartuffe" or "Quisling") to hide from the public the fact that such documents exist and, if they are revealed, to lie skillfully about their significance. It is worth recalling, incidentally, that the real Alain Duhamel is an eminent member of Siècle, a "French club that is very closed and that brings together political, financial, industrial, and media elites" (Pierre Bitouin, *Les Cumulards*, Paris: Stock, 1998, 44, 230). The way things are going, to find out the decisions being made *in their name*, ordinary people will need, not curious minds, but *secret agents*.

8.   Hans Peter Martin and Harald Schumann, *Le Piège de la mondialisation* (Paris: Solin-Actes-Sud, 1997). The following quotes all come from this first-hand witness.

9.   In practice, it is hard to be terser than John Gage, the American director of Sun Microsystems: "We hire our employees by computer, they work by computer, and they are fired by computer."

At debate's end, what was seen as the most reasonable solution was put forward by Zbigniew Brzezinski[10] and dubbed "tittytainment." This portmanteau term referred simply to a "mix of dumbed-down entertainment and sufficient food to keep the frustrated people of the planet in a good mood." This cynical and contemptuous attitude[11] has the obvious advantage of defining with much-needed clarity the mission that global elites have assigned to the twenty-first century school. It is possible, with little risk of error, to deduce the a priori forms of any plan to reconfigure the educational system according to capital's political and financial interests. Let us try our hand at this game.

First, such a system must preserve a very selective component designed to train, at the highest levels, the scientific, technical, and managerial elites that will be needed as the global economic war becomes increasingly challenging and ruthless.

These magnet schools, which must be highly selective, will continue the serious transmission of knowledge (most likely on a classical basis, at least for key disciplines)[12]—not only of sophisticated and creative knowledge, but also (despite the positivistic reservations of some of the system's defenders)

---

10. Zbigniew Brzezinski was a former adviser to President Jimmy Carter and the founder, in 1973, of the Trilateral Commission, a "club even more inaccessible than Siècle, which in 1992 consisted of 350 American, European, and Japanese members," and is a "space for developing the ideas and strategies of the capitalist International" (Bitouin, *Les Cumulards*, 44).

11. This analysis makes quite clear how intellectual and media elites see ordinary people ("moldy France," as the elegant Philippe Sollers would put it): a world full of "hicks" and "rubes," the regular butt of Cabu's cartoons or the *Guignols de l'Info* TV satire show. It is worth noting the system's extraordinary powers of appropriation: during the nineteenth century, a *guignol* was one of the few weapons available to common people to mock their masters. Now, it has become part of the heavy artillery that the elite uses to make fun of the people. It is not hard to imagine what will happen to Robin Hood the day that, to improve ratings, Vivendi asks its employees to give him a new televisual existence.

12. When serious business is at stake and real results needed, capital does not fool around. For instance, when sport ceases to be a game and a festival and becomes an industry in which winning alone is profitable, it is crucial that the training of future champions is not confined to Foucamberts or Meirieus. Liliane Lurçat writes: "Pedagogic rigor has abandoned the classroom and is now found where sports are practiced. Curiously, in these places, no one pretends to be inspired by constructivism and pedagogical rigor is not seen as hindering spontaneity" (*La destruction de l'enseignement élémentaire et ses penseurs*, Paris: Guibert, 1998, 25). And strangely, the popular origins of most sports is never described as an obstacle to traditional pedagogical rigor.

a degree of culture and critical thinking, without which the acquisition and practical mastery of knowledge has no meaning and (most importantly) no real utility.

For average technical skills—which the European Commission estimates as having "a half-life of ten years, their intellectual capital depreciating 7% per year, accompanied by a corresponding decline in workforce efficiency"[13]— the problem is quite different. They amount to *disposable knowledge*—as disposable as the human beings who temporarily embody them—in that, because they draw on more routine skills and are adapted to specific technological contexts, they cease to be operational once a field becomes outdated. Since the information technology revolution, however, these characteristics are, from a strictly capitalist standpoint, only advantages. A utilitarian and essentially algorithmic form of knowledge—one that does not depend on autonomy and creativity—can ultimately be learned[14] alone, that is, at home, on a computer, with the necessary educational software. By generalizing, for intermediate skills, the practice of multimedia remote education, the dominant class can kill two birds with one stone. On the one hand, major corporations (Olivetti, Philippe, Siemens, Ericsson, and so on) will be "asked to sell their products on the lifelong learning market, which is governed by the

---

13. Report of May 24, 1991. Cited in Gérard de Saleys and Nico Hirtt, *Tableau Noir* (Brussels: EPO, 1998). This indispensable little book consists of texts that, for the past several years, the European Commission, the OECD, and the European Round Table (one of the most discreet and efficient EU lobbies, whose tireless *passionaria* is Édith Cresson) have devoted to defining the "structural adjustment" policies required by capitalist reformers. Because these reports are not intended to be read by the sovereign people, their authors speak with a cynicism that is utterly dumbfounding.

14. "A parenthetical remark on education: people chat endlessly about the crisis in education, every minister proposes a reform of their own, and yet the essential gets left aside— and for good reason. As Plato observed 2500 years ago, at the root of the acquisition and transmission of knowledge lies eros: love for what is taught, which is necessarily contingent on an affective bond between teacher and student" (Cornelius Castoriadis, *La fin de l'histoire*, Paris: Éditions du Félin, 1992). These self-evident points remind us of the a priori limitations of all remote education. At best, machines can inculcate knowledge severed from all affective and cultural support and, consequently, shorn of human significance and its critical potential. It is essentially no different from what skillful training could "teach" an animal.

laws of supply and demand."[15] On the other, tens of thousands of teachers (whose financing comprises most of the Education Ministry's budget) will become completely useless, making it possible for them to be terminated, which will allow the state to invest the resulting savings in operations profitable to major international firms.

There remains, of course, the most numerous group—those destined by the system to remain unemployed (or to be employed on a precarious and flexible basis, in McDonald's-like jobs), in part because, to use the OECD's[16] terms, "they will never constitute a profitable market" and "their exclusion from society will increase as other [groups] continue to progress." This is fertile terrain for tittytainment. Clearly, the costly transmission of real knowledge—and particularly critical knowledge—as well as the teaching of basic forms of civic behavior and the encouragement of honest and upright conduct offer the system nothing of interest and can even, in some political situations, threaten its security. It is when educating this most numerous group that ignorance must be taught in every conceivable manner. But this task is not entirely self-evident, and is one in which traditional teachers, at least for now, have for the most part been poorly trained. The teaching of ignorance requires that teachers be *reeducated*, in other words, that they be made to *work differently*, under the enlightened despotism of a powerful and well-organized army of "education science" experts. The key task of these experts will be to define and impose (by every means available to a hierarchical institution) the pedagogical and material conditions of what Debord[viii] calls the "dissolution of logic":[17] that is, the "loss of the ability to perceive immediately what is important and what is insignificant or irrelevant, what is incompatible or, inversely, what could well be complementary; all that a

---

15. European Commission Report. See above.

16. Report of the Philadelphia Round Table, February 1996, cited in *Tableau Noir*, 43.

17. Guy Debord, *Comments on the Society of Spectacle*, available at https://theanarchist library.org/library/guy-debord-comments-on-the-society-of-the-spectacle. It is worth mentioning that the "dissolution of logic" is a genuine cultural revolution since, until recently, as Debord observes, "almost everyone thought with a minimum of logic, with the striking exception of cretins and activists." In this sense, one could say that the ideal school reform, from a capitalist point of view, would transform each student as quickly as possible into a *cretinous activist*.

particular consequence entails and at the same time all that it excludes." A student who has been trained in this way, Debord adds, will find himself "at the service of the established order right from the start, even though subjectively he may have had quite the opposite intention. He will essentially follow the language of the spectacle, for it is the only one he is familiar with; the one in which he learned to speak. No doubt he would like to show himself as an enemy of its rhetoric; but he will use its syntax."[18]

The task of eliminating common decency, arising from the need to turn students into uncivil and often violent consumers, poses far fewer problems. One simply has to ban any effective civic education and replace it with a random form of citizens' education,[19] a conceptual mush that is all the easier to spread as it simply reiterates the dominant discourses promoted by the media and entertainment industries. One could, in this way, mass produce consumers of law who are intolerant, proceduralist, and politically correct, while being, at the same time, easily manipulable—and who also have the not-negligible advantage of enriching major law firms, consistent with the American model.

Of course, the goals assigned to what remains of the public school system imply two decisive changes over time. First, teachers will have to abandon their current status as *subjects who are supposed to know*[ix] and become activity leaders of various kinds: through "consciousness-raising" or "transversal" activities, pedagogical fieldtrips, and discussion forums (conceived, needless to say, on the model of TV talk shows). To ensure that they are profitable, these activity-leaders are tasked with various material tasks and providing psychological guidance. Furthermore, schools will become democratic and joyous living spaces and civic day-care centers, in which organizing celebrations (the anniversary of the abolition of slavery, the birth of Victor Hugo, Halloween)

---

18. Ibid.

19. When the dominant class goes through the trouble of inventing a word (*citoyen* or "citizen" used as an adjective) and requiring its use, even though there exists, in ordinary language, a term that is perfectly synonymous ("civic") and whose meaning is completely clear, anyone who has read Orwell will immediately understand that the new word, in practice, will mean exactly the opposite of the existing one. For example, until recently, helping an old lady cross the street was an elementary civic act. At present, it is possible that hitting her steal her purse could be interpreted (with, of course, a little sociological good will) as an admittedly naïve way of protesting exclusion and social injustice—and thus constitute the first step towards being a "citizens'" act.

will be assigned to associations of parents eager to "get involved," and spaces that are completely open to representatives of civic life (associations, veterans, CEOs, jugglers, fire-eaters) and to the technological and cultural merchandise of large corporations—now known as "educational partners." I expect that it will also occur to someone to place, at the entrance to this great educational theme park, a few electronic devices for detecting metal objects.

ONE DOES NOT have to be an expert in the history of education to recognize, in the negative utopia I have sketched, the basic contours of the reforms that have been pursued (in different forms and at different speeds, depending on the place) for the past thirty years in most Western countries.[20] If French capitalism has displayed any originality, it is solely to the extent that, in its war against the working classes, it has shown exceptional intelligence in exploiting the ideological commonplaces that, since May '68, have overtaken

---

20. As the classic site of capitalist production, the United States obviously experimented with most of these reforms well before Europe. This explains the disastrous state in which public education there finds itself. And this confirms the fact that pedagogical methods that have led the American school system to the brink of collapse, with the full knowledge of its participants, were deliberately introduced in France. Liliane Lurçat notes: "The reading techniques recommended by Meirieu as being scientifically correct contributed to the generalization of illiteracy in the United States, where, according to Jacques Barzun, 60 million functional illiterates owe their failure to the 'look and say' method." (*Vers une école totalitaire*, 144). This does not necessarily mean that the first educational reformers were conscious agents of capitalism. By destroying, as a matter of principle, the achievements of tradition, they were simply trying, as they understood it, to expand the sphere of freedom. This was, of course, nothing more than the spirit of consumption and free trade transposed into pedagogy. But this is why each step forward taken by reform was necessarily condemned to liberate new spaces for capitalist dynamics, which contributed, in turn, to consolidating the mythologies of "new education." For the most part, it was not until 1998, under Lionel Jospin and Claude Allègre, that these educational utopias were recycled (in a way that was perfectly conscious and deliberate) in the service of the "European construction"—in other words, to prepare European companies for the global economic war. Whoever wants to understand education reform's shift from anti-authoritarian naiveté to liberal cynicism should doubtless study the role played by Inspector Foucambert (we have the Lysenkos we deserve) and his famous army of fanatics (Liliane Lurçat, *Les destructeurs de l'enseignement secondaire et ses penseurs*, Paris: François Xavier de Guibert, 1998).

the market.[21] Alain Finkielkraut[x] writes: "Revolutionary tracts of yore have become the governmental directives of the present. Thirty years ago, high school action committees proclaimed that, to fight inequality, teachers could no longer confine themselves to transmitting the culture they had acquired but had to awaken each student's personality and teach them to educate themselves. Now, teaching inspectors speak exactly the same way."[22]

In practice, the reform movement is, of course, a complex process. It must deal with the contingencies of multiple power relationships and partial road-blocks, which it makes up for with sudden, brutal accelerations. Traditional liberals get bragging rights for implementing the first wave of reforms in the wake of the events of May '68. From the 1972 regulations on teaching French[23] to the establishment in 1977 of mixed ability middle schools,[xi] this political current did its work rather well.

---

21. It must be said that when it comes to implementing this Americanized destruction of education, the dominant classes have always been able to rely on—from within the ranks of teachers themselves—the unfailing support of a very strange organization, the SGEN-CFDT. Jean-Claude Milner has described it as "a rarity: a teachers' union that systematically demands the material and moral abasement of teachers" (*De l'école,* Paris: Seuil, 1984, 30). The key to this penchant for martyrdom and crucifixion is to be found, no doubt, in the CFDT's Christian origins.

22. Alain Finkielkraut, *L'Ingratitude* (Paris: Gallimard, 1999, 153). Very curious reports now circulate in the republican school, if the November 10, 1998, *Bulletin* of *Force Ouvrière des lycées et collèges* is to be believed: "Here are a few remarks by IPR's (*Inspecteurs pédagogiques régionaux*, or Regional Teaching Inspectors): "Mr. X follows the policy line favored by the Education Minister. Mr. Y *simply teaches his classes.*"

23. Beginning in 1972, literary culture—denounced as bourgeois—ceased to be the focal point of French classes. The psycho-pedagogues of the day, who were influenced by Pierre Bourdieu's scientism—contrasted "the culture of reading, the formative role of great works, and the importance of literary heritage in the life of the mind" to "the idea that reading is used to acquire information and documentation" (Lurçat, *Les destructeurs de l'enseignement secondaire et ses penseurs,* 87). One is reminded of James Holroyd, a character from H. G. Wells's early work, who "had read Shakespeare and found him weak in chemistry." It is also easy to discern, beneath this rough leftist exterior, the seed of the cult—which would soon take over—of the successful corporation and consumer society. It is significant that the disciples of Inspector Foucambert consider advertisements—capital's self-avowed propaganda technique—to be a particularly valuable tool for reading education, in contrast to the inevitably bourgeois texts of classical literature.

Yet the problem with the liberal right is that, due to its history, a non-negligible share of its electorate still belongs to rural, Catholic France, which, for contradictory reasons, views the complete modernization of its way of life with great reticence. This *incoherent faction of the right*—which, in Russell Jacoby's famous words, "worships the market and bemoans the education it engenders"[xii]—exists just enough, despite its planned obsolescence, to compel the business-minded right to hide, moderate, or suspend its ultra-modernizing agenda.

This is obviously a problem that cannot be raised by the modern or *plural* left—that is, the *liberal-libertarian* left—in that it defines itself ontologically as the party of progress and movement—as the *avant-garde of everything*.[24]

Hence it is almost always because of the left's cultural power that the modernization of education and life—which, since the eighteenth century, is the essence of the capitalist program—has been systematically and efficiently imposed on the working classes. Indeed, one has only to consider (with a minimum of critical thinking) the never-ending initiatives of Claude Allègre and his faithful deputy, Alain Geismar,[xiii] to recognize the instructions that the global powers-that-be give their political peons at their discreet strategic gatherings. These guidelines advocate "trimming the fat"[xiv] and making schools completely accessible to the computer industry, no matter how useless their merchandise. Of course, political peons are always required to retranslate these instructions into "pedagogical" and "egalitarian" terms, which never fails to mislead the most moronic activists.

---

24. In left (or progressive or modernist) culture, a closed door is, by definition, an intolerable provocation to the human spirit. To open—and keep open—all existing doors is a categorical imperative, even if they open directly onto the tracks on a moving train. This is, at the end of the day, the metaphysical foundation for the nervous fear of forbidding anything, which characterizes so many teachers and parents, who, for their own intellectual comfort, insist on "remaining on the left," whatever the price. It is worth adding that, in keeping with the usual circuits of the unconsciousness' compensation mechanisms, this fear of forbidding turns quite quickly into a relentless need to forbid everything that is not politically correct (through petitions, street demonstration, lawsuits, and so on). One recognizes the sad and contradictory psychology of the new middle classes (of which the modern left, once its popular roots have been liquidated, has become the preferred political sanctuary).

CHAPTER 5

Autobiographical Interview

The following interview was conducted in July 2008 by the journal *À Contretemps* and *Radio Libertaire*, a radio station affiliated with the *Fédération anarchiste*, a French anarchist network founded in 1953. In this interview, Michéa discusses his upbringing, his first forays into politics and philosophy, his trajectory as a thinker, and his personal political opinions.

RADIO LIBERTAIRE: Jean-Claude Michéa, which philosophers do you most admire and what topics did your university work focus on?

MICHÉA: I studied philosophy at the Sorbonne between 1967 and 1972. Because of the time, and also because of my family's tradition, Marx was in those days the philosopher *par excellence*. Without the least bit of originality, I devoted my masters' thesis to "the status of the materialist dialectic in Marx's work." Of course, when one teaches philosophy to students, one must take an interest in other philosophers. In my personal pantheon, other highly ranked thinkers include Spinoza, Hobbes, Pascal, Rousseau, Hegel, and Nietzsche. But I was obviously marked by this early encounter with Marx, even if I subsequently became more critical of his work.

RADIO LIBERTAIRE: Did you yield to the communist temptation?

MICHÉA: "Temptation" is not the right word. The truth, quite simply, is that I was born into it! My parents—who met in the Resistance—were rank and file

Communist Party members. My father was a sports reporter for *L'Humanité*,[i] and my mother was a stenographer for the *Union française d'information*, the Party's press agency. For better or worse, communism was my political mother tongue.

RADIO LIBERTAIRE: And did you join the Party?

MICHÉA: I followed the usual path. I first made my way through the youth organizations. After two years with the *gauchiste* enemy, in a world of Oedipus and May '68,[ii] I joined the Party in 1969. My decision to join, incidentally, was more a reaction to the witch-hunt on campuses controlled by *gauchistes*[1] than a genuine endorsement of the Party's line. I finally left the Party in 1976, at the end of a process in which questions of international relations played a decisive role. Beginning in 1964, when I first visited the USSR, I took many pilgrimages to Soviet Bloc countries, including Cuba. More than any other factor, it was my discovery of "actually existing socialism" that led me to understand the nature of Stalinism and break with the worldview in which I had been raised.

RADIO LIBERTAIRE: And about the camps—that essential question of twentieth-century communism? What did you know?

MICHÉA: It won't surprise you to learn that these trips, which were obviously highly orchestrated, did not allow me to immediately grasp the essence of actually existing communism. Particularly since the Séguélas[iii] of the East were, by their own standards, pretty effective. Because I spoke fluent Russian, I gradually made it a habit to escape from the official tour routes and visit places—like Zagorsk, the religious capital—that were strictly forbidden to Western travelers. While I obviously never stumbled on a concentration camp, my surprising encounters with ordinary workers allowed me to see what their lives were really like, and thus the genuine class character of Soviet power. Unless you chose to be blind—that is, unless you were a

---

1. On the strange climate of ideological-sanguinary madness into which some *gauchiste* organizations descended after 1968, see Morgan Sportés' chilling masterpiece, *Ils ont tué Pierre Overney* (Paris: Grasset, 2008). On the human background to this collective madness, some fascinating insights can be found in Virginie Linhart's *Le jour où mon père s'est tu* (Paris: Seuil, 2008).

true believer—there was always a moment when you wound up opening your eyes. Others, like Orwell and Castoriadis,[iv] discovered this truth in different ways, simply by using their ability to think critically—and without seeing the USSR first-hand.

RADIO LIBERTAIRE: When you discovered that reality, did you break with communism?

MICHÉA: Only gradually. I know that might sound astonishing now, but you have to understand that, at the time, the nature of the French Communist Party was ambiguous. While its leadership was fundamentally Stalinist, its grassroots organizations functioned as a genuine counter-society, offering many workers and "ordinary people" (to use Orwell's term) an effective political framework that integrated them into society. In neighborhood and workplace cells one met men and women who were incredibly generous and courageous (many of whom, incidentally, had taken part in the Resistance), and who never would have dreamed of using the Party as a springboard for personal ambitions. Leaving the Party—and remember that, at the time, it was still genuinely rooted in the working class and represented nearly one out of every four voters—was not just an intellectual break-up. It meant ending friendships, which was hard, morally and psychologically.

RADIO LIBERTAIRE: Long ago, when I started working at the SNCF, I knew activists like that in the CGT.[v]

MICHÉA: My father, Abel Michéa, is a good example. He was a faithful communist activist, but he clung to his anarchist instincts, which were rooted in his connections to pacifist circles during the interwar years. Consequently, he was a merry Epicurean—a close friend of Antoine Blondin and Louis Nucéra[vi]—who was deeply allergic to ideological discipline of any kind. ("He's a political non-entity," Maurice Thorez[vii] used to say of him.) My father made it a point of pride that he refused any promotion in the Party hierarchy or opportunity for upward mobility, even though the bourgeois press regularly made it clear that it would pay handsomely for his services. While remaining sincerely attached—until the very end—to the Party he had joined during his time in the *maquis*,[viii] he passed on to me the principles of his political morality. Of these principles, first and foremost was fidelity to one's working-class origins and its political corollary: the *refusal to succeed*, to borrow a term made famous by Albert Thierry[ix] and revolutionary syndicalism. It is out of respect for this elementary moral principle that I have, for example, made it a point of honor to never abandon my high school students[x] for a university career, which is usually considered more "noble." And I have never regretted this decision. Not only because secondary education is a privileged position from which to observe young people and the contemporary world, but also because I know how difficult it is to preserve one's intellectual independence and lucidity when teaching political philosophy (and particularly the social sciences) while enjoying the material and symbolic privileges afforded *homo academicus*.

All this to say that the family education I received—which was in no way unusual for the time—made me immediately sensitive to the moral implications of political engagement. Clearly, there must be a minimum degree of consistency between the generous ideas one promotes and the way one behaves with friends and in daily life. And I say that without even getting into the key philosophical question of real income, which is the material foundation of critical activity. Obviously, there exists a threshold of material comfort below which it becomes a heroic task to think freely. This is probably what explains my instinctive distrust of the "bohemian bourgeoisie," the political and "humanitarian" activism of celebrities, and those who used to be called "socialists of the chair."[xi] On this topic, Orwell said all there is to say.

RADIO LIBERTAIRE: Do you remember books that marked you in your childhood and adolescence?

MICHÉA: Like so many schoolchildren back then, I learned to dream thanks to *Le Grand Meaulnes*, Jules Verne's *The Mysterious Island*, and the adventures of Arsène Lupin.[xii] I was also a fanatical devotee of Alphonse Allais,[xiii] who remains, in my view, one of French literature's great stylists. But the book that most marked my adolescence was—already—a political one: Anton Makarenko's *Pedagogical Poem*. I have no idea whether his name still means anything. Makarenko was a Russian educational theorist who, early in the Soviet Revolution, devoted himself with tremendous passion and dedication to reeducating delinquents and abandoned children at the famous Gorky

Colony.[xiv] In *The Pedagogical Poem*, he recounts how, with meager resources and little encouragement from the Soviet authorities (who were already very bureaucratized), he tried to teach the values of giving, friendship, and mutual aid—socialist morality, in short—to these bewildered young people, who were seen by society as irredeemable. One may of course argue over specific aspects of Makarenko's methods and beliefs. Clearly, we no longer live in the same world. But if his pedagogical experience still speaks to us, it is because Makarenko was able to imagine the principles of a socialist pedagogy in extremely difficult historical, social, and material circumstances. In any case, it was reading Makarenko that led me, as a teenager, to decide that teaching was my calling. I would add—but this won't surprise you—that his humanistic pedagogical methods would gradually be abandoned by the Stalinist regime. This is a further reason to read *The Pedagogical Poem*, which would first require it to be republished. Coline Serreau[xv]—another great admirer of Makarenko—once told me that she often fantasized about bringing it to the silver screen. Were this project ever to come to fruition, it would be a magnificent opportunity for the young generation to discover a man who embodied what the Soviet revolution might have been if the authoritarian turn of Leninism and Stalinism had not crushed all hope of building a decent society in Russia.

RADIO LIBERTAIRE: And in the realm of philosophy, who were the first thinkers you encountered, the ones that marked you?

MICHÉA: That's something I remember like it was yesterday! In our public housing unit, you could get books from Progress Publishers[xvi] at prices that beat the bourgeois competition of that era. They were the natural foundation of our family library. The first philosophy book that fell into my hands—I was fourteen at the time—was *Materialism and Empirio-Criticism*, a book that Lenin wrote shortly after the failure of the 1905 Revolution.[xvii] The mysterious title immediately fascinated me, and I threw myself into that furious polemic against Mach and Avenarius[xviii] (two philosophers whose names still send me into reveries) as one might throw oneself into a novel by Jules Verne or a comic book by Blake and Mortimer.[xix] In retrospect, I recognize that it may not have been the best way to enter into philosophy. But that reading experience had all the savor of a "first encounter," and it marked me forever. After all, in our age of manga and video games, *Materialism and Empirio-Criticism* does not seem like the worst thing for a teenager to read.

RADIO LIBERTAIRE: And what about Nietzsche, that paradoxical thinker *par excellence*?

MICHÉA: Yes, Nietzsche is an absolutely fascinating thinker, precisely because his critique of modernity is always ambiguous, even contradictory. But what I find particularly extraordinary about him is his constant—and always "untimely"—desire to hunt down the real individual that always lurks behind the seemingly disembodied thinker or moralist. "Who is speaking?" is the Nietzschean question *par excellence* (indeed, often a fatal one whenever you have the opportunity to observe an ideologue at close quarters). This is why, incidentally, he liked to define himself as an "old psychologist and ratcatcher." There is an obvious parallel with Dostoyevsky (I'm thinking here of *The Possessed*). In our positivist universe, Nietzschean philosophy is a time bomb whose effects are still being felt. But to return to your first question, I must admit that it was not until 1972, when I became a high school philosophy teacher responsible for teaching a specific curriculum, that I really became interested in non-Marxist thinkers in their own right.

RADIO LIBERTAIRE: Quite late, then . . . .

MICHÉA: I'm not proud of it! Of course, during my years at the Sorbonne, I had to read the great philosophers. But like a good dogmatist, I had placed a cordon sanitaire between Marx and other authors in the curriculum. In the best case, the latter were honorable "precursors" to the author of *Das Kapital*. I am ashamed to admit it, but it took me a long time to understand that these two worlds were not alien to one another. Clearly, Spinoza, Hegel, and Pascal—a writer whose subtlety never ceases to amaze me—are, as thinkers, at least as important as Marx. If reading them always elicits feelings of freedom and freshness, it is precisely because they were not ideologues. By which I mean, they were not intellectuals entirely subservient to partisan discipline and who, consequently, had first and foremost to defend a line, before even considering the option of thinking for themselves. As a result, classic philosophers are usually much further removed from the conflicts over ego (and thus power) that now infest most debates between institutional intellectuals. Interestingly, Marx himself—unlike Lenin—was not really an ideologue. More than anything, he was a free spirit (as was, at a later point, Antonio Gramsci), a man far more concerned with whether an idea was true or false than whether it was politically correct. Like Nietzsche, his great misfortune was to have disciples. It is well known that, towards the end of his life, he was in the habit of declaring: "I know only one thing: that I am not a Marxist." Marx's curse is the existence of Marxism, or, more precisely, Marxism-Leninism.

RADIO LIBERTAIRE: His analysis of surplus-value is, in any case, still valid. Two hundred years later, if you want to understand how a company works, you must still refer to it. No?

MICHÉA: The analysis of commodities (and the theory of exploitation that accompanies it) is one aspect of Marx's oeuvre that is alive and well, as Anselm Jappe[xx] has so valuably reminded us. You have only to walk five minutes in a modern big-box store to understand immediately the philosophical interest in the distinction between use-value and exchange-value or the merit of the theory of commodity fetishism. I would not say the same for the theory of historical materialism, which is ultimately just a radicalization of liberal claims about the primacy of the economy, of the kind found in Adam Smith's work. On this topic, Cornelius Castoriadis has shown the limits of Marx's economic determinism as well as his positivistic idealization of growth and technological and industrial progress. These limits naturally have a lot to do with the later failures of Leninism and explain, among other things, the latter's inability to create anything other than a *state imitation* of capitalism.

But I agree with you regarding the analysis of exploitation itself. Despite all the elegant talk tossed about these days concerning the "immaterial economy" and "cognitive capitalism," it is clear that *man's exploitation of man* has not disappeared in the least. Just visit a Chinese factory or a cotton plantation in equatorial Africa if you need evidence that the world Dickens described is still with us. If anything, man's exploitation of man has everywhere increased, including in Western countries, though not always in the forms Marx imagined. For instance, consider "stress management," which is rapidly expanding in modern companies, as the wear and tear on workers' nerves and psychological wellbeing gradually becomes more profitable, economically speaking, than physical exhaustion. While I have long stopped identifying as a Marxist, Marx still occupies an important place in my library, alongside the classic thinkers I mentioned, as well as more contemporary thinkers such as Castoriadis, Clastres, Debord, and a few others.

RADIO LIBERTAIRE: And contemporary writers who are still living?

MICHÉA: Before turning to the living writers, I would like to mention one other author, who died not so long ago—Christopher Lasch . . .

RADIO LIBERTAIRE: . . . To whom you often refer in your books.

MICHÉA: Yes. He is quite an extraordinary writer. Each time I revisit one of his books, even if it was written thirty years ago, I am awestruck by the contemporary relevance of his analyses. If the development of liberal society obeys a certain logic—which it does, in my view—it is hardly surprising that old Europe should always wind up experiencing, a little later, the various cultural revolutions that have marked the history of American capitalism.

But since you asked me to mention a few authors who are still alive, I will say that the philosophical movement that has most influenced me—with the exception, of course, of the Situationist International and its various heirs—is the *Mouvement anti-utilitariste dans les sciences sociales* (Anti-Utilitarian Movement in the Social Sciences, or MAUSS), which has, since 1981, under the leadership of Serge Latouche and Alain Caillé,[xxi] brought together dozens of scholars and activists from different countries—and scholars of markedly divergent (to put it mildly) political sensibilities. It is through their work, inspired by the foundational writings of Marcel Mauss and Karl Polanyi[xxii] (work that was long ignored, rejected, or just misunderstood, due to the popularity on campuses of structuralism and postmodernism), that I first came to understand the anthropology of gift-giving and the birth of economic ideology. I also have huge admiration for René Girard,[xxiii] without always really knowing how to integrate him into my analyses. Finally, I must mention the free spirit that is Slavoj Zizek. He is one of the most stimulating contemporary thinkers—his political use of Lacan[xxiv] is fascinating—even if I often struggle to follow him all the way in his turbulent philosophical expositions. Those are the living ones.

RADIO LIBERTAIRE: Jean-Claude Michéa, I want to ask you a two-part question: why do you write and why do you publish?

MICHÉA: Let me tell you a secret: I've always hated writing. Even if it's just a postcard—not to mention a letter! Like any good Mediterranean, I am convinced that you must be a masochist to enjoy spending month after month in a *tête-à-tête* with your computer while a magnificent sun waits outside. My first essay, *Orwell, anarchiste Tory*, was published when I was 45 years old. The need to scribble on paper and see my name on a book cover was not particularly important to me. Indeed, I belong to that category of normal people—fortunately, the majority—who are convinced that to be happy, you must remain hidden.

Everything began, as has often been the case in my life, with a friendship. In 1988, Alain Martin, whom I had known in the 1970s when he was working for the publisher *Champ Libre*, created *Climats Éditions*, headquartered at Castelnau-le-Lez. At the outset, it was a small-scale operation, with offices at the home of Martin and his wife, Françoise. One day, completely by chance, Alain found a short text on Orwell's essays that I had written about ten years earlier for the journal *Critique*, and of which we both had only a vague memory. This essay had been rejected at the time by Jean Piel—the journal's editor—on the grounds that it was of dubious political orthodoxy. Martin, who found the little text interesting and relevant, decided to publish a few hundred copies, asking me only for a brief afterward. Thus was born, in 1995, *Orwell, anarchiste Tory*. It goes without saying that, for Alain, this publication was primarily a gesture of friendship and a way of symbolically marking the occasion. I played along because I was convinced that this first book would also be my last and that, once the parentheses had been closed, I could return to the important things in life—which, as far as I was concerned, did not include writing books and giving talks.

But against all expectations and entirely by word of mouth, that little book ended up striking a chord. If I remember correctly, the turning point was a review in *Le Canard enchaîné*, written in the combative prose of Jean-Luc Porquet.[xxv] From that point on, one thing led to another in a way that I can't quite reconstruct. All the books I've subsequently *had* to write—with a gun to my head—began in circumstances at least as arbitrary—and extraordinary—as the first. Looking back, the only common denominator connecting these circumstances was Martin's mysterious shadow. If it were up to me, I would never have written another line. I much prefer the pleasures of soccer, friendship, and Montpellier's beaches. Every time I find myself in an office with a punishing computer, I feel that I've been trapped yet again by a cruel torturer—who also happens to be my friend, Alain Martin. [. . .]

RADIO LIBERTAIRE: Several different sensibilities seem to dwell within you, Jean-Claude Michéa. I must ask: politically, how do you situate yourself?

MICHÉA: Yes, you're right. I must be built like a Russian doll! I would define myself, first, as a "socialist" in the sense that the word still had in the early nineteenth century, in the work of Pierre Leroux[xxvi] or the young Engels, before he was contaminated by Marx's progressive teleology. In other words, I remain convinced that there is nothing utopian about defending the idea of a classless society, founded on the traditional values of gift-giving, mutual aid, and *philia* (to use the Greek term for all forms of reciprocal benevolence). I am, consequently, decidedly hostile to any project that would "modernize" or "rationalize" human existence and, in one way or another, promote a calculating egotism and purely antagonistic form of rivalry. As a sports lover, I know that positive and friendly forms of emulation are possible in life.

Next, I would define myself—and this is obviously not incompatible with my first point—as a radical democrat. In other words, as someone who thinks that democracy cannot be equated with the representative system.[2]

---

2. The first liberals were perfectly aware of this fundamental distinction. And they still had the intellectual honesty to acknowledge it. Sieyès, for instance, wrote: "Citizens can place their trust in a few in their midst. Without alienating their rights, they assign the exercise [of these rights to others]. It is for the common utility that they name representatives far more capable than themselves of knowing the general interest and interpreting in this way their will. Another way of exercising one's right to formulate the law is to participate immediately in its making. Such immediate participation is what characterizes true democracy. Mediated participation refers to representative government" (Speech of September 7, 1789). We note that the foundational principle of the representative regime was, from the beginning, a capability granted to an elite to "interpret" the people's will in its stead, better than it could itself. Just as any macho guy knows that a woman who says "no" really means "yes," so a modern European leader knows that the people's "no" is a "yes" that has misunderstood itself—and that, consequently, there is no point in paying attention to it and that it is absurd to trouble the

The latter leads inexorably to dispossessing the people of any real sovereignty and handing over power to a caste of *professional* politicians benefiting from the technical assistance of self-proclaimed "experts." The referendum on the European Constitution[xxvii] offers a perfect illustration of this model. In representative (or liberal) systems, referenda represent a final remnant of the people's direct powers. Because the French people chose to unambiguously reject a treaty[xxviii] that sought to constitutionalize capitalism's key dogmas, nearly all the "people's representatives"—on the right and the left—decided that the popular will had to be blocked and that the treaty that had just been rejected implemented indirectly. This shows, once and for all, the true weight of the will of the people in liberal "democracies." One would have to be incredibly naïve to believe that, were the will of the people to threaten the capitalist system, the European nomenklatura would stand by and do nothing. Cohn-Bendit, member of the European Parliament, put it succinctly: "National referenda are inadequate tools for deciding European questions."[3]

If democracy means "government of the people, by the people, and for the people," it is clear that modern representative regimes are no more than an extremely impoverished and, in some cases, purely formal version of democracy. From a strictly philosophical standpoint, it would be more precise to define these regimes as "liberal oligarchies," to use a felicitous expression coined by Castoriadis, or even "elective aristocracies," if one prefers Rousseau's terminology.

That said, I would add that liberal oligarchies cannot be equated with dictatorships—as some far-left activists are increasingly inclined to assert, due notably to the influence of theorists like Alain Badiou[xxix]—Guy Debord's great contempt for his work is well known—or Parisian associations that

---

people for so little. Like Pascal Perrineau, we will describe as "populist" any alternative opinion on this question. Admittedly, this noble champion of liberalism believes that "the anti-capitalist far left should be banished just like the far right, including at the local level." See *Le Nouvel Observateur*, July 3, 2008. With such precautions, bad election surprises will surely become less frequent.

3. Whoever understands the essence of liberal logic will find certain political predictions childlike in their simplicity. If, for example, the Irish people (or any other) were to reject once again the Lisbon Treaty, it can be immediately asserted, with zero risk, that the European nomenklatura will quickly find the legal means to bypass it and impose its unilateral will.

are extreme and poorly educated enough to believe that the current French state is "fascist" or "racist." It would be absurd to deny that a liberal oligarchy guarantees its subjects—even as they are exposed to increasing abuse—personal freedoms of which North Koreans and Saudi Arabians can only dream. It is obviously a major political advantage to be able to talk here, among ourselves, without having to worry about the police randomly showing up and sending us to reeducation camps. Yet it would be just as absurd to maintain that, in liberal society, political power is really exercised by the people. As Debord wrote, the rights available to us are essentially those of the "human spectator." In other words, we are generally free to criticize the movie the system plays for us (which, for a troublemaking people, is no mean right). But we have no right to change the movie's plot, whether by voting for the right or for the left. On this matter, the referendum business should have convinced anyone who was still naïve enough to believe the contrary.

Yet even in the hypothesis that actual democratic institutions were established (which would require the complete abolition of corporate control over the media), a few unresolved questions would remain. It is at this level that the genuinely anarchist dimension of the problem—using "anarchism" in Orwell's sense—comes into focus. To grasp this point, one could, for example, draw on Pierre Clastres' analysis of so-called "primitive societies" in South America.[xxx] These societies are indeed extremely egalitarian (leaving aside the question of the status of women) and organize themselves in all kinds of ways—including ritual warfare with their neighbors—to prevent the emergence of a state and a political divide between dominators and dominated. Yet Clastres was forced to recognize that, even in such societies, one inevitably meets people whose obsessive need for admiration and obedience compels them to be "number one" (and because the social structures are egalitarian, it seems far more likely that this need is rooted in these individuals' *personal* stories).[4] Clastres was thus led to examine the various strategies that such societies use to tame the desire for power of ambitious narcissists and *neutralize* their most corrosive political effects.[5]

---

4. In traditional warrior societies, for example, the premature death of the father occurs frequently.

5. It is quite symptomatic that one of the most violent attacks against Clastres' anarchist anthropology comes from Emmanuel Terray (see "Une anthropologie politique?" in

In these situations, the political question does not simply concern the institutional mechanisms that make the collective exercise of power possible. The question, rather, is clearly moral and psychological—or, if you will, Nietzschean. It is a question that will *always* be asked by any society, even an egalitarian one, due to the existence of individuals who cannot exist on their own, but who have a constant need to be recognized, defy their peers, and try to dominate, exploit, or simply use other people. It was precisely this crucial question that Stendhal raised with remarkable insight in his *Mémoires d'un touriste* ("Memoirs of a Tourist") when critiquing the ideas of Charles Fourier[xxxi]—an author, incidentally, whom he admired greatly. This critique was not at all about the organization of phalansteries (on this point, Stendahl was rather amused and intrigued). What he objects to in Fourier is that, even in the hypothesis of a perfectly socialist society (presuming such an idea even makes sense), there will always be a "Robert Macaire" (a character who, in nineteenth-century French literature, is the prototype of the unscrupulous social climber) who manages to seize power and become president—or secretary general—of the association. (. . .)

I insist on this point because, from my perspective, it affects everything else. It is generally because people neglect this question or (more seriously) because they refuse to address it that most revolutions self-destruct or deviate from their initial goals. This was Orwell's thesis in *Animal Farm*. Remember how, at the novel's beginning, an animal revolution manages to get rid of the

---

L'Homme 110, April 1989), the former dean of Abidjan's Faculty of Letters (the white man always knows how to position himself), a major figure in "new Parisian radicalities" and the author, during his Stalino-Althusserian period, of a particularly nonsensical work entitled *Le Marxisme et les sociétés primitives* ("Marxism and Primitive Societies," Paris: Maspero, 1969). To those who might be surprised at the vehemence of this ideological attack against an anthropologist who gives the "desire for power" essential explanatory power, one must recommend the astonishing *Lettres à la fugitive* ("Letters to the Fugitive," Paris: Odile Jacob, 1988), which Terray wrote a year earlier, in the (very adolescent) hope that he might convince the woman who had just left him that she was wrong to prefer someone else. Once one realizes that *malicious jealousy* (a particularly pronounced form of egoism, which results in the subject preferring that the other be unhappy by his side rather than happy without him) is a classic form of the desire for power, Terray's visceral anti-anarchism becomes clearer, psychologically speaking. Rarely does one have such an opportunity to peer inside the mind of one of the liberal far left's main lesson-givers.

farm's owner, Mr. Jones. As soon as they have freed themselves, the animals decide, amidst general enthusiasm, to build a model socialist farm on which all animals will be equal. The problem is that a few animals—symbolized, in the novel, by the pigs—are not prepared to live in a society that is "free, egalitarian, and decent" (which is Orwell's definition of socialism). It is psychologically impossible for them to adapt to a world in which they no longer control other people's lives, make decisions for them, or are simply the center of attention. It is thus the pigs who, naturally, come up with the famous slogan that "all animals are equal, but some animals are more equal than others" (an expression that, if you think about it, is a great definition of "positive discrimination").[xxxii] At this moment, Orwell concludes, the revolution's fate is sealed: when no one stands up against the pigs' seizure of power (with "pigs" referring to anyone who *takes pleasure* in power, in every sense of the term), nothing can prevent class domination from reconstituting itself, albeit in historically unprecedented forms. In this wonderful political tale, we see that, for Orwell, the question of the will to power was not just a problem concerning the dominant class. It was as much—and perhaps even more so—a concern for revolutionary activists. A political organization is always a machine for conquering and exercising power and distributing positions, even when it is in the opposition. Consequently, it is logical and inevitable that, just like a lamp attracts moths, political parties attract "Robert Macaires."

This is where things get complicated, of course. For the problem would be fairly easy to resolve if the need to dominate others—which is the genuine psychological motivation of some "comrades"—always presented itself as such, in a visible and transparent manner, with childlike naiveté, as it were. It must not have been too difficult to have noticed Stalin's will to power from the outset, for instance—or since we are in Montpellier, that of Georges Frêche.[xxxiii] Such individuals have a relatively simple psyche. They are clearly seeking personal revenge for childhood experiences. The model with which they identify politically lies somewhere between Nero and Caligula. The consequences are perfectly clear: those who agree to support these individuals, to collaborate with them (or to have careers alongside them) have no moral excuse. They are either accomplices, blind devotees, or disgusting courtesans. Yet what complicates this issue is that, more often than not, the will to power manifests itself in far more subtle and indirect ways—to the point that the love of power almost always remains invisible even to those who are deeply motivated by it. One has only to consider the way in which public debate takes place in practical terms—at general assemblies, at organizational meetings—to immediately identify recurring behaviors that acquire their full meaning only in light of this analysis. The most classic forms of the infantile desire for prestige and autonomy are to be found, for instance, in the way some people (usually men) monopolize speech or speak just to hear themselves talk and draw attention to their precious egos. And yet, even at this elementary level, it is still quite rare for those who operate in these ways to have the slightest awareness of what is really at stake (leaving aside, obviously, the case of perverts).

But this is just the tip of the iceberg. In practice, the pathological need to always be centerstage and ensure one's ability to control others can assume far more complicated and troubling forms. This is precisely what led me, in my book, to describe the unexpected and often oblique paths (in this instance, psychoanalysis helped me greatly)[6] by which some individuals ultimately end up acquiring de facto control over a group or an organization

---

6. In *L'Empire du moindre mal*, I suggested that, alongside "paternalistic" forms of domination (which are very easy to identify: fantasizing about or staging the death of the father can be achieved by anyone with an Oedipus complex), there exist "maternalistic" forms of control that are far more difficult to recognize, if only because they are usually invisible to those who wield them. From this perspective, the oeuvre of Saint Francis of Assisi is particularly illuminating. Though the Franciscan order was supposed to embody absolute equality (rooted in Francis' desire to eradicate every trace of patriarchal domination, to the point of absolving Eve of any role in original sin), power games were gradually reintroduced through a curious "matriarchal" angle. For Saint Francis, according to Jacques Dalarun, "the only mode of government that can be reconciled with the fraternal principle is partial maternity. Francis' wide range of *gendered transgressions* have been listed elsewhere. He addresses Leon as a mother (*sicut mater*), is called 'dear mother' by Saint Pacific, dreams that he is a black hen struggling to gather her chicks beneath her wings, presents himself as a desert pauperess impregnated by a king and as the statue of a great lady whose metallic composition recall Nebuchadnezzar's dream, and is greeted as 'Lady Poverty'" (Jacques Dalarun, *François d'Assise ou le pouvoir en question. Principes et modalités du gouvernement dans l'ordre des Frères mineurs*, Brussels: De Boeck Université, 1999, p. 36). When one realizes that the theme of the "abbey as mother" is omnipresent in monastic literature, the time has come to consider what the far left's unconscious owes to Franciscan and monastic spirituality. On the psychoanalytic aspects of this issue, see Jean-Pierre Lebrun, "Une économie de l'arrière-pays," *Che vuoi?* 29 (2008) (the concept of *arrière-pays* or "backcountry" refers, for Lebrun, to the subject's original relationship with the mother in the pre-oedipal world).

without overtly violating its rules and, indeed, while still genuinely believing that their stifling interventions are nothing more than evidence of exemplary devotion to the cause. Daily experience provides plenty of evidence that these exhausting, maniacal, and quarrelsome individuals (who are usually past masters in the art of making others feel guilty), but who also, when necessary, can be charming and even charismatic, are generally just as dangerous, for the proper functioning of democracy in any community, as a Stalin or Georges Frêche.

It is at this level that my "anarchist" sensibility kicks in. I am convinced that, as long as no way can be found to neutralize the various manifestations of the will to power (institutional or otherwise) in a manner that is at least as intelligent as that of the Amazonian Indians described by Clastres, we are in danger of confronting the same political problems indefinitely. And the risk will grow greater and greater that the inevitable "Robert Macaires" will get the better of the collective desire for equality.

CHAPTER 6

The Unity of Liberalism

The following text is arguably Michéa's most important theoretical statement. In his earlier, more occasional pieces, he explored the themes of common decency, its destruction by experts, the central role of free-market liberalism in contemporary society, and the seduction of the left by liberalism. This essay brings these concerns together, by way of an historical argument. Michéa argues for the fundamental unity of liberalism—that is, the inseparability of political and cultural liberalism from economic liberalism—by showing that these two strands arose from a common historical root, specifically, the desire for a pacified society governed by a "value neutral" state that emerged in the wake of the religious wars of the seventeenth century. Michéa delivered an earlier version of this essay at a conference for philosophy teachers in Montpellier in January 2007. It later became the first chapter of his book, *L'Empire du Moindre Mal* (2007).

THERE IS LITTLE DOUBT that were Adam Smith or Benjamin Constant to return among us (which would raise the level of political debate considerably), they would find it very difficult to recognize their rosy view of liberalism in the *cross of the present*.[1] This would seem to be the reason the

---

1. Adam Smith's famous pin factory employed only ten workers. The author of *The Wealth of Nations* did not for a moment contemplate what it would mean, in practical terms, for

word "liberalism" is at present accompanied by such extraordinary intellectual confusion. For many, all that is needed is a distinction between "good" political and cultural liberalism and "bad" economic liberalism. Even the critique of the latter requires nuance, depending on whether one is dealing with "true liberalism," "neo-liberalism," or "ultra-liberalism." In what follows, my thesis at least has the merit of simplifying the question. I maintain that the historical trend that has profoundly transformed modern society must be understood as the logical realization (indeed, the truth) of the liberal philosophical project, as it has gradually defined itself since the seventeenth century, and especially since the Enlightenment. This amounts to asserting that the soulless world of contemporary capitalism constitutes the only historical form in which liberalism's original doctrine could, in practice, realize itself. Put differently, contemporary capitalism is *actually existing liberalism*. And we see this as much in liberalism's economic version, traditionally preferred by the right, as in its cultural and political version, the defense of which has become the specialty of the contemporary left, particularly the far left, that restless locus of modern spectacular culture.

In defending this thesis, which no doubt will meet with far from unanimous approval, some preliminary clarifications are needed. To speak of a "liberal logic" implies that one can distinguish the *intentions* of various classical authors from the political and civilizational effects that their systems of

---

pension funds and major transnational corporations—not to mention shell companies and the illicit economy—to rule the planet. On this point, Matthieu Amiech offers very interesting insights in a study of "The United States Before Major Industry," which appeared in the December 2006 issue of the journal *Notes & Morceaux choisis* (Éditions La Lenteur). [Translator's note: Michéa's reference to "rosy" liberalism and the "cross of the present" is an allusion to a theme in Hegel and Marx's writings. In his preface to the *Philosophy of Right* (1820), Hegel discusses a quote from Aesop, "*Hic Rhodus, hic saltus*" ("Rhodes is here, jump here"), as a way of emphasizing that reason displays itself in experience rather than abstractions. He observes that to recognize "reason as the rose in the cross of the present, and to find delight in it, is a rational insight which implies reconciliation with reality." This statement is interpreted as a critique of the view that the world is driven by obscure truths that are only understood by an initiated few—that is, a position associated with Rosicrucianism, an esoteric school of philosophy that adopted a rose or rosy cross as its symbol. Marx alluded to this passage from Hegel in *The Eighteenth of Brumaire of Louis Bonaparte* (1852).]

thought helped bring about in ways that were, in my view, inevitable. This exercise should not disorient liberals, given that many presumably agree with Adam Ferguson[i] that real social change is first and foremost the "the result of human action, but not the execution of any human design."[2] It is, in any case, an exercise as old as philosophy itself. After all, it is the method that Plato employed in *Gorgias* to unveil the issues at stake in sophism. Plato's critique, it will be recalled, unfolded in three stages. The first part of the dialogue introduces us to the axiomatics of Gorgias, who is, one might say, the Adam Smith of rhetoric. This initial sparring is followed by a critical examination of the views of Polus, a disciple of Gorgias who makes the most of the philosophical implications of the axiomatics that his master, for reasons of personal decency, was reluctant to draw out. This second moment shows us "actually existing rhetoric" in fourth-century BCE Athens. The dialogue concludes with an intervention by Callicles, a character who is necessarily imaginary in that he, for Plato, symbolizes everything that sophism *could* become were it to one day realize—tragically, for the polis—the possibilities inherent in its project. The implication of this conclusion is that while Gorgias cannot be conflated with Callicles, Gorgias is, in a sense, intellectually responsible for all the conclusions that a potential Callicles might draw from his postulates.

But to speak of a "liberal logic" also implies that, over and above the many authors associated with liberalism and their many specific disagreements, it is possible to deal with it as a school whose principles not only can but *must* be philosophically unified. Obviously, this is the point that many readers will have trouble conceding. For if I am right, it makes it much harder to contrast—as do many on the contemporary left and far left—political and cultural liberalism, defined as unlimited advances in rights and the constant liberalization of behavior, and economic liberalism, as if the emancipatory achievements of the former were essentially independent of the harm caused by the latter.

I am fully aware of the risk involved in this undertaking, which, in the history of ideas, arises whenever one attempts to define an "ism." This is

---

2. Adam Ferguson, *An Essay on the History of Civil Society*, 1767. See version available at the Liberty Fund's Online Library of Liberty, https://oll.libertyfund.org/titles /ferguson-an-essay-on-the-history-of-civil-society.

particularly true when the school in question has a pedigree extending over several centuries. Any attempt to shed light on a *philosophical logic* always entails an effort at conceptual reconstruction and thus a set of simplifications and interpretive choices that are anything but ideologically neutral. Needless to say, I take full responsibility for this position. I only hope that, in proceeding this way, I will not be accused of giving undue weight to liberalism's Callicles as opposed to its Poluses and Gorgiases.

A final, terminological difficulty must be addressed. In 1928, Carl Schmitt wrote that there is "absolutely no liberal politics, only a liberal critique of politics." If by "liberalism," one refers to a strictly *defensive* political posture—one that supports struggles for fundamental *democratic* freedoms wherever they are threatened, distorted, or abolished—then I obviously have no objection to "liberalism" thus defined. Even Orwell, when he happened to use the word in this very specific sense, did not hesitate to refer to the legacy of the "old liberals" of nineteenth-century England. But the liberalism that is debated at present represents a much more specific political ideal, and one of far greater philosophical scope. It refers to a project of radically transforming the human order, the implementation of which must necessarily rely on specific government policies. It is surely significant, from this perspective, that the terms "liberal ideas" and "liberalism" did not appear, at least in French, until *after* Thermidor, when Benjamin Constant published his *Des réactions politiques* (1797),[ii] a foundational text if there ever was one. Moreover, it was not until *after* 1815 that these terms permanently entered the political vocabulary, where they were for many years used to describe the parliamentary opposition on the left[iii] to the reactionary powers on the right. The *positive* project of a liberal society (and, consequently, of a "liberal government") would thus seem inseparable from the new ideological framework that was defined around the same time by Auguste Comte. How is it possible to establish a modern social order—that is, one consistent with the basic aspirations of a humanity that has reached its 'adult' stage—once it is acknowledged that the French Revolution had rendered impossible any return to the traditional Old Regime, except in purely imaginative terms? In recalling this point, I am, of course, not overlooking the first partial experiments with liberal government that occurred in France during the monarchy itself. (Notably, Laverdy and Maynon d'Invault's policies to deregulate the grain trade between 1764 and 1770,[iv] of which Diderot's critique, "Apology for

Abbey Galliani," remains instructive.)[3] Nor have I forgotten the first phase of the French Revolution and, in particular, the decisive roles played therein by the Allard Decree and the Le Chapelier Law.[v] Even, so, it was primarily as a *postrevolutionary project*—that is, one made possible by the old regime's definitive destruction—that philosophical liberalism became historically active, to the point that it is now, in our day, the dominant and perhaps sole dynamic political and civilizational principle—one that is transforming the West and, by extension, the entire planet. It is in this sense, and this sense only, that we use the term "liberalism."

The liberal doctrine did not make its historical entrance like a thunderclap disrupting a serene sky. Its inner logic acquires its full meaning only once it is understood as part of the Western modernizing project and the questions that define it. Not only is liberalism inseparable from this project; it is, in truth, its only coherent theoretical elaboration. Unlike the republican ideal, which continued to assign an important role to ancient virtues, or early socialism, with its ideas of morality and community, liberalism does not borrow any of its major claims from earlier philosophical traditions. Contrary to the absurd view, particularly widespread on the left, that liberal policies are inherently "conservative" or "reactionary" (terms that—in a great historical irony—mostly date back to Constant), liberalism must be seen as *the modern ideology par excellence*. To lay bare this logic, it is thus essential to briefly revisit the origins of the modern project itself.

To understand the nature of modern liberalism, one must be careful to avoid anachronistic or ethnocentric illusions (a methodological precaution that is often neglected). One must resist the temptation to explain foundational moments in terms of ideological frameworks that emerged *because of* these moments and that primarily serve a self-justifying role. Consequently, one should not assume that the European modernization project was an *historically necessary* stage in the progress of reason (or in "the development of productive forces"), nor that this movement was inevitable and irreversible, turning it into a trend that no civilization had the right or ability to oppose.

---

3. Diderot's text was reedited in 1998 and introduced with a remarkable preface by Michel Barrillon, entitled "Diderot dans la première bataille du libéralisme économique" (Diderot in the First Battle over Economic Liberalism). *Apologies: Apologie de l'abbé Galiani & Lettre apologétique de l'abbé Raynal à M. Grimm* (Paris: Agone, 1998).

Once this naïve mythology has been deactivated (though it is essential to modernity's self-understanding), a genuinely philosophical examination of liberalism becomes possible. We can at last stop coming up with endless "roadblocks" and "obstacles" that supposedly cause "premodern" societies to deviate from the "normal" path to civilization. Instead, we can ask what "fortuitous concurrence of many foreign causes" (as Rousseau puts it) led to the *Western exception*, rendering intelligible the historically unprecedented, though not necessarily exemplary, path that, beginning in the seventeenth century, European societies chose to take.

In the complex array of contingent causes, and without overlooking the historical specificities of earlier times (such as the theological-political problem bequeathed by the conflict between the Empire and the Church),[4] a key role must be assigned to the invention of the natural sciences, which depended on a wide range of political and intellectual circumstances and constitute one of the modern West's most distinctive features.[5] The crucial importance of the *scienza nuova* lies in the fact that it rendered the modern project of making human beings "masters and owners of nature" philosophically conceivable. Yet it is above all as a new symbolic authority—that is, as a *scientific ideal* challenging the Church's authority—that Galilean physics produced its two most important effects. First, it provided the concept of progress with a robust metaphysical foundation (a point that Pascal also recognized).[6] Second, it promoted the belief—whose implications were first explored by Hobbes and Spinoza—that the extension of the Galilean method to the study of human nature could make possible a "social physics," which, in turn, would create the conditions for an approach to political problems

---

4. See Pierre Manent, *An Intellectual History of Liberalism*, trans. Rebecca Balinski (Princeton: Princeton University Press, 1995 [1987]), chapter 1.

5. On this topic, one will find particularly stimulating philosophical insights in Olivier Rey, *Itinéraire de l'égarement* (Paris: Seuil, 2003).

6. Hence Blaise Pascal's efforts, in his preface to the *Treatise on the Vacuum*, to draw a preventative demarcation line between "subjects that fall under the senses and under reasoning," that is, in which the authority of the moderns will henceforth prevail, and all the other "matters" (including, of course, theology) that cannot be conceptualized in terms of the category of progress. Pascal is thus one of the first philosophers to be both modern and anti-modern, or, alternatively, one of the first modern critics of modernity.

that would, at long last, be "scientific" and "impartial."[7] The implications of this remarkable paradigm were limitless.

The intersection of this new conception of reason as perpetual progress with the discovery of America (another event that was clearly accidental) results in a remarkable series of effects. Whereas for Strabo and Herodotus the encounter with other civilizations implied geographic coexistence, such encounters would now be conceived in terms of historical succession. It is interesting to note, moreover, that Adam Smith was one of the first thinkers to take advantage of the new model, proposing, on the basis of the anthropological evidence available to him, a systematic theory positing that humanity develops through "stages," with economic growth serving as foundation and motor of this process.[8] If it is agreed that one should not speak of "modernity" except where people have begun to view their way of life as no more than a specific historical *moment* within a broader historical evolution,[9] it is undeniable that most of the philosophical tools deployed

---

7. Auguste Comte would later write: "When politics becomes a positive science, the public will necessarily grant publicists the same trust in political matters as it now gives astronomers in astronomical matters, doctors in medical matters, etc." (*Séparation générale entre les opinions et les désirs*, 1819). This is the metaphysical foundation of the contemporary authority of "experts," which has become ubiquitous.

8. See Christian Marouby, *L'Économie de la nature. Essai sur Adam Smith et l'anthropologie de la croissance* (Paris: Seuil, 2004). It was by taking as his privileged reference point the anthropological material available from the Iroquois and Hurons of the Five Nations confederacy that Adam Smith was led to imagine a "necessary" trend that led all human societies from the "hunters' stage" to "commercial society," by way of "pastoral society" and the "agricultural stage." Marouby carefully identifies the deviations from empirical observation and logical reasoning upon which Smith's thesis depends, as well as the anthropological postulates upon which *The Wealth of Nations* is based (along with all of contemporary economic "science," as it hardly need be point out).

9. See C. A. Bayly, *The Birth of the Modern World, 1780–1914: Global Connections and Comparisons* (Malden, MA: Blackwell, 2004, 10–11): "In the first place, this book accepts the idea that an essential part of being modern is thinking you are modern. Modernity is an aspiration to be 'up with the times.' It was a process of emulation and borrowing. It seems difficult to deny that, between about 1780 and 1914, increasing numbers of people decided that they were modern, or that they were living in a modern world, whether they liked it or not . . . It was also the modern age because poorer and subordinated people around the world thought that they could improve their status

by the modern imagination were first formulated and circulated during the Galilean revolution.

Though the scientific ideal played a key role in the formation of the modern imagination, it did not trigger the modernization process. The Galilean revolution could be quickly invoked as a model for resolving a political problem only because this problem had no historical precedent. In this "fortuitous concurrence of many foreign causes," the most decisive catalyst for the modern response to the crisis of European society was (as contemporaries saw it) the traumatic experience of the period's long and extensive wars.

In his classic study on the problem of war and peace from Machiavelli to Hobbes, Georges Livet maintains that "all texts from this period long for peace."[10] The dramatic wars that, throughout the sixteenth and seventeenth centuries, defined the contours of people's daily lives had two profoundly original characteristics. First, the introduction of new weapons and corresponding tactical and strategic innovations (such as the dominant role of the infantry) made conflict far more deadly and devastating than ever before. Second and most importantly, a form of war emerged in the late sixteenth century that was entirely new, at least in terms of intensity:[11] *ideological civil war*, the main form of which, during this period, was *religious war*. This does not mean that every conflict contributing to Europe's disorder was the result of civil war. But the latter was always in the background, so that even the seemingly more traditional wars that pitted the great powers of the time against one another—such as the Thirty Years War in the first half of the seventeenth century—were always overdetermined, in their origins as well as their specific trajectory, by the logic of this new form of conflict. It is well known, of course, that civil war does not simply determine how people fight. It affects, far more radically, the very nature of human relationships. Like Hobbes, Pascal considered civil war *the greatest evil*[12]—an expression also

---

and life-chances by adopting tokens of this mythical modernity, whether they be fob watches, umbrellas, or new religious texts."

10. Georges Livet, ed., *Guerre et paix de Machiavel à Hobbes* (Paris: Armand Colin, 1972), 50.

11. Early on, Plato made the distinction between *stasis* (civil war) and *polemos* (war against foreigners).

12. Pascal's expression is in obvious allusion to Erasmus (who, in *The Education of a Christian Prince*, observed that "war is the source of all misfortunes to the state"). It must be noted

found, in the same period, in Nicole's *Moral Essays*.[vi] Whereas traditional war strengthened communal bonds, civil war, by definition, tended to bring about the most de-socializing divisions imaginable. Those who set parents, neighbors, and friends against one another risk undoing the traditional cycle of solidarities based on gifts and counter-gifts—cycles that are the essence of "primary sociality" (as Alain Caillé dubs it) and the essential matrix of daily relations of trust, without which no lasting historical community is possible.[13] Corneille, whose work is a celebration of warrior and heroic virtues, does not hesitate to define civil war as the "reign of crime."

This *dread of civil war* most likely explains why seventeenth and eighteenth-century philosophers (particularly those of Protestant origin and inclinations) almost always described the "state of nature" as characterized either originally or derivatively by *the war of all against all*. Clearly, this was a philosophical transposition of the contemporary condition of civil war, pushed hypothetically—like any thought experiment—to an imaginary limit, at which individuals, assumed to be free of any allegiance to others, have no other value to defend than their own lives, in a world suffused with defiance and the fear of death. This hyperbolic formulation of a political problem contains its own solution.[14] To borrow again from Rousseau, it is only when

---

that Erasmus already recognized the central role of civil war ("What term should we apply, then, when Christians engage in battle with Christians, since they are united by so many bonds to each other? What shall we say when on account of a mere title, on account of a personal grievance, on account of a stupid and youthful ambition, a war is waged with every cruelty and carried on during many years?").

13. On the nature and scope of primary sociality in the early modern period, the standard work is the book by the historian Nathalie Zemon Davis, *The Gift in Sixteenth-Century France* (Oxford: Oxford University Press, 2000).

14. At a metaphysical level, Cartesian doubt must in a similar way assume a hyperbolic form to imperiously found the possibility of the cogito. It is worth noting that modern solutions must always be deduced from philosophical situations that are not only negative and often desperate (such as absolute doubt and total violence), but also fictitious (the dreaming and evil genius hypotheses, in the case of Descartes; the state of nature, in that of Hobbes; the myth of original bartering, for economists). It is by no means the least paradoxical aspect of a society that seeks (for the first time in history) to be completely "realistic" and procedural—founded on the purely mechanical protocols of law and the market—that it requires such foundational myths.

the obstacles resulting from the endless rage of mimetic rivalries "show their power of resistance to be greater than the resources at the disposal of each individual for his maintenance in that state" that these same individuals prove capable of understanding that "the human race would perish unless it changed its *manner of existence*" (*The Social Contract*, book 1).

The fear of violent death, suspicion of one's fellow man, the rejection of ideological fanaticism, and the desire for a calm and peaceful existence: here we have the historical horizon of the new "*manner of existence*" for which moderns, from this point on, would constantly strive. From this perspective, it is one and the same thing to establish a society promoting the progress of reason and to define the conditions that would allow humanity to end war once and for all ("the conditions of Society, or of Humane Peace," as Hobbes solemnly puts it at the beginning of *De Cive*). This configuration, which is inextricably political and psychological, clarifies the central role played in modern Western culture by the repression of everything related to death and a deeply rooted sense of the horror and absurdity of war, which is seen as the worst of all evils. This feeling, which is essential to liberalism's genesis, was forged in a particularly terrible prism: that of ideological civil war, whether in the form of unbridled religious fanaticism or revolutionary terror. This also explains why the only "war" that remained conceivable, in this philosophical framework, was that of a war between man and nature, waged with the weapons of science and technology. Moderns would use this displaced war to redirect energies previously devoted to wars between men to work and industry. Christopher Lasch, with his usual insight, grasped this point perfectly. The modern belief in progress, he argued, must not be understood as a "secularization of the Kingdom of God." Fundamentally, progress is evidence of a prosaic aspiration to live at last in peace, free from the deadly turmoil of history, and to devote oneself (according to Adam Smith) to "improving [one's] condition" by calmly tending to *one' own business*.[15] In this sense, the modern ideal of progress was, at its inception, rooted

---

15. Christopher Lasch, *The True and Only Heaven: Progress and its Critics* (New York and London: W. W. Norton, 1991) 52, 54. This weariness and profound desire for peace bring to mind the curious lines that Benjamin Constant wrote in an unfinished project for a preface to his novel *Adolphe*: "I wanted, with *Adolphe*, to depict one of the main moral illnesses of our age: the fatigue, anxiety, absence of strength, and perpetually analytic

far less in a longing for some earthly paradise than in a desire to escape at any price from the hell of ideological civil war—to extricate oneself from the "greatest of all evils."

Once one has recognized the ideological pacification of society as the key issue, it becomes possible to consider the modern project's absolute originality and the anthropological principles it presupposes, as well as the profound unity of the two philosophical frameworks that liberalism will use to take this project to its logical conclusion. First, let us consider its originality. In a remarkable essay, Éric Desmons shows that the ability to sacrifice one's life for one's community when circumstances demand it was always the *avowed* morality of traditional societies—that is, societies that prioritized face-to-face relations and thus feelings of *shame* and *honor*. From the primitive warrior to the ancient Roman citizen (remembering, as Quentin Skinner reminds us, that the republican ideal never fits perfectly into the modern paradigm),[vii] from the Christian martyr to the medieval knight, this permanent disposition to sacrifice was, for better or worse, the basis for self-esteem and the warrant of eternal glory, whether sacred or profane.[16]

Like Hegel's slave—who, at the decisive moment, feared for his biological life and preferred it to the honor of a heroic death—Western modernity appears to be the first civilization in history to have made *self-preservation* the primary and even sole concern of the rational individual and the foundational ideal of the societies that individuals form with their peers. Constant insists on this point: "The aim of the moderns is the enjoyment of security in private pleasures; and they call liberty the guarantees accorded by institutions to these pleasures."[17] There is no better way to express the idea that the liberty celebrated by liberals, unlike the obscure liberty of republicans, was

---

state of mind that results in every feeling have an ulterior motive, so that each feeling withers at birth." Adolphe's moral illness is clearly the liberal syndrome itself.

16. Éric Desmons, *Mourir pour la patrie?* (Paris: Presses universitaires de France, 2001). Desmons provides a fascinating analysis of the two-part movement whereby Saint Augustine first transferred the love for one's city that was expected of ancient citizens to the city of God, and then how the nations born in the late Middle Ages reclaimed the Augustinian ideal of the Christian martyr to infuse a new patriotism.

17. Benjamin Constant, *The Liberty of Ancients Compared with that of Moderns* (1819, available online at https://oll.libertyfund.org/titles/constant-the-liberty-of-ancients -compared-with-that-of-moderns-1819).

initially just *another word* for a peaceful—and, if possible, enjoyable—life and a desire for an historically well-deserved rest. In 1755, Francis Hutcheson called it "the calm desire for wealth."

The philosophical habit of prefacing political theory with a supposedly objective (or "materialistic") description of human nature—a habit we owe to Hobbes—can be explained by this desire for pacification. The purpose of this practice is to declare that the anthropological conditions necessary for peace are valid from the outset, by inscribing them into one's philosophical premises. Yet according to the prevailing philosophical view of the time, the two main causes of warmongering were great men's desire for glory and man's claim to be the sole possessor of truth and goodness (which was seen as the cause of civil war), allowing him to sit in judgement over others. On this basis, it is easy to lay out the answers that moderns concocted in response to the question of civil peace. First, one must assume that the desire for glory and the cult of heroic virtues are simply masks for pride and self-interest. This argument exemplifies what Paul Bénichou[viii] called "the demolition of heroes," in which La Rochefoucauld and Port-Royal played a major role. Second, one must demonstrate that human convictions about the true, the beautiful, and the good are not universal and amount to little more than habits and tastes. Phrased in more contemporary terms, these two arguments consist in a *philosophy of suspicion* (deconstructionism) and *cultural relativism* (multiculturalism). Together, they form the two pillars of the post-modernist temple. The emphasis that, since the seventeenth century, moderns have placed on the philosophical necessity of considering men, not as they should be, but *as they are* ("to treat of human vice and folly geometrically," as Spinoza put it) should fool no one. Appearances to the contrary, this view has much less to do with a hard-won lucidity acquired through the new "human sciences" than with theoretical constraints internal to the project of modernity itself. Ultimately, it consists of an anthropology of weariness (an early iteration of the "never again" mindset), which is eager to define what individuals *must be* so as to activate the mechanisms that will devalue and neutralize the two most bellicose passions: the claim to possess the truth and the claim to embody virtue. Within this very framework, human nature will be interpreted in a way that emphasizes the bourgeois model, conveniently symbolized by the merchant, whom the entire period sees as plain, peaceful, and inoffensive. From this perspective, it can be said that the ideological effects of modernity only began to manifest themselves once (to borrow Marx's play on words) "civil society" (*die burgerlische Gesellschaft*) came to be thought of as "bourgeois society."

It is now possible to present, in its core logic, the parallel movement that led philosophical liberalism to propose the utopia of a rational society, grounding its pacified existence exclusively upon the impersonal structures of the market and law.[18] Whatever solution is reached, the approach remains the same. It always consists in discovering or imagining the mechanisms (that is, the system of weights and counterweights, conceived on the model of equilibrium theory in physics) that are capable, entirely on their own, of engendering political order and harmony, without ever appealing to individual virtue. This renunciation is, admittedly, of little psychological import, given that for the modern mind, "virtue" (whether it draws its official inspiration from religious faith, custom, morality, the civic ideal, or the spirit of giving) is now seen as little more than hypocrisy or self-deception, a constant source of ideological dispute and conflict that constantly threatens to deregulate the subjectless process needed to establish a peaceful society.

In proposing this thesis, it is not, of course, my intention to deny the different philosophical emphases that make it possible to distinguish a liberalism of rights (or political liberalism) from a a liberalism of markets (or economic liberalism). From the standpoint of the history of ideas, it is crucial to keep this distinction in mind. But from a philosophical standpoint, it must be recognized that, most of the time, these parallel versions of liberalism are connected in practice. Moreover, to escape their respective contradictions, each is driven by a structural necessity to seek theoretical support from the other. Marx captured this need in his famous reformulation of the revolutionary motto: "Liberty, Equality, Bentham."

If, at its origins, liberalism was a philosophical ledger with two columns,

---

18. [TR: Here and throughout the essay, Michéa refers to "*le Marché et le Droit*." *Droit* is difficult to translate as it means both "law" and "right." In the sense of "right," it means both individual rights (i.e., the right to free speech) and an order based on well-defined procedural rules (close to the German notion of *Recht*). *Droit* in this sense also overlaps with the idea of "justice," particularly as defined in the deontological ethics of Immanuel Kant and John Rawls. Depending on the context, *droit* has thus been translated alternatively as "law," "right," or "justice."]

it matters little whether, when explaining its principles, one starts with its strictly political dimension or its strictly economic one. Even so, it would seem logical, from a pedagogical perspective, to start with *political* liberalism, since unlike its economic counterpart, it addresses the modern political problem directly, by theorizing an extremely precise power mechanism that did not initially assign a metaphysical role to the market.

The fundamental axiom of political liberalism is well known. If the main reason for human violence is the conviction of some individuals (or associations of individuals, like a church) that they alone possess the truth about the good life, then members of a society cannot live in peace unless the authority responsible for organizing their coexistence is philosophically neutral—that is, if it refrains, as a matter of principle, from imposing a particular conception of the good life. In a liberal society, everyone is thus free to adopt the lifestyle they consider most appropriate to their conception of duty (if they have one) and happiness. There is, however, one and only one caveat: these choices must be compatible with the freedom of others. This requirement implies the existence—over and above the individuals engaged in their separate pursuits of happiness and the good life—of an authority responsible for harmonizing these competing freedoms and that, through the definition of shared rules, is uniquely capable of limiting the scope of personal freedoms. This authority is the law (the state, according to this perspective, having no other function than that of ensuring the law's effective application). In liberal terminology, the principle that guides law is justice. Once again, Constant formulates the matter with exemplary clarity: "Let them confine themselves to being just. We shall ourselves assume responsibility for being happy."

The liberal thesis of the *primacy of justice over the good* (as British and American philosophers put it)[19] must be properly understood. If, for political liberalism, right constitutes the ultimate regulative authority that must replace all others, it does so not in the manner of older normative mechanisms, such as custom, morality, religion, or republican virtue, which liberalism finds arbitrary and stifling. The "theory of justice" on which the new authority of right is based has little in common with what traditional phi-

---

19. See Michael Sandel, *Liberalism and the Limits of Justice* (New York: Cambridge University Press, 1998 [1982]).

losophy meant by this term. It no longer concerns itself with defining ideas or grasping essences—that is, with expressing some "truth," whatever its metaphysical status. Rather than a "theory of justice," it would be far more appropriate to speak of a theory of "adjudication" or "adjustment." This theory seeks to develop the most efficient institutional combinations possible. It calculates as accurately as it can a system of weights and counterweights ("checks and balances," in the British and American tradition) that will preserve the balance between rival freedoms by imposing minimal demands—the lowest possible existential taxes. As a matter of principle, a liberal theory of justice should not even consider the best way to live. To the contrary, it must confine itself to defining the technical conditions of a *modus vivendi*, one that will be imposed on a multitude of perpetually moving elementary particles to reduce the risk of shocks and collisions to an absolute minimum. In practice, this means that liberal justice should resemble traffic laws. How these particles might view their duty or happiness is a question that must be banished from political philosophy. Paraphrasing Heidegger's famous remark about science, it could be said that for liberals, the just state—or, in any case, the state that asks the least of us—is a state *that cannot think*. A state without ideas—or, as liberals would say, without ideology—takes pride, through a kind of inverted Platonism, in never inquiring into the best way to live or make use of one's freedom. Taken to its logical extreme, this state without ideas or values (which forbids itself from judging and hence from even considering issues that are not technical) should no longer even understand itself as a "government of men." It represents, to invoke Saint-Simon's famous distinction, a pure "administration of things," requiring no genuine political convictions, but rather the competence of "experts" and shrewd managers. No one has expressed this idea of absolute value neutrality,[20] which lies at the heart of the liberal project, better than Immanuel Kant, who observed, in *Perpetual Peace*, that, were a perfect legislative system to exist, the mechanisms of law would alone suffice to ensure peaceful coexistence—"even for a race of devils."

Yet it is at this point that political liberalism's troubles really begin. Except for the Marquis de Sade (whom Lasch, Lacan, and Pasolini, each

---

20. [TR: "Value neutrality" has been systematically used to translate what Michéa calls "*neutralité axiologique*."]

for their own reasons, saw as the dark side of Enlightenment philosophy),[21] none of the early liberals would have celebrated the advent of a "race of dev-ils" as liberty's logical culmination. The problem is that nothing in liberal-ism's political logic protects it from such an outcome. As we have seen, the authority of liberal right is legitimate only to the extent that it limits itself to adjudicating competing liberties, without appealing to any criteria other than liberty itself, which can generally be reduced to the imperative of not harming others. The latter criterion, which is of crucial importance to liber-als, proves difficult to implement in practice, as John Stuart Mill made clear in the mid-nineteenth century. By what right indeed can a liberal society, for example, prevent an individual from harming himself? (It is well known that many liberals, from Milton Friedman to Daniel Cohn-Bendit,[ix] have called for the decriminalization of drugs). How is one to decide whether criticiz-ing (or mocking) a religion does not interfere with the freedom of believ-ers? Conversely, to what extent do certain religious teachings about women and homosexuality threaten "minority rights"? Faced with these questions, which can be extended indefinitely, liberalism finds itself in a difficult posi-tion. If it forbids itself, when deciding such matters, from drawing on meta-physical ideas (such as salvation, common decency, or human dignity) then it is destined, due to the constant evolution of social mores (a process that moderns believe is "natural"), to encounter an increasing number of "social problems" that cannot be coherently resolved within liberalism's narrowly technical framework. Liberalism's logical tendency is thus to move gradu-ally towards mass acceptance of every possible behavior imaginable.

Consider, for instance, the exemplary case of prostitution. If the only criterion for distinguishing legal from illegal acts[22] is individual *consent*, then by what right indeed could anyone deny that prostitution, so long as it is practiced voluntarily, is *a job like any other*, one that will probably be

---

21. Christopher Lasch, *The Culture of Narcissism: American Life in an Age of Diminishing Expectations* (New York: W. W. Norton, 1979); Jacques Lacan, "Kant with Sade" in *Écrits: The First Complete Edition in English* (New York, W.W. Norton & Co, 2006), and, of course, *Salò, or the 120 Days of Sodom*, Pier Paolo Pasolini's unbearable cinematic master-piece, filmed in 1975, which shows Sade's world (which was, for a time, one of the far left's "revolutionary" reference points) reaching its apogee in fascism's terminal moment.

22. See Michela Marzano, *Je consens donc je suis . . . Éthique de l'autonomie* (Paris: Presses universitaires de France, 2006).

classified under the economically promising category of "home care"? From the moment that one refuses to base one's opinion on a critique of the commodification of the body (since it is a partial and anti-capitalist philosophy), it is hard to disagree with the liberal legal scholar Daniel Borillo, who concludes: "The state should not promote a specific sexual morality lest it become itself immoral. Only adults can determine what is appropriate for them . . . . By what right can the state prevent an individual from having sexual relations in exchange for compensation and making such conduct a regular job?"[23] This irrefutable legal argument, presuming one holds liberalism's foundational dogmas as sacred, provides liberal "feminists" with ideological armor, especially when, like Marcela Iacub and Catherine Millet,[x] they assert: "As women and feminists, we oppose those who would tell women what they must do with their bodies and sexuality. We oppose those who would repress prostitution rather than seeking to destigmatize it, so that those who have chosen what they consider an authentic profession can practice it under the best conditions possible." This minimalistic style of reasoning can, of course, be extended to *every possible demand*, including those that are totally opposed to common sense and "common decency," as examples from the United States regularly demonstrate. One has only to be a clever practitioner of "deconstruction," a technique that, due to its seductive conceptual simplicity, is now available to anyone, even the average reader of *Libération*. Deconstruction makes it possible, without much intellectual effort, to transform every ethical scruple into another arbitrary and historically determined taboo.

There will, of course, always be people—or associations of people—who believe that each new "advance" in the realm of rights threatens their freedom by *hurting* their feelings and *damaging* their "self-esteem"—which, by general consensus, has become one of freedom's main ingredients. This infinite

---

23. Ibid., 145. It is worth noting that Daniel Borillo, due to his very liberal suspicion of "collectively decreed norms" (see his interview in *Marianne*, February 10, 2007), displays the prudence of a positivist in maintaining that the differences between "male" and "female" rest on clever metaphysical constructs. "The legal scholar should not be concerned with such things"—a point that explodes, incidentally, the principle of parity between the sexes. It is no surprise that Jack Lang was eager to write the preface of the latest book by this Milton Friedman of law.

extension of individual rights (or the liberalization of behavior) inevitably winds up unleashing a *new war of all against all*, driven by a dialectic in which provocation produces stubbornness. This time around the war is waged in the courtroom and through lawyers.[24] The advocates of "political correctness" have become, as everyone knows, its professional soldiers. And because the self-proclaimed neutrality of liberal law prevents it from turning to philosophy for help in dealing with these contradictory claims, no other solution is available than a passive acknowledgement of the constantly shifting balance of power between different opinions. Today, we ban tobacco; tomorrow, we may legalize drugs; and, soon, we will most likely ban tobacco and legalize drugs. Of course, the strange climate that will then prevail, favoring ever-more frequent legal crusades (characterized by the disturbing pleasures of secret denunciation, generalized surveillance, and the inevitable extension of censorship, monitoring, and prohibitions), would seem the exact opposite of the peaceful and tolerant world imagined by liberalism's founders. What would Montesquieu, Constant, and Tocqueville have thought of ACT UP,[xi] the *Chiennes de garde*, or the *Indigènes de la République*?[25] Yet it is precisely in the name of their theory of law and freedom that this fanatical need to legalize, exclude, and prohibit is now expanding without restraint. Once the liberal state has become, as Pierre Manent puts it,[xii] "institutionalized skepti-

---

24. As even the most forgettable American television series reminds us, the lawyer is, with the entrepreneur, liberalism's emblematic figure.

25. The "value neutrality" demanded by liberalism often has curious consequences. There is no logical reason to prohibit racism, for pedagogical purposes, if one has reason to believe that using racism is a politically effective way to achieve the equality of rights (this is the principle of all forms of "affirmative action"). This is why Houria Bouteldja, the spokesperson of *Indigènes de la République*, could calmly declare, on Fréderic Taddeï's show on France 3, the TV station—without eliciting the slightest political or media reaction—that the first condition for "reeducating the rest of Western society" was to consider "whites" as "less than dogs" (see *Marianne*, June 30, 2007). This is the perfect moment to make a point about vocabulary, which is ignored by most political and media professionals: "*indigene*," in French, does not mean "savage," "primitive," or "colonized," but "to be originally from a place" (it is an exact synonym of "native populations"). The term's antonym is "*allogene*," which means, conversely, "to be from somewhere else." One does not have to have read Orwell to guess what hides behind the political and media decision to require the public to use a word in a way that is directly contrary to its true meaning.

cism," there can be no coherent firewall preventing the methodical dismantling of what Orwell called "common decency"—or even common sense.

Is it even necessary to recall that it was precisely this crucial question— that of the difference between a *just* society and a *decent* society[26]—that gave rise, in the early nineteenth century, to the first socialist critique of liberalism? Socialism originated in the lived experience of the working classes confronting the first forms of dehumanization engendered by the new industrial order and the boundless egoism of its new proprietors. Its guiding principle was that a society which in practice[27] encourages behavior that is indecent and clearly op- posed to human dignity could not be morally acceptable, meaning that there was no sense in defining it as "just." The early socialists believed that it was necessary for the community to deliberately organize itself to achieve a decent standard of living and a minimal degree of solidarity, without which the rule of law, whatever its advantages, would be deprived of any human content.

It is especially interesting to analyze the answers to these problems pro- posed by Frédéric Bastiat in 1848.[28] In the history of French liberalism, Bastiat occupies a key place for at least two reasons. First, he was one of the first liberals to engage overtly with the early socialist critique. ("Our adver- saries," he wrote, "are the communists, the Fouriérists, the Owenists, Cabet, Louis Blanc, Pierre Leroux, and many others.")[xiii] Even more importantly, Bastiat was (with his "economist" friends) one of the movement's first ideo- logues to embrace, without the slightest reservation,[29] the dialectical unity of liberalism's two facets. Bastiat thus heralds the future philosophical course of *actually existing liberalism.*

---

26. On this distinction, which originates with Orwell, see Avishai Margalit, *La Société décente* (Castelnau-le-lez: Climats, 1999/Paris: Champs-Flammarion, 2007).

27. It is known that, for early socialists, the critique of liberalism always began with the contradiction between the formal principles of law and reality (hence the distinction between "formal freedom" and "real freedom"). Leaving aside the political problems it raised, this philosophical stance opened the door to the social question. These days, however, left intellectuals see reality as the exception that confirms the (preferably "sociological") theory.

28. Frédéric Bastiat, "Justice et fraternité" (*Journal des économistes*, June 15, 1848). [Trans: For this quote and subsequent ones from this text, I have drawn on the translation available at https://www.econlib.org/book-chapters/chapter-chapter-4-justice-and-fraternity/]

29. This was not the case, as is well known, for Constant, Tocqueville, or even Adam Smith.

Yet what immediately strikes the contemporary reader is how carefully Bastiat explains that, far from defending the calculating egoism denounced by the "socialist schools," he personally embraces the same ideal of a decent and solidarity-based community as his adversaries: "Are we to be reduced to speaking of ourselves? In that case, let our actions be subjected to close scrutiny. Certainly we should like very much to grant that the numerous political theorists who in our day wish to stifle even the feeling of self-interest in men's hearts, who appear so pitiless toward what they call individualism, who incessantly repeat the words 'devotion,' 'sacrifice,' 'fraternity,' are themselves actuated exclusively by those sublime motives that they recommend to others . . . but, in the last analysis, we may venture to say that we do not fear comparison in this regard." What is at play in this foundational debate is not, in Bastiat's eyes, the question of whether "fraternal" or solidarity-based behavior is worth more than egotistical behavior. On this point, Bastiat, unlike most modern liberals,[30] claims to have not the slightest doubt: he declares himself in total agreement with the socialists. Consequently, his critique of early socialism is far more subtle. He contends that fraternity cannot be practiced "on command" lest it lose all meaning, and that an act is not truly generous unless it is performed spontaneously, with no expectation of reward.[31] Consequently, because they wish to enshrine in law the duties that individuals alone can impose on themselves, the socialists' mistake is to render genuine fraternity impossible. Bastiat writes: "[H]ence these efforts to mobilize labor; hence these declarations that the state owes subsistence, well-being, and education to all its citizens; that it should be generous, charitable, involved in everything, devoted to everybody; that its mission is to feed the infants, instruct the young, assure employment to the able-bodied,

---

30. When contemporary liberals assert, for example, that every attempt to limit the *indecent* profits of the great predators of the business world would necessarily force them to leave the country or outsource their companies, they take *for granted* their indifference to civic duty, morality, and even human feeling. As Laurence Parisot proudly declared, "a salary scale has nothing to do with morality."

31. Bastiat's critique makes perfect sense when applied exclusively to the daily relationships between individuals (that is, everything that relates to "primary sociality"). His error—or sophism—consists in transposing, without any serious discussion, this basic anthropological truth onto the very different level of public policy and what Alain Caillé calls "secondary sociality."

provide pensions for the disabled; in a word, that it should intervene directly to relieve all suffering, . . . balm for all wounds, refuges for all the unfortunate, and even aid, to the point of shedding French blood, for all oppressed people on the face of the earth." The desire to implement this generous program through "laws and taxes" (as Bastiat puts it) can only undermine itself. While establishing only a caricature of genuine fraternity, the socialist program would inevitably lead to a regime of terror and misery.

Yet the problem remains. If fraternity only makes sense as an individual choice and the state is forbidden from intervening in this realm, how is one to inject into daily life the moral rectitude and spirit of solidarity that Bastiat recognizes as essential to a genuinely human society? What authorizes, in short, a political liberal to believe that people will, on their own, make desirable choices and not act selfishly or cynically, like "demons"? If Bastiat's answer is telling, it is because it clearly marks the (philosophical and historical) moment when liberal philosophy's unity *in itself* becomes *for itself*—the moment when liberalism, in response to the socialist critique, recognizes that there is no other coherent option than *subcontracting to the market* the task of resolving the contradictions inherent in its conception of right.

"After mature consideration," Bastiat writes, "it must be recognized that what God has done He has done well, so that the best chance of progress lies in justice and liberty." This curious way of broaching the topic, which seems so unmodern, need not concern the liberal reader. We learn that this *deux ex machina*, charged with finding a definitive solution to the moral question, can assume no other form than Adam Smith's "invisible hand." Bastiat's point was simply that the total liberation of economic exchange (as well as the nearly total abolition of taxation)[32] would, by placing all of society under the tutelary protection of the laws of supply and demand, assume the role of creating a community that is peaceful and solidarity-based—the ideal, in short, that true liberals and socialists share. Granted, Bastiat is perfectly aware of the massive and already familiar objection of contemporary socialists. "What could result," asks Victor Considerant,[xiv] whom Bastiat cites at

---

32. For Bastiat, this condition rises to the level of a personal obsession. In this respect, he is one of the first writers to have articulated with true conviction the major grievance of contemporary liberals: "The rich are the true poor, as the state takes all they have." Hence his great popularity, particularly with employers' organizations.

length, "from that industrial liberty on which so much reliance had been placed, from the famous principle of *free competition*, which was believed to be so eminently democratic in character? Nothing could come of it save the general enslavement, the collective subservience, of the masses, deprived of capital, of industrial arms, of the tools of production, and, above all, of education, by the well-armed industrial class. We are told: 'The lists are open; every individual is free to enter the fray; the conditions are equal for all combatants.' Very good. Only one thing is forgotten—that on this great battlefield some are trained, disciplined, equipped, armed to the teeth, that they have in their possession a vast store of provisions, materiel, munitions, and engines of war, that they occupy all the strategic positions; and that others, plundered, destitute, ignorant, and hungry, are obliged, in order to live from day to day and keep their wives and children alive, to implore their *adversaries* themselves for any kind of work whatsoever at a meager wage."[xv]

If Bastiat was outraged that one could use such aggressive language to describe the fundamentally peaceful world of industry and *doux commerce*[xvi] (what is more unthinkable than economic war?), he recognized that Considérant at least grasped the stakes of the debate. "The profound, irreconcilable disagreement on this point between socialists and economists consists in this: the socialists believe that men's interests are essentially antagonistic. The economists believe in the natural harmony, or rather in the necessary and progressive harmonization, of men's interests. This is the whole difference." It so happens, however, that on this key question, Providence is not neutral and has long since chosen sides: "Providence is not mistaken," Bastiat explains, "it has arranged things in such a way that men's interests, under the rule of law, tend to adjust themselves naturally in the most harmonious combinations." He adds: "And this is precisely the conclusion at which political economy arrives."

All the ingredients for a miraculous solution have come together. Political economy, as both the new Newtonian science and Providence's authoritative interpreter, can now announce the eagerly awaited good news. Only political economy has the power to reveal, with its theorems, the magical equations that prove that free and unhindered trade will automatically result in unlimited growth and that the latter will, just as automatically, "relieve the suffering classes in two ways: first, by reducing the cost of living; second,

by raising wage rates." Yet according to Bastiat—and this is the real core
of his argument—"it is not possible for the condition of the workers to be
thus naturally and doubly improved without a corresponding improvement
and refinement in their moral condition." For moral capacities are directly
proportional to the material property at their disposal, as it provides security against the two eternal wellsprings of the inclination towards evil: envy
and resentment. Hence there is no reason to fear a race of demons. It is the
economy, free at last to develop according to its natural laws and protected
by the judicial system of an ideologically neutral state (since any ideological intervention could deregulate the market's providential order), that will
be responsible for moral education and gradually instill fraternity into the
hearts of the people, under the eye of an amazed God. All this will happen,
of course, without the slightest need for legal constraint or appeals to duty.
Economic growth is the solution to the enigma of history; it is the secret,
according to Bastiat, of "Progress" and the way a society can "ceaselessly
perfec[t] itself."[33] For a consistent liberal, authority must, of course, remain
within its bounds, contenting itself with being just. It is up to the economy
to make us happy, fraternal, and good.[34]

We started with liberalism's antinomies in dealing with Kant's demons

---

33. In a speech delivered at Silver Spring, Maryland on February 14, 2003, George W. Bush
    expressed with the utmost clarity the shared assumption of all liberals, be they on left
    or right: "Growth is the solution, not the problem."

34. Bastiat does not seem to have realized that his solution was contradictory. If, due to
    the "creation of jobs and wealth" through unlimited growth, people gradually became
    more honest, generous, and communal (which, incidentally, is also the postulate of
    state sociologists when they claim that transgressive and delinquent behavior are exclu-
    sively the result of poverty), the equilibria that make growth possible would be quickly
    compromised, as they are premised, by definition, on each individual's pursuit of their
    own egotistical interest. One would immediately find oneself in Mandeville's para-
    dox: a hive cannot be economically profitable if filled with honest and virtuous bees.
    The rise of selfishness and "private vices" remains the only cultural basis for economic
    growth (*The Fable of the Bees*, 1714). It is worth noting in passing that Bastiat's thesis
    (and that of far-left liberal sociologists) also presupposes that the rich are necessarily
    honest. Because they are, by definition, free from need, they would never dream of
    breaking the law (by defrauding the revenue service, for instance, or exploiting their
    employees).

but find ourselves thrown brutally back into the world of Adam Smith and Turgot. Yet there is nothing about this oscillation between two liberal moments that should surprise us. We must remember that the ideal of *doux commerce*—a centerpiece of Enlightenment philosophy and the basis of early modern political economy—was not formulated through learned reflection on the allocation of scarce resources or the optimal combination of the factors of production. From the beginning, its project was the systematic pacification of society, which is the true origin of modern institutions. It is significant that the first known plan for universal peace, *Le Nouveau Cynée* by Émery de Lacroix (also known as Crucé), published in 1623, connected the question of peace to the entirely new issue of free trade—as evidenced in the book's subtitle, "Discourse on the Occasions and Means to Establish General Peace and Free Trade Throughout the World." In this curious treatise (which proposes to bring together "the Turk and the Persian, the Frenchman and the Spaniard, the Chinese and the Tartar, the Christian and the Jew or the Mahometan"), one finds an early rehabilitation of the once universally scorned figure of the merchant, in a way that makes its political stakes particularly transparent: "There is no trade of comparable utility," Crucé writes, "than that of the merchant, who legitimately increases his means at the expense of his labor, and often at the risk of his life, without harming or offending anyone: *in this respect, he is more praiseworthy than the soldier, whose advancement depends on spoils and the ruin of others.*"[35] It only took Boisguilbert[xvii] in the following century to formulate the concept of a natural economic order, transposing a Cartesian model based in physics onto the sphere of commercial activities, for the conjunction of modernity's two motifs—the pacifying role of trade and the self-regulating market—to render philosophically conceivable Adam Smith's project: that is, to demonstrate that the free market can, without state intervention or the elusive virtue of individuals, generate entirely on its own a world that is as peaceful, prosperous, and happy as a world of egoists can be—the perfect *mechanical imitation* of the hopes that morality and religion once placed in collective goodness. If political liberalism ultimately always finds its natural center of

---

35. Crucé Émeric, *Le Nouveau Cynée ou discours d'État* (Rennes: Presses universitaires de Rennes, 2004).

gravity in economic liberalism, it is because the latter, from the very beginning, constituted a parallel political response to the modern problem.

The dialectical movement that inevitably reduces political liberalism, whatever its initial intentions, to free-market liberalism owes nothing to chance.
It is clearly the only philosophically coherent solution available to this doctrine whenever it tries to escape its inherent contradictions—the conjunction of "just" authority and the demons of freedom—without renouncing its
core conviction, which was inspired by the trauma resulting from the Wars
of Religion and the Jacobin Terror: the idea that a state that prohibits moral
judgments about the good life is the only one that will never attempt to impose salvation or happiness on people against their wishes.

It was all very well for early socialists to object that a society that demands nothing of its members but respect for their mutual indifference is
not a true society, and that the maxim "live and let live" always ends up,
wherever no modicum of common decency (that is, a minimum of shared
values and collective solidarity) is to be found, becoming "live and let die."
To remain faithful to itself, political liberalism has no choice but to step
aside. At this point, the *visible hand* of the state—which should have confined itself to establishing the rules of the game—finds itself repeatedly compelled to cede its unresolved problems to the market's *invisible hand*. It is, of
course, at this very point that the liberal right's methodical doubt finds its
truth in the arrogant dogmatism of economics.

It remains to be seen if this solution *is* a solution, and if it really lays the
socialist objection to rest. There is reason to fear that the "moral order" that
so terrifies political liberals was run out of town by the state, only to reenter
by way of the market. For if the mission of the economy, now that it has replaced theology, is to determine the path that humanity must follow—that
of unlimited growth, the new "balm of all wounds"—it is because, in reality, beneath the intimidating banner of "necessity," it is nothing other than
an invisible ideology and *religion incarnate*.[36] Is it not the market that now
monopolizes—through the massive entertainment industry and the ubiquitous propaganda of advertising—the right to teach humans, starting with

---

36. On this point, I recommend Pierre Legendre's magnificent analyses in *Dominium
    mundi. L'Empire du management* (Paris: Mille et Une Nuits, 2007).

children, what they can know, what they must do, and what they may hope for? To teach them, in short, how they must live and why "scientific" reasons render any other perspective meaningless? In short, things are as they should be. If the liberal state is destined to be philosophically empty, what other force than the market can fill in its blank pages by teaching humans how to live? Constant's political liberalism was never a one-way ticket. It always included a return trip to Adam Smith.

CHAPTER 7
Modern Society's Unconscious

In this essay, Michéa turns away from his usual concerns to consider psychology. Blending insights from anarchism and psychoanalysis, he investigates the psychological origins of the will to power. Throughout his work, Michéa shows how ordinary people, left to their own devices, will gravitate towards what Orwell calls "common decency." Yet if this is the case, why do certain individuals, even in the most egalitarian and communitarian societies, display an insatiable need to control others and make themselves the center of attention? Drawing on the thought of Jacques Lacan and Slavoj Zizek, Michéa probes this question in a way that allows him to theorize the nature of "modern society's unconscious." This essay was first published in *L'Empire du Moindre Mal* (2007).

IN HIS LETTER to Humphry House of April 11, 1940, George Orwell summarized his position on socialism. English intellectuals, he wrote, "have been infected with the inherently mechanistic Marxist notion that, if you make the necessary technical advance, the moral advance will follow of itself. I have never accepted this . . . A year ago, I was in the Atlas Mountains, and looking at the Berber villages there, it struck me that we were, perhaps, 1000 years ahead of these people, but no *better* than they, perhaps on balance rather worse. We are physically inferior to them, for instance, and manifestly less happy. All we have done is to advance to a point at which we *could* make a real improvement in human life, but we shan't do it without the recognition that common decency is necessary. My chief hope for the future is that the common people have never parted company with their moral code."[1]

In this passage, the conservative dimension of Orwellian socialism appears with particular clarity.[2] Its true principle lies less in nostalgia for a vanished world than in resolute opposition to the moral pessimism of the moderns. It is the insistent refusal to drown the "common man" in the icy waters of egotistical calculation that allows Orwell to criticize both liberalism and totalitarianism. In this regard, it has not been sufficiently emphasized that these two rival ideologies draw upon *the same negative vision of man* that was forged, as we have seen, in seventeenth-century Europe. Only against the background of this common starting point is it philosophically possible to grasp what truly distinguishes these ideologies from one another. From the moment that one posits that men are solely motivated by "love of themselves and forgetfulness of others,"[3] there can indeed only be two coherent solutions to the modern political problem. Either one decides to accept men "as they are," in which case one must resign oneself to making the most of their selfishness in an *empire of lesser evils*, or one clings to the project of an *empire of the good* (in other words, the utopia of a perfect world) whose triumphal advent depends on the creation of a *new man*. The Orwellian idea of a decent

---

1. George Orwell, "Letter to Humphry House," *Collected Essays, Journalism and Letters*, vol. 1, *An Age Like This, 1920–40*, ed. Sonia Orwell and Ian Angus (New York: Harcourt Brace Jovanovich, 1968), 529–532, at 532.

2. It is well known that, in order to provoke the prickly left intelligentsia, Orwell liked to present himself as a Tory anarchist. One finds the same attitude in Paul Goodman, an important figure in the American anarchist movement and one of the founders of the gay rights movement, who defined himself as a neolithic conservative: "As a conservative anarchist," he wrote, "I believe that to seek for Power is otiose . . . I am eager to sign off as soon as conditions are tolerable, so people can go back to the things that matter, their professions, sports, and friendships. Naturally, politics should not be for me." *New Reformation: Notes of a Neolithic Conservative* (Oakland, CA: PM Press, 2010), 189.

3. "We should not be angry with men when we see their harshness, their ingratitude, their injustice, their pride, their self-love and forgetfulness of others; they are made thus, it is their nature; we might as well protest because a stone falls or because the sparks fly upward." La Bruyère, "On Man," in *Characters* (1688). [TR: I have drawn from an English translation of this text available athttps://www.ourcivilisation.com/smartboard/shop/bruyere/chap11.htm]

society largely escapes these contradictions because it is rooted in a far more nuanced—and more realistic—understanding of human nature. For the self-institution[i] specific to this society necessarily entails a constant reliance on already existing moral possibilities. These possibilities are radicalized, internalized, and universalized, but not eliminated in the name of the "progressive" struggle against *every* aspect of tradition, each of which is seen as *equally* repressive. Only on this "conservative" foundation can the various inventions of human genius (notably science and technology) acquire human meaning and contribute, within appropriate limits, to improving collective life.

Yet Orwell's definition of socialism is also an invitation to clarify its "anarchist" dimension. Indeed, Orwell always considered the *desire for power*—that is, the sense that people can only realize themselves by controlling others—as the major psychological obstacle to a decent society and the ultimate source of all the political perversions authorized by ideology.[4] This crucial point is worth clarifying, for it sheds light on key aspects of *modern society's unconscious*.

It is well known that Stendahl held in high regard the work of Charles Fourier—that "sublime dreamer who uttered a great word: association." In his *Mémoires d'un touriste* ("Memoirs of a Tourist"), Stendahl nevertheless raises a fundamental objection against the idea of the phalanstery, one that, in his view, undermined every attempt at "association" put forward by the various currents of early socialism. Fourier, he writes, "did not see that, in each village, a mischievous and smooth-talking rascal (a Robert Macaire) would place himself at the head of the association and pervert all of its happy outcomes."[5] All appearances to the contrary, this critique is very different

---

4. "The growth of 'realism' has been the great feature of the intellectual history of our own age. Why this should be so is a complicated question. The interconnection between sadism, masochism, success-worship, power-worship, nationalism, and totalitarianism is a huge subject whose edges have barely been scratched, and even to mention it is considered somewhat indelicate." George Orwell, "Raffles and Miss Blandish" (1944), *A Collection of Essays* (Garden City, NY: Doubleday, 1954), 139–154, at 151.

5. Robert Macaire is the hero of *L'auberge des adrets*, a successful play written by Benjamin Antier in 1823. The role of Macaire was played by Frédérick Lemaître, one of the great actors of the age. Popularized by Honoré Daumier's caricatures, Robert Macaire became the symbol, throughout the nineteenth century, of the unscrupulous, wheeling and dealing scoundrel, the perfect embodiment, as James Rousseau puts it, of "our positive, egotistical, miserly, mendacious, and boastful age."

from that of the liberals. Stendahl does not maintain (at least in this text) that it is human nature that renders the project of a solidarity-based society utopian. He simply observes that socialists, probably because of their excessive optimism, have systematically forgotten that the will to power found in some people will always undermine the best-intentioned political endeavors. If "anarchism" means the project for a world in which "Robert Macaires" would be, if not impossible, at least prevented from seizing power to achieve their ends, it can be said that Stendahl raises the *ultimate anarchist question*.

Admittedly, the concept of the "desire for power" (or "will to power") usually elicits little interest among modern critics of liberal society. Those who have been trained to view matters in purely sociological terms (which, at present, is pretty much everybody) usually discount such explanations, relegating them to the realm of "psychologism."[6] This criticism contains, of course, a kernel of truth. The desire for power is tied to specific social and historical conditions. It is thus tempting to consider it as a secondary psychological effect of class relations and the institutional forms that facilitate man's exploitation of man. Yet it is impossible to completely dissolve the will to power into these relationships and forms. On the one hand, the question of power (that is, of control over others) extends across the entire range of human relationships, including everyday and private ones. On the other hand, as Pierre Clastres demonstrated,[7] the need to impose one's ego on other

---

6. Christopher Lasch writes: "The left has too often served as a refuge from the terrors of the inner life. Another ex-radical, Paul Zweig, has said that he became a communist in the late fifties because communism 'released him from . . . the failed room and broken vases of a merely private life.' As long as political movements exercise a fatal attraction for those who seek to drown the sense of personal failure in collective action—as if collective action somehow precluded rigorous attention to the quality of personal life— political movements will have little to say about the personal dimension of social crisis." *The Culture of Narcissism: American Life in an Age of Diminishing Expectations* (New York: W. W. Norton, 1979), 46. The *imperative* of seeking a purely sociological explanation for all human behavior (including delinquency, relationships at school, and personal life) can, to a considerable extent, be explained by this analysis.

7. For years, Pierre Clastres studied, using South American Indians as his example, the political strategies employed by "primitive" societies to prevent the desire for prestige that occasionally motivates tribe members from turning into coercive power. Their solution is to turn these individuals into symbolic "chiefs," bound by an obligation to show

people (treating them as means to one's own ends or mirrors of oneself) can emerge at any moment, *even in the most egalitarian societies.* And everyone knows—except, perhaps, activists themselves—that the world of parties, labor unions, and associations is no better protected from power struggles and conflicts over egos than any other (and perhaps less so).[8] On this point, one must acknowledge the anarchists' philosophical lucidity and accept that the history of individual subjects and their relation to the unconscious be reintroduced into the political realm.

The problem's premises can be formulated quite easily. It involves considering simultaneously two seemingly contradictory facts. First, we know that there is no reason to consider the desire for power (understood as a higher form of selfishness and the negation of others) as part of human nature itself, lest one fall back on the naïve cynicism of the seventeenth-century moralists.[ii] Second, it must be admitted that such a desire is, to a degree, universal, as it can manifest itself in any social and cultural context, no matter how egalitarian (even if some contexts are obviously far more favorable to it than

---

unlimited generosity to their community. "What does the 'big man' receive in exchange for his generosity? Not the achievement of his desire for power, but the tenuous satisfaction of a point of honor; not the ability to command, but the innocent pleasure in glory that he must exhaust himself to preserve. He works, literally, for glory: society readily gives it to him, as it busies itself enjoying the fruits of its chief's labor. Every flatterer lives at the expense of those who listen to him" (*Recherches d'anthropologie politique*, Paris: Seuil, 1990, 139). This wonderful anarchist lesson is also discussed in *Society against the State* (Paris: Éditions de Minuit, 1974) and in the volume dedicated to Clastres' oeuvre (edited by Miguel Abensour), *L'Esprit des lois sauvages* (Paris: Seuil, 1987).

8. This point was made by Claude Alzon in 1974 when he analyzed, with his usual energy, the then-flourishing phenomenon of communes. "I am perfectly aware that these little bastards swear only by Marcuse and Deleuze, without having read them. They are experts in making the weakest feel guilty, they can't say three words without brandishing the specter of repression—a useful argument that makes it possible, on the pretext that one's freedom is being threatened, to squeeze those around them like lemons. And this is without mentioning the sexual exploitation to which the commune's girls are subject and the criticism that they pile onto others, whom they claim are solely responsible for failures that they were the first to provoke." *La Mort de Pygmalion* (Paris: Maspero, 1974), 154. Thirty years later, one can measure the paths traveled by these "little bastards," many of whom found in the scintillating worlds of politics, business, and communication far more remunerative satisfaction for their unaltered desire for power.

others). In other words, even though most human beings clearly do not be-have like Robert Macaire,[9] the fact remains—and in this respect Stendahl was absolutely right—that, wherever there are human beings, you can expect to find a Robert Macaire. I see only one logical and empirically verifiable way to resolve this apparent contradiction. A philosophical distinction must be made between adult selfishness, which is always contingent, and the selfish-ness of children, which, to the contrary, seems inevitable, not because it is "natural" but because it is *primary*,[iii] which is very different.

There is no need here to review the vast literature that psychoanalysis has devoted to this topic, notably in its reflections on narcissism. Casual ob-servation (so long as it is not blinded by the most possessive forms of paren-tal love) shows that the desire for omnipotence is a primordial stage in the development of any individual mind.[10] This desire lies at the root of what Christopher Lasch calls the "the child's rage against those who do not re-spond immediately to his needs."[11] If education has any meaning, it precisely resides in offering the child a way of overcoming this initial egocentrism and acquiring a *sense of the other*, which is both evidence of and condition for true autonomy (or, what amounts to the same thing, psychological matu-rity). Only once this stage is achieved do individuals become capable of hold-ing their own in human affairs—that is, of entering, in turn, the socializing chains of gift-giving and reciprocity. If a failure on the part of "paternal"

---

9. "It is, therefore, a just *political* maxim," David Hume wrote, "*that every man must be supposed a knave*" ("On the Independency of Parliament," 1741). Admittedly, Hume's empiricism leads him to immediately correct his liberal premise: "Though at the same time, it appears somewhat strange, that a maxim should be true in *politics*, which is false in *fact*" (*Essays Moral, Political and Literary*). On this point, see Didier Deleule, *Hume et la naissance du libéralisme économique* (Paris: Aubier, 1979).

10. Commenting on the work of Susan Isaacs, Claude Levi-Strauss observes that the child's initially possessive attitude "is felt not only for material objects, but also for immaterial rights, such as the hearing or singing of a song. Furthermore, 'taking turns' is one of the hardest lessons for children under five years to learn." He adds: "It can thus be said that the capacity for sharing or 'taking turns' is a function of the growing feeling of reciprocity, itself the result of a living experience of the collective fact, and of the deeper mechanism of identification with another." *The Elementary Structures of Kinship*, trans. James Bell Harle, John Richard von Sturmer, Rodney Needham (Boston: Beacon Press, 1969), 85, 86.

11. Christopher Lasch (quoting Thomas Freeman), *The Culture of Narcissism*, 79.

or "maternal" functions prevents the autonomization process from occur-ring (with all the necessary acts of self-denial it implies), the subject, with-out subsequent liberating encounters, will remain bound to his initial desire for omnipotence and find himself deprived of the ability to grow up.[12] He will remain a selfish monad, incapable of giving, receiving, and giving back, except in purely formal ways (that is, purely for "propriety's" sake, when it is required by social theater, which depends on training rather than genu-ine education). The ego's pathologies—from the will to power as such to its multiple offshoots, such as the pathetic desire to be rich and famous—must appear for what they are: the effects of unresolved childhood dependency, which leads the subject to view his life as an occasion for personal revenge (a debilitating outlook, as it automatically turns life into a "career," pathologi-cally organized around the desire to succeed and live one's life as a perfor-mance).[13] This is why the will to power is always a gloomy passion. As Plato understood, tyrants are never happy, no matter the realm or level at which their need to dominate others is exercised. From an anarchist perspective, the ruling classes are above all to be pitied.

There is thus nothing surprising about the importance that anarchists have traditionally placed upon education (at home and at school) or their unwavering sensitivity to the moral and psychological dimension of politi-cal activity. To the extent that the repression of these key issues is the root of all the revolutionary movement's misfortunes, from the inevitability of

---

12. The idealization of the child, which is central to modern liberal culture (though not for Hobbes) is, in the first place, evidence of fascinated admiration for his or her initial ego-centrism. This is why the principle of liberal education is not to help the child grow but to let its "nature" freely express itself. The most radical literary critique of this illusion is William Golding's *Lord of the Flies* (1954). It is worth noting that Peter Brook, in his remarkable film adaptation of the novel (from 1963), thought it necessary to discreetly alter the final scene, which suggested that the child's initial egoism was perhaps also humanity's. No doubt his leftist sensibility forbade him from admitting to so radical a critique of liberalism.

13. The "refusal to succeed" (*refus de parvenir*) was one of the main slogans of intellectuals who supported anarcho-syndicalism (like Albert Thierry and Marcel Martinet). This maxim followed logically from their attraction to common decency. Experience shows that those who dedicate their "lives" to climbing rungs on the social ladder never do any-thing other than (to use Georges Elgozy's wonderful expression) "crawl vertically."

bureaucratization to the slide into totalitarianism, anarchism appears less as just another political ideology than as a *moral propaedeutic* to any possible revolution (and perhaps a "metapolitics"), provided that, by "revolution," one understands, not the conquest of power by interchangeable Robert Macaires, but the creation, by the once dominated classes, of a free, egalitarian, and decent society.[14]

One mystery remains to be dispelled. Given that it is the great merit of the anarchist movement to have shed light on the origin of the desire for power in individuals, how does one explain that this tradition's valuable analytical work so often seems to have been cut short? Since the nineteenth century, every form of "patriarchal" domination has been widely described and denounced, to the point that these arguments have become hackneyed platitudes of social criticism and gender studies. The same cannot be said, however, of forms of subjection and the manipulation of others that are unconsciously modeled on *maternal control*. This oversight is particularly odd. For it is at the very moment that the development of modern society began to undermine the cultural foundation of longstanding patriarchal structures[15]—by discrediting all references to a symbolic law[iv] and privileging rights and the market—that social criticism began to focus almost exclusively on patriarchal domination.[16]

What makes this modern mystery even stranger is the blatant denial on

---

14. Emphasizing the "metapolitical" dimension of anarchism makes it possible to resolve a number of philosophical difficulties. It is possible to identify the existence of an "anarchist" critique in third century China, even though this civilization did not, as François Jullien has shown, develop a typology of political regimes comparable to ancient Greece (as is also the case, of course, for the "anarchism" of the South American Indians analyzed by Pierre Clastres). See François Jullien, *Éloge de l'anarchie par deux excentriques chinois* (Paris: Éditions de l'encyclopédie des nuisances, 2004).

15. In the *Communist Manifesto*, Marx reminds us that "wherever it has got the upper hand," the bourgeoisie "has put an end to all … patriarchal … relations." One wonders how some so-called Marxists can see the "patriarchy" as the necessary condition for everyday capitalist relationships.

16. We must salute the courageous analyses of Michel Schneider, even if his inadequate definition of liberalism leads him, curiously, to see the triumph of "big mother" as the achievement of "socialism" rather than "liberal modernity. To the contrary, as Slavoj Zizek points out in his ferocious analysis of Bill Gates' liberalism, "the dominating

which it depends. As we have all observed, the elimination of the symbolic law never leads automatically to the triumph of joyful and all-conquering freedom. As Slavoj Zizek rightly reminds us, "the decline of traditional patriarchal authority (the symbolic law) is accompanied by its disturbing double, the superego."[17] This latter concept, which, in Zizek's thought, owes more to Jacques Lacan than to Sigmund Freud, is particularly interesting. "The superego," Zizek writes, "must be strictly contrasted with the symbolic law. The symbolic law tolerates silently, between the lines. It even encourages the very things that the letter of the law forbids (like adultery). Due to its very clarity, however, the superego's injunction to *enjoy* is far more effective than any prohibition at preventing the subject from accessing enjoyment." To illustrate this fundamental distinction, Zizek offers the following example: "A parental figure that is simply 'repressive,' assuming the form of a symbolic authority, will tell their child: 'You must go to your grandmother's birthday whether you like it or not and behave, even if you're bored to death. I don't care if you want to or not, you're going anyway!' By contrast, the superego figure will tell the same child: 'Even though you know perfectly well how much your grandmother wants to see you, you should only do it if you really want to—otherwise, you're better off staying at home.'" The ruse of the superego consists in encouraging the idea that this is a free choice, when, as every child knows, it is a forced choice, implying an even more coercive command: not just "you must visit your grandmother, no matter how you feel about it," but "you must do so, and *you must be thrilled about it!*" The superego orders you to *enjoy* doing what you have to do. Proof of this may be found in what would happen if the poor child, believing that he or she really could choose freely, replied 'no!' One may easily enough imagine the parent's response: 'How can you refuse? Why are you so mean? What has your grandmother done to make you not like her?'"[18]

After such evocative descriptions, it is surprising that Zizek confines himself, in this text, to invoking a generic "parental figure," even though the "superego figure" he describes is best represented by a more specific type: *the*

---

figure with which we must contend is no longer the good old patriarchal Oedipal master."
Le Spectre rôde toujours (Paris: Éditions Nautilus, 2002), 20.

17. Zizek, *Le Spectre rôde toujours*, 29.

18. Ibid., 29, 30.

possessive, castrating, "bad mother." Whereas the "patriarchal" abuse of paternal authority orders the subject to *obey* the law that the tyrannical father claims to embody, the "matriarchal" desire for power takes on different and far more stifling forms. It imposes unconditional love on the subject as its due and, consequently, relies primarily on guilt and emotional blackmail, in an infinite variety of modes: grievance, criticism, accusation, and so on. Patriarchal control establishes an order that is primarily disciplinary, demanding that the subject exhibit complete submission in his external behavior. Matriarchal control establishes a far more radical form of control, as it has no definable limits. It demands that the subject give up his desire[v] and fully accept the submission demanded of him, lest he lose all self-respect, since any refusal to accept total control over his life can only imply a blameworthy inability to reciprocate in a way that is worthy of the "sacrifices" made for him. This difference alone is reason enough to explain why it is so hard to grasp the experience of domination as such when it assumes a maternal form. Whereas the disciplinary order is always direct—which simultaneously brings about awareness of its oppressive character and makes rebellion possible—matriarchal control exercised "for one's own good" and in the name of "love" operates in more all-encompassing and insidious ways. The upshot is that the subject will almost inevitably blame himself for his ingratitude and moral failings. The resulting consequence is crucial to understanding modern politics. The mechanisms of patriarchal control (which mimic paternal authority in its function as a separating third)[vi] can generally be perceived by all involved without difficulty. Anyone (be they a man or a woman) operating in a patriarchal mode has no doubt that they *enjoy* power. But those over whom this power is exercised are not taken in by this pleasure. By contrast, matriarchal forms of control (of which many men have become past masters) are far more difficult to perceive and name, both by those who are subject to them and by those who exercise them. As experience constantly shows, it is psychologically impossible for a possessive mother (or any subject functioning in this way) to experience her will to power as anything other than an exemplary form of love and sacrificial devotion.[19] It is thus inevitable that the *visible hand* of patriarchal domina-

---

19. What modern political philosophy has usually failed to see, literature has always managed to unveil with its unique abilities. There probably does not exist a more precise (and disturbing) description of the *unconscious* will to power of the woman-mother

tion ultimately obscures the *invisible hand* of matriarchal domination, ensuring that every challenge to coercive power focuses on the former. It is likely in this major difference that one must seek the ultimate explanation for the age-old political repression of the rule of mothers.[20]

These brief remarks allow us to raise a corner of the ideological veil behind which the dark continent of modern society is concealed. Liberalism's inner logic objectively entails the dismantling of all norms that explicitly reference the symbolic law and their replacement by the "value neutral" mechanisms of market and law. For this reason, liberalism is condemned to induce the unrestricted development of new norms that are anchored primarily in subjects' imaginaries—and that are thus governed directly by the unconscious itself (and particularly what Zizek, following Melanie Klein[vii] and Christopher Lasch, calls "ferocious superego figures"). This is why the slow historical dismantling of disciplinary societies, which is late modernity's main achievement, never results in large numbers of people acquiring the incredible autonomy they have been promised. Without a total critique of the mechanisms of domination—a critique that liberal materialism excludes on principle—this methodical dismantling leads to the gradual establishment of control societies relying on the ever-increasing authority of experts[21]

---

than Ludwig Lewisohn's magisterial novel *The Case of Mr. Crump* (which Freud called an "unrivaled masterpiece"). Written in the mid-1920s, this astonishing work was immediately rejected by every American publisher and its author's name dragged through the mud, on the grounds that he was undermining married couples and national values. Finally published in France in 1931, with a preface by Thomas Mann, the book was not allowed to appear in the United States until 1947 (and even then, only in expurgated form). The way in which the period responded to this novel (and its discreet fate down to our own time) clearly merits psychoanalysis.

20. See François Vigouroux, *L'Empire des mères* (Paris: Presses universitaires de France, 1998).

21. "'Adulthood' in the last generations has had very little to do with 'adulthood' as that word would have been understood by adults in any previous generation. Rather, 'adulthood' has been defined as 'a position of control in the world of childhood.' Ambitious Americans, sensing this, have preferred to remain adolescents, year after year." George Trow, "Within the Context of No-Context," *The New Yorker*, November 8, 1980. This is why Trow concludes: "In the absence of adults, people came to put their trust in *experts*." This point sheds light, among other things, on the importance of schools to liberal society and the contemporary proliferation of coaches.

and suffused with a peculiar ambiance of self-censorship, repentance, and generalized guilt. In such societies, a new war has been added to the "war of all against all": the war of each against themselves.[22] In the final analysis, such indeed seems to be the unconscious anthropological foundation of this regressive civilization of "progress," which Lasch was among the first to recognize as the culture of narcissism.

---

22. David Fincher's film *Fight Club* is, from this perspective, one of the most representative films of our liberal age, as Slavoj Zizek (*La Subjectivité à venir*, Castelnau-le-Lez: Climats, 2004, and Paris: Champs-Flammarion, 2006) and Stanko Cerovic have argued (*Comment maigrissent les ombres*, Castelnau-le-Lez: Climats, 2003).

CHAPTER 8

Egoism and Common Decency

In this essay, Michéa examines liberalism, not from the standpoint of psychoanalysis, as in the previous chapter, but from that of anthropology—that is, the theory of human nature. He considers whether liberalism can sustain the very conception of human nature that made it possible in the first place. This essay was first published in *L'Empire du Moindre Mal* (2007).

THE LIBERAL WAGER is biblical in its simplicity. It rests on the conviction that, even if one assumes that individuals act only in their private interest, it always remains possible to avoid a war of all against all and establish a free, peaceful, and prosperous society. To do so, it suffices to channel the energy of "private vices"[i] towards the community's benefit by delegating the task of harmonizing individual conduct to the neutral and impersonal mechanisms of law and the market. This solution, in turn, implies that moral values—from which past civilizations partly drew their raison d'être—must be cast out of the public square. As anyone can see, most of today's liberals have fully adapted themselves to this foundational exclusion. Like Lysander Spooner,[ii] they are convinced that it is impossible for anyone, "except each individual for himself," to "dra[w] any accurate line, or anything like any accurate line, between virtue and vice." Rather, they see this foundational sacrifice as an opportunity to bid good riddance to "the old Morall

Philosophers."[1] From this standpoint (and excepting economists narrowly construed, whose primary activity consists in mathematizing egoism), Ayn Rand is probably the twentieth-century thinker who endorsed most resolutely the liberal paradigm's moral implications. A coherent capitalist ethos, she writes, "*proudly* advocates and upholds rational selfishness." The clear conscience with which modern economic princes exploit and lay off their precarious employees, reap staggering profits, move their companies offshore, negotiate with dictators, plunder the environment, cook their books, and then open wide their golden parachutes, finds in the theory of "rational egoism" valuable psychological sustenance.

Yet it might seem unfair to reduce the moral philosophy of liberalism to this icy defense of individual egoism (even if its intellectual preconditions were already present in Jeremy Bentham's utilitarianism).[2] Was not liberalism's initial concern to banish from political life any reference to a shared conception of morality and the good life? Strictly speaking, this position required only that moral, religious, and philosophical values be *privatized*, not that they be abolished. In theory, everyone remained free (as we saw with Bastiat) to have a *personal preference* for generous rather than selfish behavior, to the extent that such a distinction still made sense. Yet it is worth asking how coherent this solution really is. From a liberal standpoint, an altruistic individual concerned with the common good is necessarily an *exception to human nature*.[3] A private choice of this kind—presuming that it is not itself

---

1. "For there is no such *Finis Ultimus*, (utmost ayme) nor *Summum Bonum*, (greatest good) as is spoken of in the Books of the old Morall Philosophers." Thomas Hobbes, *Leviathan*, Book 1, chapter 11.

2. At first glance, Adam Smith's liberalism seems difficult to dissolve into the radical theory of rational egoism. Trained in the school of Frances Hutcheson, Smith tried, throughout his life, to preserve a role for "sympathy" in the formation of social bonds and personal morality. This is the origin of what German commentators called *das Adam Smith Problem*—that is, the question of the relationship between *The Theory of Moral Sentiments* (1759) and *An Inquiry into the Nature and Causes of the Wealth of Nations* (1776). It is, however, important to note that the balance between egoism and the sympathy always ends up tilting towards the former. In any case, this is the thesis that Serge Latouche convincingly (and, in my view, definitively) defends in *L'invention de l'économie* (Paris: Albin Michel, 2005; see pages 191 to 223).

3. Using the language of liberal economic analysis, one could say, with Kenneth Arrow, that altruism is a "scarce resource."

a mask for self-interest or self-love—is already destined to remain the (rather mysterious) privilege of a narrow elite. But most importantly, such a choice would be of little consequence. If the best way to serve one's community is to pursue one's enlightened self-interest (which, since Adam Smith, has been liberalism's creed), a liberal concerned with the common good should, logically speaking, force himself to behave selfishly to confer real content upon his moral convictions. In any case, liberals with a human face are condemned to get with the program.[4]

Yet these internal difficulties are not the most troubling ones. Even more fundamental problems arise with the ideal of "value neutrality," which is liberalism's philosophical foundation. For if liberals resign themselves so calmly to eliminating traditional values once and for all (since liberalism always presents itself as a war machine against conservatism in all forms), it is because they are convinced that the balancing mechanisms of the modern market and law are sufficient to generate the cultural dispositions needed to integrate individuals into communities. This deeply held conviction is based upon two ideological postulates that are not always made explicit (except by economists). First, it presupposes that the necessary and sufficient condition for establishing an efficient human order resides in the ability of individuals to embrace the logic of the market and law—that is to make deals and honor contracts. It further presupposes that this salutary ability is natural, since it requires nothing more than the faculty (which is also held to be natural) of acting consistent with one's enlightened self-interest. Yet there is nothing self-evident about the axiom of interest, which was forged in circumstances specific to seventeenth-century Europe. When considered from the

---

4.   Hence all the apparently insoluble psychological contradictions of those who, like Constant or Tocqueville, resign themselves to the triumph of commercial society even as they remain deeply alienated from its spirit. In the case of Constant, literature was the privileged means for grappling with these contradictions. A far simpler solution is, of course, to adopt the schizophrenic position of partisans of the traditional right, who, as the American critic Russell Jacoby observes, "worship the market and bemoan the education it engenders" (the exact ideological counterpart being the contemporary left, which claims that it is fighting the market's logic—though less and less—only to yield enthusiastically to the culture it engenders). For decades, we have all been aware of the political effects of this fake alternative and of the capitalist system's interest in presenting itself as "unsurpassable" and necessary for "the clarity of democracy debate."

standpoint of modern anthropology's core insights, its psychological naiveté (and, even more so, its ethnocentrism) is astonishing.

The market and the law (and the state itself) are necessarily *secondary* forms of socialization. Not just in the obvious sense that they appeared relatively late in humanity's history, but above all and more significantly because they can only function and reproduce themselves on the basis of existing anthropological conditions—conditions that the market and the law are structurally incapable of reproducing in modern form. Even the practical possibility of economic exchange and legal contracts (the two principal modalities of reciprocal exchange) presumes that individuals who prioritize such relationships already share a degree of preexisting trust and are thus endowed with a minimal psychological and cultural disposition towards honesty. Yet as the sprawling literature devoted to the prisoner's dilemma makes clear (though we have known this since Hobbes), no rational calculation—that is, no calculation based exclusively on considerations of interest—can ever allow supposedly selfish individuals to enter the enchanted circle of trust and agree upon the best solution for them (that is, the system of reciprocal exchange mentioned above). As the economist Ian O. Williamson acknowledges, "calculative trust is a contradiction in terms."[5] The true psychological and cultural conditions for trust, which plays a central role in traditional communities, as seen in the practice of oaths and the importance of "giving one's word," are only to be found in the infinitely complex and varied games of *primary* sociality (to use Alain Caillé's term). These games are essentially founded on the traditional obligation (which is neither economic nor legal) of giving, receiving, and giving back. The logic of the gift, which Marcel Mauss was the first to make central to sociology, lends itself to multiple and even contradictory interpretations.[6] Yet it al-

---

5. Quoted by André Orléan, "Sur le rôle respectif de la confiance et de l'intérêt dans la constitution de l'ordre marchand," *Revue du MAUSS* 4 (1994): 17–36.

6. The common root of these interpretations is the idea that gifts exist only when a gift given in return is not a legal or economic obligation. The freedom to give back or not give back (whatever the modalities and motivations) is central to how the cycle works and makes it unthinkable as a purely deterministic structure. We should add that the "spirit" in which something is given must also be considered (which rules out, once again, mechanistic approaches) as well as the fact that gift-giving can obviously assume

ways implies the primacy of cycles or relationships (whether conscious or unconscious) over individuals, thus inscribing *symbolic indebtedness*—an essential form of humanity's constitutive incompleteness—into the very heart of the human subject.

The gift cycle, which defines "society's foundational moment," should naturally not be confused with morality narrowly construed. But, as Jacques T. Godbout[iii] observes, the gift cycle is, in a sense, morality's "foundation."[7] What Orwell calls "common decency"[8] becomes philosophically coherent only when it is situated in this anthropological context. Orwell's concrete examples clearly show that this politically decisive concept never refers to a metaphysics or theology of the good—that is, to a particular *moral ideology*. To the contrary, in using this deliberately vague and imprecise concept, Orwell's enduring concern is to deeply root socialist practice in *basic human virtues*, which have always looked upon forgetting, neglect, and disdain as the distinctive mark of ideologues and men of power. These virtues or psychological and cultural dispositions towards generosity and loyalty (and which can ultimately be summarized in our personal ability to give,

---

antagonistic forms (from vendettas to potlatch by way of prestige gifts and "poisoned pills"). On this topic, see Jacques Godbout's critique of Alain Testart's ambiguous theories, "Ni égoïsme ni altruisme. Don et théorie des jeux," in *La Revue du MAUSS* 20 (2002): 286–299.

7. Jacques T. Godbout, *Ce qui circule entre nous*, 230. One of the great merits of Godbout's work is that he always bases his critique of liberal egoism on specific studies and experiments. Summarizing the countless experiments conducted in relation to the prisoner's dilemma, Godbout observes that they massively contradict the liberal ideological postulate of Robert Axelrod, "which maintains that generosity is very rare and almost always leads to exploitation. We are approaching, perhaps, the true contradiction of this approach: founded initially on selfish interest in the name of realism, these experiments show that, in fact, this postulate provides only a weak explanation of actors' behavior" (p. 270). Godbourt's method is the same as Joseph Henrich's, whose team had the inspired idea of asking some fifteen hunter-gatherer societies to conduct tests comparable to the prisoner's dilemma. Their conclusions were clear: "The axiom of selfishness is verified in none of the societies studied." Godbout, *Ce qui circule entre nous* 271.

8. A good summary of this topic can be found in an article by Bruce Bégout, "Vie ordinaire et vie politique. George Orwell et la common decency," in *L'Ordinaire et le politique* (Presses universitaires de France 2006), 99–119.

receive, and return)[9] naturally allow for an indefinite number of particular expressions, varying from one civilization and one historical context to the next. In the last analysis, however, it is precisely their enduring amenability to translation that renders them universalizable, as opposed to ideologies of the good, which cannot extend beyond their particular domain or establish their universality other than through crusade or conversion. The negation of these elementary virtues, by contrast, always takes the same form: egoism and the spirit of calculation, those historically unchanging preconditions for the will to power and, by extension, for all the betrayals that inevitably accompany it.

It is therefore not difficult to predict the kind of civilizational impasse into which any program for the thoroughgoing modernization of life will necessarily place humanity in the future. By generalizing the logic of "give-and-take" (which, to avoid the worst, must always choose the lesser evil) to all human behavior, such a program can only encourage the systematic dismantling of every anthropological condition that, within very specific limits, had allowed the mechanisms of the modern market and law to function in the first place, consistent with liberal theory's expectations. Moreover, this explains how, until relatively recently, the capitalist system was able to function somewhat efficiently, producing quality goods that at times were useful to humanity. As Cornelius Castoriadis observes, this stems from the fact that capitalism "inherited a series of anthropological types that it did not create and could not have created: incorruptible judges, honest, Weberian-style civil servants, teachers devoted to their vocation, workers who went

---

9. What differentiates moral behavior narrowly understood from traditional behavior founded on the sense of honor and custom is the internalization of the obligation to give, receive, and give back—in other words, the acquisition of the ability to act "in good conscience" and not simply because others are watching, or one's reputation is at stake. In this sense, an ethical disposition implies that the individualizing process and the "care for the self" has reached a certain level of historical development. The individual's reappropriation of the gift-giving spirit (which is morality's essence, in the modern sense of the term) is what endows the autonomous subject with a capacity for resistance and revolt that is no doubt considerably greater than that available to individuals in traditional society. Hence liberalism's need to constantly deconstruct the subject in all its forms—so as to neutralize the effects of "moral conscience" that modernity, against its will, made possible.

about their work with at least a minimum of conscientiousness, and so on. These types did not arise by themselves nor could they have done so. Rather, they were the creation of previous historical periods and in reference to values then considered at once sacrosanct and unquestionable: honesty, service to the State, the transmission of knowledge, craftsmanship, and so forth. Yet we now live in societies where these values are a notorious laughingstock and where all that counts is the amount of money you have pocketed, no matter how, or the number of times you have appeared on television. The sole anthropological type created by capitalism, the one that was indispensable for its establishment at the outset, was the Schumpeterian entrepreneur: someone who cares passionately about the creation of this new historical institution, *the company*, and who strives constantly to expand it via new technologies and new methods of reaching markets. Yet even this type is now being destroyed. As far as production is concerned, the entrepreneur is being replaced by a managerial bureaucracy. As for making money, stock-market speculation, hostile takeovers, and financial intermediation earn much more than 'entrepreneurial' activities. Therefore, even as we witness, due to privatization, the increasing dilapidation of public space, the anthropological types that were necessary to the system's very existence are being demolished."[10] By constantly urging people to become "rational actors," all of whose existential choices are to be modeled on the axioms of interest and strategic calculation (for that is indeed the ultimate meaning of all those never-ending calls to "bring mentalities in line with the development of the modern world"), the logic of liberalism does not just constantly destroy the conditions of any form of civility and common decency; it also paradoxically jeopardizes the effective operation of its own foundational constructs, at the risk of reinstating the war of all against all at every level of society— that is, the very thing liberalism was initially meant—at least in theory—to overcome once and for all.

Yet to the extent that a society bereft of any normative framework

---

10. Cornelius Castoriadis, *La Montée de l'insignifiance* (Paris: Seuil, 1996), 68 [TR: I have used the translation published as *The Rising Tide of Insignificance (The Big Sleep)*, trans. anonymous, available at https://web.archive.org/web/20180422000233id_/http://www.costis.org/x/castoriadis/castoriadis-rising_tide.pdf. The quote comes from the essay called "The Dilapidation of the West"].

remains—until proven otherwise—an anthropological impossibility, the old "god-making machine" will inevitably be hauled back out. There exists, however, only one means that is compatible with liberalism for restoring something like a common framework that would not infringe upon the value neutrality of market and law. It consists of deriving from these very mechanisms the human need for meaning and normative frameworks. In an advanced liberal society, it is thus inevitable that growth (another name for climate change) ends up acquiring the status of a modern categorical imperative ("always act in such a way that you consume infinitely more while working infinitely more"). By the same token, the icy mechanism of abstract law necessarily becomes the preferred basis for a new and particularly stifling moralism (that of the "politically correct" individual), in which the Other in all its singularity is replaced by the *man without qualities*—that ridiculous metaphysical residue of the struggle "against discrimination of all kinds."

Yet does the mystique of market and law, summoned forth by the cold mechanics of liberalism, provide the soul that is missing from a system whose negative ambition has, from the outset, been a quest for the lesser evil? There are plenty of reasons to doubt it. The transformation of market and the law into cult objects can only give rise to theological commandments of rather limited cultural interest (Compete as you consume! Come together in good conscience!). It is quite clear that this "anthropological" foundation is far too limited to entirely supplant the creative dialectic of primary sociability and the human norms that take root in it. In the long run, every effort to repress the latter can have but one consequence: the return of the anthropological repressed in the form of permanent psychological suffering, which is destined to grow at the same rate as capitalist globalization. This uniquely liberal form of civilizational discontent must not be conflated with unprecedented forms of social deprivation. But, in terms of scale, it surely constitutes an altogether new historical phenomenon,[11] from which the ruling classes

---

11. On this point, one might consider many works inspired by psychoanalysis—such as those by Jean-Pierre Lebrun, Charles Melman, and Dany-Robert Dufour—which attempt, in various ways, to circumscribe the "new psychic economy" brought about by the lifestyle characteristic of generalized liberalism. Clearly, the repression of primary forms of relationality must have specific effects in subjects' unconscious. It is well known, for example, that those who, in the name of their own difference, systematically

and their pathetic "celebrities" (the ersatz modern form of what were once called courtesans) are, if one considers how impoverished their lives have become, the last who should expect to be spared. One must recall George Sand's socialist lesson: "There is no true happiness in selfishness."

refuse to bow to the slightest custom (that is, any shared way of living) generally tend to develop a large number of personal manias (which are simply private customs and ceremonies) and have considerable potential for (self) destructive hatred and anger. From this perspective, Jean-Pierre Lebrun, in *La Perversion ordinaire. Vivre ensemble sans autrui* (Paris: Denoël, 2007), offers an illuminating analysis of the case of Richard Durn, a telling example of the men without qualities that liberal society now mass produces. One can also find valuable information in Eva Illouz's essay (*Les Sentiments du capitalisme*, Paris: Seuil, 2006), which seeks to describe the new emotional configuration introduced by the liberal paradigm (among other topics, she examines the new kinds of relationships that are the structural consequences of the internet). From this perspective, it would be interesting to study the way in which the repression of primary sociality (in which face-to-face relationships prevail) leads a growing number of individuals to seek a compensatory second life in virtual universes, the price of which is the disappearance of the real subject in relation to its avatar. On such topics, the work of reference remains Christopher Lasch's *The Culture of Narcissism*.

CHAPTER 9

Doublethink

The following essay appeared as the forward to Michéa's 2008 essay, *La Double pensée: retour sur la question libérale*. Here he returns to the theme of the connection between economic and cultural liberalism, arguing that these opposed forces are in reality two poles of the same dynamic, which Orwell characterized as the ability to believe contradictory ideas simultaneously, known as doublethink (*la double pensée*).

Winston sank his arms to his sides and slowly refilled his lungs with air. His mind slid away into the labyrinthine world of doublethink. To know and not to know, to be conscious of complete truthfulness while telling carefully constructed lies, to hold simultaneously two opinions which cancelled out, knowing them to be contradictory and believing in both of them, to use logic against logic, to repudiate morality while laying claim to it, to believe that democracy was impossible and that the Party was the guardian of democracy, to forget whatever it was necessary to forget, then to draw it back into memory again at the moment when it was needed, and then promptly to forget it again: and above all, to apply the same process to the process itself. That was the ultimate subtlety: consciously to

induce unconsciousness, and then, once again, to become
unconscious of the act of hypnosis you had just performed.
Even to understand the word 'doublethink' involved the
use of doublethink.

GEORGE ORWELL, *1984*

One too often forgets that the modern world is, on the flip
side, the bourgeois world, the capitalist world. It is even an
amusing spectacle to see how our anti-Christian and, in
particular, anti-Catholic socialists, unconcerned with contradiction, shower with praise a world they call 'modern'
even as they denigrate the very same world by calling it
bourgeois and capitalistic.

CHARLES PÉGUY, *DE LA SITUATION FAITE*
AU PARTI INTELLECTUEL (1907)

In the nineteenth century, socialism was invented to replace
capitalism. But we must fully accept the market economy.
I would rather speak of 'the left.'

MANUEL VALLS, *FRANCE-SOIR*, MAY 19, 2008

THE INFLUENCE OF LIBERAL dogma over "news" and entertainment is so
obvious (and accepted so naturally by professionals of that world) that some
analysts have, to explain this phenomenon, proposed the term "monothink"
(*la pensée unique*).[1] This concept's descriptive merits cannot be denied. The
term, in any case, captures with particular accuracy the appalling *ideological
uniformity* of the contemporary media landscape.[2]

---

1.   The first two authors to have used the term seem to have been Alain de Benoist (in 1993
     in the journal *Éléments*) and Ignacio Ramonet (in 1995 in *Le Monde diplomatique*).

2.   This ideological uniformity attains a maximal degree of intensity every time capital-
     ist institutions face threats that are real (for example, with the referendums on the
     Maastricht Treaty and the European Constitutional project) or imagined (as with the
     presidential elections of April 2002). The absolute harmony between political commen-
     tators, the scale of their deception, and the inevitable mobilization of official artists
     can be compared, without any exaggeration, to the propaganda typical of totalitarian

Even so, the very fact that the term could be adopted so easily is troubling. It implies that the word means something to everyone. Those who oppose economic liberalism will maintain, with good reason, that any criticism of the ideology of growth, global trade, budget austerity, retirement reforms, and the indecent wealth of rich people will never be granted more than a marginal role in the mainstream media. Conversely, those who oppose cultural liberalism will contend—just as reasonably—that it is difficult to imagine a TV anchor being openly racist or homophobic, criticizing abortion, proclaiming men's superiority over women, speaking approvingly of a remark by the pope, or calling for the expulsion of immigrants who cross our borders illegally. In this way, "monothink" seems oddly double: the economically correct (usually favored by the right-wing bourgeoisie) always intersects with the politically correct (typically favored by the left-wing bourgeoisie).[3]

The larger question is whether the inner duality of "monothink" is philosophically coherent. The answer is surely "yes." Since the eighteenth century, liberal philosophy has always presented itself as twofold or, put differently, as a double-entry ledger: on the one hand, political and cultural liberalism[4] (of the kind associated, for instance, with Benjamin Constant and John Stuart Mill) and, on the other, economic liberalism (associated, among others, with Adam Smith and Frédéric Bastiat). These two liberalisms represent, in fact, two *parallel* and *complementary* versions of one and the same intellectual and historical rationality.

This philosophical complementarity can be easily explained. The purely "formal" and negative liberties that the liberal state guarantees individuals ("everyone should be free to lead their own life as they see fit") can never

---

states. It is precisely in such privileged moments—when people howl with the wolves and masks come down—that one gets a true sense of the courage, probity, and moral worth of media and entertainment professionals.

3.   The same division of labor can be seen in academia. The role of economics departments is primarily to train readers of *L'Expansion* (and after graduation of *Le Point* and *L'Express*); that of humanities and social sciences departments is to train readers of *Libération* (and post-doctoral, of *Inrockuptibles* and *Télérama*). In this way, each sector of the university world has its own distinct orthodoxy and corresponding ways of defining "incorrect" ideas.

4.   Political and cultural liberalism are logically connected. If everyone is free to fully choose the way of life that suits them, traditional norms immediately lose their prescriptive power and can be legitimately deconstructed. And vice-versa.

serve as even the most innocuous basis for collective life, apart from the negative principle of not harming others. Political and cultural liberals thus find
themselves compelled, sooner or later, to take their bearings from the prosaic
world of *doux commerce*. With its exclusive appeal to motives, notably the
selfish pursuit of individual interest, presumed to be shared by all, only the
marketplace is thought to provide the privatized (or atomized) subjects of
political and cultural liberalism with an effective framework for daily life.[5]
This is ultimately the reason why most political liberals have, since the nineteenth century, logically concluded that the market economy is the natural
complement of their initial ideological premises.[6]

To refer to this fundamental dialectical circularity[7]—or philosophical
shift—between two essential moments in liberal rationality, I have chosen the
expression "doublethink," first coined by George Orwell in his novel *1984*. Its
first merit is to render immediately intelligible the paradox of "monothink":
in principle, there is no contradiction between the liberal economic system's
struggle to achieve the globalization of exchanges and the abolition of all borders,
on the one hand, and liberals' war on arbitrary moral "taboos" and "discrimination in all its forms," on the other. The Cannes Film Festival is not the majestic
negation of the Davos Forum; it is, on the contrary, its philosophical truth.

Yet in George Orwell's novel, the term doublethink has a much more
specific meaning. It refers to a distinct way of functioning psychologically
that supports totalitarian thought. (Orwell was, of course, inspired by the
Stalinist intellectuals of his time). These astonishing mental gymnastics,
made possible primarily by lying to oneself, allow those who grasp the con-

---

5.   It is well known that in the eighteenth century, the term "commerce" still referred to
    any form of exchange favoring civilized social bonds (such as, for example, pleasant
    conversation).

6.   Some, like Benjamin Constant and Tocqueville, reached this conclusion with resigna-
    tion. Others did so with considerable enthusiasm, such as Frédéric Bastiat.

7.   Of course, this dialectic has its counterpart: when the development of the market
    economy achieves the stage of consumer capitalism (or "the society of the spectacle"),
    it finds its logical complement in the transformation of human beings into infantilized
    consumers, subject only to greed and their own whims. It is in this new context that
    generalized cultural liberalism appears as the ideological form that is best suited to the
    demands of a limitless economy.

cept to simultaneously embrace two logically incompatible propositions.[8] This allows them, for example, as Orwell explains in *1984*, "to repudiate morality while laying claim to it, to believe that democracy was impossible and that the Party was the guardian of democracy."

This meaning of "doublethink" fits the new left and far left[9] liberal intelligentsia that emerged during the Mitterrand era like a glove. Its abandonment of socialism (which is now described as totalitarianism or "populism") and its embrace of political and cultural liberalism has placed the intelligentsia, for well over twenty years, in a particularly maddening double bind. The fact that in France, since the Dreyfus Affair, the term "the left" implies a

---

8. "Simultaneously" is a key distinction. For example, when, in 1967, Michel Foucault said: "What I have tried to do, is to introduce structuralist-like analyses into realms where they had not yet reached, that is, the history of ideas, the history of knowledge, the history of theory"; and then, in 1976, when he observed "I have no ties to structuralism, and I never used structuralism for historical analyses. Even more, I would say that I know nothing about structuralism, and it does not interest me." See Foucault, "La philosophie structuraliste permet de diagnostiquer ce qu'est 'aujourd'hui'" (1967), in *Dits et Écrits, 1954–1988*, ed. Daniel Defert and Francois Ewald, vol. 1, *1954–1969* (Paris: Gallimard, 1994), 580–584, at 583; and Foucault, "Le savoir comme crime" (1976), in *Dits et écrits*, vol. 3, *1976–1979* (Paris: Gallimard, 1994), 79–86, at 80. This double game has nothing to do with doublethink. It simply means that nine years after the first text, references to "structuralism" had become unfashionable, making it more profitable—in terms of one's academic image—to distinguish oneself overtly from it. On the other hand, when a contemporary intellectual maintains, in one book after another, that the concepts of "national borders" and "national identity" are inherently fascistic and, consequently, that the Tibetan and Palestinian peoples should at last be granted national borders that are precise and consistent with their national identity, we are clearly dealing with a case of (regrettably widespread) doublethink.

9. It would be helpful to distinguish a radical position from a "far" or "extreme" position (in the same vein as one speaks of "extreme" sports). A radical critique should refer to any critique that can identify evil at its root and propose an appropriate solution. An extreme position, to the contrary, refers primarily to the well-known (and usually Oedipal) psychological configuration that requires a subject—in a desperate move to maintain a positive self-image—to constantly overcome existing limits (mimetic one-upmanship being the extremist ritual *par excellence*). These two phenomena are, of course, very different. Were someone to propose, for instance, amputating the right leg of a patient with the flu, no one would describe this remedy as radical: it would simply be called "extreme." Hence an extreme (or "far") left is by no means ensures a radical one.

significant dose of anticapitalism (which was enhanced for decades by a power-ful Communist Party) prevented it from calmly accepting the ultimate eco-nomic consequences of its cultural liberalism. To maintain a semblance of philosophical coherence, this intelligentsia is constantly condemned to lie to itself and invent suitable ideological enemies (to whom it refers by the men-acing term "new reactionaries.")[i] Marx accurately recognized that the devel-opment of capitalism necessarily meant that "all fixed, fast-frozen relations, with their train of ancient and venerable prejudices and opinions, are swept away, all new-formed ones become antiquated before they can ossify. All that is solid melts into air, all that is holy is profaned." This is why the new left intelligentsia had to lay down the law: a liberal society based on fashion, spec-tacle, consumption and unlimited growth had only one conceivable oppo-nent: neoconservatism, a subtle mix of religious austerity, rigid control over children, the continual reinforcement of patriarchal institutions, and com-mitment to patriotic and military duties.

One has only to spend ten minutes in a classroom or in front of a TV screen to realize the extent to which this new vision of contemporary liberal society is truly *delirious* (and the extent to which Marx had by 1848 grasped the essence of the world being born before his eyes). Paradoxically, this delirious perspec-tive seems essential to the psychological stability of the new left intellectuals. Without it, it would be impossible, in practice, to continue to follow their re-lentless injunction to transgress every boundary and established cultural and moral limit as if it were a magnificent subversion of consumer capitalism.[10]

---

10. Marx perfectly grasped the structural relationship between illusion and the dominant class. In *The German Ideology*, he observes that the modern bourgeoisie has its own "di-vision of labor." On the one hand, there are "active, conceptive ideologists" (*die aktiven konzeptiven Ideologen*), whose main livelihood (that is, their academic careers) comes from "perfecting the illusions of the class about itself"; and, on the other, the "active members of this class" (*die aktiven Mitglieder dieser Klasse*)—that is, those who are di-rectly involved with the economic world—who "have less time to make up illusions and ideas about themselves." Marx adds that this "cleavage" between left-liberal intellectuals and right-liberal businesspeople "can even develop into a certain opposition and hostil-ity between the two parts." Yet, he observes, "in the case of a practical collision, in which the class itself is endangered, [this cleavage] automatically comes to nothing, in which case there also vanishes the semblance that the ruling ideas were not the ideas of the ruling class and had a power distinct from the power of this class."

Clearly, *doublethink*, as Orwell understood the term, is the only plausible way of experiencing such a strange situation while retaining a semblance of good conscience.

In employing the concept of *doublethink*, I have set my sights as much on the philosophical nature of liberalism as on the left's psychological defense mechanism.

CHAPTER 10

Can Common Decency Be Universalized?

This essay is the response to the third question Michéa poses in his 2013 book, *Le complexe d'Orphée: La gauche, les gens ordinaires et la religion du progrès* (The Orpheus Complex: The Left, Ordinary People, and the Religion of Progress). In Greek mythology, Orpheus was a musician who, after rescuing his wife Eurydice from the underworld, made the mistake of looking back at her. As result, Orpheus lost Eurydice forever. For Michéa, the "Orpheus complex" is the blackmail of progress that pervades contemporary culture, particularly on the left: the risk that whoever is tempted to "look back" to earlier times, and their associated morals and forms of solidarity will be condemned as unenlightened, reactionary, or "deplorable." In this essay, Michéa examines the political implications of Orwell's notion of "common decency," in particular whether it necessarily entails a particularistic way of thinking or whether it might not serve as the inspiration for a universalist politics and a reinvigorated form of socialism.

[QUESTION:] You claim that "common decency" is, for Orwell, "simply the necessary starting point for socialist politics" and not an "end in itself"—one that could easily lead to communitarianism or nationalism. How should one understand the concept of common decency in relation to the two major questions it raises, namely the connection between morality and politics and the relationship between the people and elites?

"MY STARTING POINT," Orwell wrote in 1946, is "always . . . a sense of injustice." By rediscovering the moral and intuitive foundation of socialism in its original form (according to Orwell, common decency warns us that "there are things one does not do"), he immediately abandons the ideological terrain shared by liberals and defenders of "scientific" socialism. Orwell rejects liberalism because its proponents believe that morality is entirely a matter of private opinion, meaning that people can only debate about and agree on strictly procedural legal norms. (One has only to watch an American courtroom drama to see how this works). Orwell rejects scientific socialism because it sees morality as, at best, petit-bourgeois sentimentality, which will vanish as soon as one achieves a deeper understanding of "history's direction" and the laws that, according to Marx, obey an "iron necessity."

Yet the notion that the socialist revolt begins with a *moral* demand for dignity and justice rather than in a cold and academic assessment of facts must be clarified. First, it is necessary to distinguish *common decency*—which "belongs to the realm of sentiments that are the deepest and most essential to man"[1]—from what I have elsewhere called *moral ideology*, or, alternatively, the *ideology of the good*. By the latter, I mean a particular type of

---

1. I borrow this phrase from Bruce Bégout's excellent study, *De la décence ordinaire* (Paris: Allia, 2008, 26). Let me use this moment as an opportunity to recall that, for Orwell, the idea of ordinary (or common) decency is as much opposed to the moral indifference of liberals (of the left or the right) as to the heroic virtue of Neo-Roman republicans (to use Quentin Skinner's terms). Concerning this republican ideal, Michel Terestschenko rightly emphasizes the degree to which it is "dangerous to confine oneself to a heroic conception of resistance to evil. By creating perfect and inaccessible icons, one is led not only to ignore the profound meaning of ordinary gestures that nonetheless testify to a rejection of moral depravity, but also to the belief that our humanity reveals itself more in our disposition towards evil than in our capacity for good. The former would seem to be our common lot, the latter the exception. Yet this is not true. The 'trivialization' of goodness is a far more fruitful heuristic than its heroization. Terestschenko, "Contre l'héroïsation de la résistance au mal." *Revue de MAUSS* 29 (2007): 321–331, at 331. This was exactly Orwell's point of view when he put forth the concept of common decency.

catechism whose alienating commandments make sense only within a given metaphysics (religious, political, or of some other nature) and that leads the faithful to adopt an automatic form of behavior which they cannot imagine being subject to internal debate. Those for whom moral ideology is a stand-in for honesty can in good conscience declare that "homosexuality is a sin" and "adulterous women must be stoned" or—to consider a more modern example—"whoever says something politically incorrect must be immediately denounced to the appropriate authorities."

What Orwell called common decency is obviously light years away from these moralizing and puritan constructs—and particularly the kinds of psychological perversions that usually underpin them. (The character of Tartuffe[i]—the unparalleled model of an ideologically correct devotee—is the best possible description of this perversion.) By committing us to loyalty and disinterestedness, common decency, to the contrary, draws on the basic virtues that humanity has always valued and that exist transversally in relation to ideological constructs. It is precisely this "transversality" (another name for universality) that led me to posit a philosophical rapprochement between these basic human virtues and the anthropological invariants to which Marcel Mauss first called attention in his *Essay on the Gift*.[2]

If one accepts the idea that the obligation to "give, receive, and give back" constitutes the original foundation (the "fundamentals," as Mauss calls them) of all human relationships, then it is not hard to identify, by way of anthropology, most of the moral dispositions that Orwell praised as "common decency." We have virtues revolving around the *obligation to give* (governing various forms of generosity), virtues revolving around the *obligation to give back* (relating to various forms of gratitude and appreciation), and virtues revolving around the *obligation to receive* (making us capable of accepting a gift as a gift, not as an entitlement or a right). And the foundation of this

---

2. "This morality is eternal; it is common to the most advanced societies, to those of the immediate future, and to the lowest imaginable forms of society. We touch upon fundamentals. No longer are we talking in legal terms: we are speaking of men and groups of men, because it is they, it is society, it is the feelings of men, in their minds and in flesh and blood that at all times spring into action and that have acted everywhere." Marcel Mauss, *The Gift: The Form and Reason for Exchange in Archaic Societies*, trans. W. D. Halls (New York and London: Routledge, 2002/Taylor & Francis e-Library), 89.

inherently ethical and anthropological system of obligations[3]—its corner-stone, which is nothing other than *human virtue as such*—is the psychologi-cal and moral capacity to set limits and keep at bay what Marx called "the most violent, mean and malignant passions of the human breast, the Furies of private interest."[4]

The historical originality of capitalism is to have transformed "the Furies of private interest" into the official engine of its development. At the heart of this project—without parallel in the history of civilization—lie the pessi-mistic convictions of the early liberals that any desire to establish a common life on shared moral and philosophical norms can only throw humanity back into a never-ending cycle of murderous religious wars. (One must never forget that cultural relativism—the idea that "everyone has their own morality"—is the foundation of liberal metaphysics and its postmodern permutations.) At first, it was in the name of civil peace and individual freedom that it became necessary to impose the principle of an ideologically neutral (that is, fully secularized) society, in which any reference to shared moral values was gradu-ally eliminated from major institutions (including the procedural rules of law and the self-regulating laws of the market). In this new context, morality be-came a merely private affair—along with religious belief—and enlightened self-interest became the "open" society's last shared language.

It is this explicit, constitutive amorality of liberal politics that explains why the first workers' protests arose from a simple moral demand for dignity and jus-tice. (It is this publicly proclaimed amorality that the industrialists of London and Manchester were eager to implement, convinced, in de Toqueville's words, that "individual egotism [could be made] the source of general happiness.") The workers involved in these protests were, as Orwell once put it, "generously

---

3. In so-called primitive societies, it is generally the concept of honor that makes it possible to conceive the unity of these two dimensions. This does not mean that these societ-ies are entirely unaware of the "ethical" dimension, in the modern sense of the word (in other words, conscience's debates with itself and the interpretive quarrels about the conduct a community should pursue). Wonderful illustrations of such thinking (no-tably in relation to the Yanomani Indians) can be found in Christian Geffray, *Trésor. Anthropologique analytique de la valeur* (Strasbourg: Arcanes, 2001).

4. Marx, Preface to the First German Edition, *Capital: A Critique of Political Economy*, vol. 1, trans. Samuel Moore and Edward Aveling (Moscow: Progress Publishers), avail-able online at https://files.libcom.org/files/Capital-Volume-I.pdf.

angry." This anger was unmistakably caused by the development of a new economic and social system that, in the name of free enterprise and the struggle against "bureaucratic" regulations, liquidated, without the slightest scruple, every principle of shared morality. "One may be aware that this isolation of the individual, this narrow self-seeking is the fundamental principle of our society," Engels wrote in 1845. Even so, it is clear that these feelings of anger and injustice could by themselves lead in most cases only to isolated revolts or forms of organization, such as mutual aid funds, that remained essentially local and defensive, similar to what the English historian E. P. Thompson, writing about the grain wars of the eighteenth century, called "the moral economy of the crowd." To extend this "spontaneous moral economy" in a socialist direction (which implies a minimal understanding of capitalist dynamics), it was necessary to rethink the latter at a higher level and on philosophical grounds that could both universalize and radicalize its principles.[5] From this perspective, the socialist project or, to use Orwell's terms, the project of a decent society, does appear as a continuation of popular morality by other means[6]—the very means that politics makes available to human action.

------

5.   Lucien Sève articulates with particular lucidity the never-ending dialectic between workers' experience and socialist theorizing: "That the worker's *spontaneous consciousness* is still nowhere close to implying by itself true knowledge of capitalist exploitation is an experience and an idea upon which Marx constantly insisted . . . But this absolutely does not mean that there is not an *immediate experience* of objective exploitation, the human effects of which may not be spontaneously *understood* but which are nonetheless *lived.*" *Structuralisme et dialectique* (Paris: Éditions sociales, 1984), 57. Sève's analysis helps us to understand, incidentally, the decisive political role played by Althusser's concept of "epistemological break" in delegitimizing the lived experience of the working classes and establishing, in the name of "science" (and the mastery of official statistics), the academic authority of the new middle classes. It would be easy to show that the imagination of contemporary official sociology rests entirely on Althusser's regrettable legacy.

6.   We can get a sense of some of the work involved in the philosophical translation required to make the shift from sensibility to concepts by reading these lines from Orwell: "There is probably no one capable of thinking and feeling who has not occasionally looked at a gas-pipe chair and reflected that the machine is the enemy of life. As a rule, however, this feeling is instinctive rather than reasoned. People know that in some way or another 'progress' is a swindle, but they reach this conclusion by a kind of mental shorthand; my job here is to supply the logical steps that are usually left out." Orwell, *The Road to Wigan Pier* (New York: Berkley Medallion Books, 1961 [1937]), 160.

The need to take up the principles of common decency at a political level (and not, as Marx wished, to replace them with scientific socialism) results, first, from the inevitable limits and ambiguities of any revolt that remains purely moral in nature. If the virtues that characterize common decency are universal (on this point, Orwell was surely not mistaken), it is only, as we have seen, to the extent that these values are "transversal"—that is, to speak philosophically, to the extent that they constitute the gift's transcendental conditions. As such, the eternal obligation "to give, receive, and give back"— the anthropological foundation of any subsequent ethical constructs— cannot dictate any *specific* empirical conduct, save for the obvious stipulation that the content be compatible with the three obligations, which excludes purely selfish behavior such as greed, ingratitude, cowardice, and treachery. In practice, the concrete nature of the duties required by the ethos of the gift (what a friend owes a friend, a young person an elder, a man his wife, a samurai his shogun, and a tribe its god) depends on symbolic constructs unique to each civilization. To mention just one example, every known culture emphasizes the obligation to be generous and loyal—even pirate culture, which closely resembles capitalism's predatory spirit. And there are none (except, once again, contemporary liberal culture) that officially encourage greed,[7] treachery, and cynicism. Even so, the obligations found in all traditional societies never specify who benefits from this generosity and loyalty, in what circumstances, and in what form. And the answer will obviously not be the same whether one is dealing with an Inuit tribe, North African nomads, Dickensian England, or a society practicing human sacrifice (this is relativism's rational kernel).[8] This means that the obligation to be generous, loyal, and grateful, while shared by all people, can, in practice, adapt to amicable and egalitarian relationships as well as to agonistic ones (as with potlatch or vendettas) or relations based on a feudal hierarchy or caste system.

To the extent that what Orwell calls "common decency" is simply a

---

7. "Greed is good": this was the slogan that Milton Friedman—the guru of modern liberals— exhorted his disciples to put into practice (originally, the line was used by Gordon Gekko— the unprincipled businessman played by Michael Douglas in Oliver Stone's *Wall Street*).

8. See the exquisite pages that Orwell, in *Homage to Catalonia*, devotes to different ways of interpreting the traditional obligation of punctuality, whether in the sense of British common decency or its Spanish counterpart.

modern reappropriation of the traditional spirit of the gift—in the form of internalized rules of the individual "moral conscience"—it alone cannot bring about socialism. The socialist project rests, in the first place, on social equality (according to Orwell, this "would have been accepted by Marx, or Lenin, or Keir Hardie, or William Morris,[ii] or indeed, by any representative Socialist prior to about 1930").[9] This idea of equality must be understood—as it has now become necessary to explain—not as "everyone's right over everything" (the *jus omnium ad omnia* that makes every difference seem like a "discrimination" or a hidden hierarchy), but, far more radically, as the abolition of all structures that make class domination and the exploitation of other people's labor possible by allowing the concentration of the necessary means for existence in the hands of a privileged few. It was precisely this organized dissolution of the basis for the moral and material autonomy of individuals and local communities—for example, during the enclosure movement[iii]—that ultimately engendered the proletarian condition and modern salaried labor. Yet the project of social equality is completely alien to most precapitalist societies. In the latter, the system of reciprocal obligations defined by the logic of the gift—like those, for instance, that traditionally bind the liege to his vassal or a man to a woman—are usually asymmetrical and inegalitarian, as long as one sets aside so-called "primitive" societies in which people were already mostly living on egalitarian terms.[10]

---

9. Orwell, "James Burnham and the Managerial Revolution," in *Collected Essays, Journalism and Letters*, vol. 4, *In Front of Your Nose, 1945–1950*, 160–181, at 164. In the political platforms of the contemporary left, one would search in vain for any reference to a "classless society" (or to the concepts of the bourgeoisie or the working class)—despite the fact that *never* in human history have class inequalities been as great (and indecent) as today.

10. That said, not every form of asymmetrical obligation merits condemnation. To take but one example, civility (or politeness) is based on the idea of effacing oneself for another's benefit ("please, after you"). But anyone can see that the daily application of this principle (which is completely contrary to the procedural character of law) implies no renunciation of personal dignity, nor of the idea of dignity in the socialist sense (though one must not, of course, confuse genuine civility with the social comedy—the icy and hypocritical world of "bourgeois propriety"—characteristic of class domination and which is no more than a strategy for social distinction). Orwell is right to include politeness in the list of positive qualities (alongside "affection, friendship, and goodwill") that allow people to neutralize "the struggle for power."

For early socialist theorists to posit the ideal of a classless society (and consequently the idea of autonomous individual and collective life) as the horizon of their struggles, they needed—deliberately or not—to borrow principles from other historical and cultural sources besides the spirit of the gift. These include the collective memory of earlier popular struggles (such as the English Levellers[iv] or the French Republicans of 1793) and the distant echo of certain religious and philosophical debates. One must not forget that memories of practices of mutual aid unique to traditional village communities—from which the emerging proletariat typically hailed—clearly played an important role in the creation of a socialist imaginary (as did habits of solidarity distinct to the old corporate system of labor organization).

If it is clear that the popular sentiment that "certain things aren't done" or that they dishonor whomever does them is sufficient to lay bare the immorality of a world based on selfish calculation and the perpetual transgression of all limits, then it is just as obvious that this sentiment could never, on its own, establish anything other than a negative political ideal, such as the desire "to not be oppressed" that, according to Machiavelli, motivated commoners in Italian city-states. And this is why—Orwell always insisted on this point—it is essential to ensure that this sentiment has time to develop politically, giving it specific philosophical foundations, which alone make it possible to universalize this principle and lay the foundations of a decent society.

The necessity of a political elaboration of the original kernel of common decency is all the more daunting for the socialist project in that the ideal of a classless society necessarily has a universal dimension. If the emancipation of workers is to coincide with that of humanity as such, then it is indispensable to extend its principles to the entire planet. Yet this goal presupposes that the socialist movement can subsume every local emancipatory program under the aegis of universal values—values, that is, that apply to all human beings, regardless of the diversity of cultures in which they are entrenched. Such a task is, however, extraordinarily complex. The implications and stakes of this task have often been underestimated by the European workers movement, due, in part, to the cultural legacy of the Enlightenment.[11]

---

11. A particularly tragic example can be found in the history of New Caledonia. In 1878, most of the Communards who had been deported to the Dacos prison participated without reservation in crushing the great Kanak insurrection at Atai. Of thousands of

A genuine "international workers association" (which is indispensable to fighting globalization at the global level) would indeed be condemned to remain a utopian project (or, even worse, to be based on one civilization's hegemony) if it were not accompanied by a parallel project of philosophical "translation,"[12] which seeks to identify the universal foundations of a truly shared world. Such an endeavor requires, on the face of it, far more resources than the good will of a particular country's working class. For in order to translate (or transpose) the socialist ideal of emancipation—born in the particular circumstances of nineteenth-century Europe—into a political language that can indeed speak to everyone, it is not only necessary to recognize the specificities of each particular civilization (including their religious aspects), but also and especially to be able to build, on the basis of these specificities, the philosophical and political mediations that will allow working classes in every nation to raise themselves to a universal standpoint without having to renounce the essential foundations of their culture and identity.

In the absence of such dialectical mediations (in other words, of a genuine international consciousness), the struggle for a decent socialist society will be hopelessly dependent on the limits of one's home continent—along the lines of the Western, liberal conception of "human rights" and the "humanitarian" conscience that usually accompanies it—and it is unlikely to be understood and embraced by different peoples, except for the most Westernized (and thus most alienated) segments of their middles classes. So vast an undertaking cannot, of course, be achieved by a single nation. To the contrary, its practical conditions depend on promoting collective action by workers across the world against what is becoming the common enemy of all peoples: the vast, humanity-crushing machine that is capitalism without borders—a machine whose rootless, uncultivated, and perpetually mobile elites are busy, as they have been for decades, dissolving the

---

deportees, Louise Michel was one of the few who saved the honor (and philosophical coherence) of French socialism by supporting with all her might this revolt of an indigenous people, whose culture she had come to respect and appreciate. In 1885, she even published a book on Kanak legends.

12. See François Jullien, *De l'universel, de l'uniforme, du commun, le dialogue entre les cultures* (Paris: Fayard, 2008).

extraordinary diversity of existing cultures into the icy abstraction of the global market, the uniformity of its "international" law, and its hypnotic and alienating "mass culture."

My point is not to defend a purely ethical and abstract conception of socialism. It is precisely the recognition of moral conscience's political limits that justifies Orwell's interpretation of fascism as a perverse form of socialism. If common decency is the socialist sensibility's only legitimate starting point—Orwell was completely allergic to the idea of an "intellectuals' socialism"—this by no means implies that this starting point already contains within it the future socialist project in its totality. Once again, it is only in their universalized form (that is, as they have developed gradually in a simultaneously egalitarian and internationalist direction) that the principles of a concrete popular morality (what Hegel called *Sittlichkeit*)ᵛ can become the common ethical denominator of a pluralistic socialist humanity. The fact remains that the idea of a moral starting point for revolutionary struggle is all that is needed to distinguish the socialist idea of a *common world* (universal values dialectically rooted in the concrete diversity of civilizations) from the liberal *uniformization* of the world (the systematic eradication of all collective identities opposed to the two-headed reign of market and law).

Even if the dialectical universalization of common decency was achieved, a purely ethical socialism would still encounter a final obstacle. The edification of a decent society (locally or globally) necessarily implies the implementation of a degree of technical knowledge that cannot be deduced from common decency alone—even if it were universalized and politically elaborated. For example, a socialist ecological policy (or a comparable monetary policy or public health policy) would still depend on specific knowledge. The cynicism of a company like Monsanto, which seeks to control humanity's food resources to enhance its own profits, probably offends the moral sensibility of most ordinary people (assuming they are aware of the problem). But the impact of this moral sensibility will be limited when it becomes necessary to define, in concrete terms, the practical measures required to rebuild agricultural practices that are respectful of the microbiology of soils, people's health, and the taste of food. Yet such a policy, which implies a radical rethinking of capitalist urbanization, with its overpopulated megalopolises, never-ending immigration, and the corresponding destruction of natural sites and arable land,[13] is meaningless unless it draws upon—in addition to the peasantry's crucial know-how—a wide array of practical scientific and technical knowledge. (Organic fertilizers, the relationship between livestock farming and agriculture, and the adaptation of crops to soil, are but a few of the issues involved.) Moreover, and the fact that it is impossible to eliminate technical considerations from the socialist project compels any decent society to reckon with a problem of particular complexity: that of training experts, determining how independent they should be, and cultivating their intellectual honesty (remember the fabulous destiny of that walking caricature, Claude Allègre)[14] and, by extension, the forms of supervision citizens should have over their activities. It is at this precise juncture that moral and political thinking can—and must—reclaim its rights.

To speak, like Orwell, of socialism's moral foundation (which, he observes, "never fail[s] to draw a snigger from anyone of intellectual pretensions") never meant that the good will of ordinary people was enough to regulate all the problems a decent society must face. It is simply a way of recalling, first, that the ends of socialism always draw their primary impetus from the moral experiences of ordinary people, not a university-based education or historical materialism. Second, it means that once these ends have been posited, they must never legitimize, in the name of political realism, the use of such notoriously immoral methods as "mass bombing of civilians, the use of hostages, torture to obtain confessions, secret prisons, execution without trial, floggings with rubber truncheons, drownings in

---

13. Some Asian countries, like South Korea, have already pushed their capitalist urbanization programs so far that they are reduced to subletting or buying entire regions of Africa to establish full-blown offshore versions of their own farming units (over the last ten years, rich people in rich countries have taken away some 50 million hectares of arable land from poor countries). It is clear, of course, that this kind of "solution" cannot continue indefinitely. Humanity must choose, sooner or later, between the economic profitability of building (which is too often disguised as "housing rights") and the demand for non-toxic food.

14. One gets an idea of Claude Allègre's working methods (and, more generally, the way that major lobbies cynically organize "climate-skeptic" disinformation) by reading Sylvestre Huet's, *L'imposteur, c'est lui* (Paris: Stock, 2010), Stéphane Foucart, *Le populisme climatique* (Paris: Denoël, 2010), and Florence Leray, *Le négationnisme du réchauffement climatique en question!* (Villeurbanne: Golias, 2011).

cesspools, systematic falsification of records and statistics, treachery, bribery, and Quislingism."[15] These are, I admit, thoroughly modest philosophical propositions. Yet they were sufficient to unleash against Orwell the holy rage and calumnies of the ideologues of the twentieth-century *bien-pensant* left.

As for the question of the relationship between different social classes and common decency, Orwell has, once again, said all that matters. For if every human being is capable of acting decently, it is undeniable that the practical aptitude for decency remains the privilege of ordinary people. This populist (in the term's original sense) conviction is by no means an "idealization" of the working classes.[16] At Wigan and on the Spanish front, Orwell was able to see the world of workers up close. (Much closer, in any case, than university professors who comment ironically on his "Rousseauism.") Orwell's belief was based on the fact that social dispositions to decency (that is, to overcoming egoism) are always born with collective practices and systems of solidarity that, until this day, still shape much of the life in working-class communities and small towns. By the same token, it is clear why the progress of liberal capitalism (particularly in the tentacular form of urbanization, characterized by the perpetual mobility of individuals and the transformation of old working-class neighborhoods into mosaics of solitary lives), as it

---

15. Orwell, "Raffles and Miss Blandish" (1944), *A Collection of Essays* (Garden City, NY: Doubleday, 1954), 139–154, at 153.

16. In the world of official media (on the left and right), it is very frowned upon to celebrate the decency of ordinary people and their ability to govern themselves directly. These beliefs are seen as a "Rousseauist" illusion (everyone "knows" that humans are naturally evil and thus always ready to harm others) and, in the worst cases, as an instance of *populist thinking*—"and who knows where that could lead." Even so, it is curious that media zealots never consider applying this negative anthropology to elites. They always take for granted that those who govern us—or who manage major international institutions (from the IMF to the World Bank by way of the UN) are admirable people always intent on fulfilling their duties to the best of their abilities. The maxim "they're all crooks" is, in short, outrageous when applied to the dominant classes but completely plausible when applied to ordinary people. Indeed, no word exists, in the official vocabulary of politics, to refer to the attitude that is symmetrical to "populism," that is, the tendency to idealize the world of elites and to constantly safeguard their reputation (which is a good summary, I think, of the modern journalistic profession, whether they work for TF1 or Canal Plus). Except, perhaps, the verb *to grovel*.

systematically destroys the material and symbolic foundation of traditional solidarities can only undermine, little by little, the most essential conditions of common decency and common life. It is thus less because of their "nature" that the working classes are relatively protected from liberal egoism than because of the existence and preservation of a type of *social fabric* ("family life, the pub, football, and local politics," Orwell notes, prefiguring Ken Loach) that, on a daily basis, keeps the most voracious forms of possessive individualism at bay. (One has only to read Orwell's writings on colonial Burma or London's ghettos to realize that he was never tempted by the theory of the "noble savage.") This is why the planned destruction of working-class neighborhoods (which planners proudly call "urban renewal"), the spread of unemployment and precarity (which complicate practices of gift-giving and counter-gift-giving), and the entertainment industry's control over "available brain time" (which is always focused on the myth of individual success) automatically increase the *lumpenization* of the least conscious and most socially fragile segments of the working classes, thus contributing to the slow erosion of common decency—one of the most troubling trends in contemporary liberal society.[17]

Yet despite the absurd political hopes that far left liberal "sociologists" have attached to this *lumpenization* (consider all the academic foolishness uttered in the aftermath of the 2005 riots),[vi] everything suggests that the working classes' capacity for intellectual and moral resistance remains infinitely greater than is commonly believed and that most ordinary people (even in "tough" neighborhoods) have, at least for now, "never parted company with their moral code" (Orwell, letter to Humphrey House, April 11, 1940). Clearly, capitalism has not yet managed to fully transform the people into a "multitude" (much to Toni Negri's regret, no doubt).[vii]

The relationship between elites and common decency is obviously very different. As Bruce Bégout writes, "There clearly exists among the higher levels of society factors that inhibit the development of common decency."[18]

---

17. On how unemployment and precariousness, by tearing apart the social fabric and local life, gradually disorganizes even the very personalities of their victims (their relationship to time, space, others, and so on), see the remarkable study by Jean Peneff and Mustapha El Miri, "Les pauvres à l'abandon," *Le Sarcophage* 23, March 12, 2011.

18. Bruce Bégout, *De la décence ordinaire*, 21.

The first factor pertains to the very nature of the capitalist system and its *principled amoralism* (the case of former aristocracies is undoubtedly somewhat different in that their power was partially offset—at least in theory—by the idea of *noblesse oblige*). To take just one example, those involved in the world of finance—the sector of the modern economy in which the logic of liberalism operates in its purest state—cannot afford the luxury of even a smidgen of personal honesty, despite the best efforts of their publicists and economists to hide their sadly ordinary tale. As Paul Jorion comments, "decision-makers like determining the membership criteria of their clubs in terms of competence; my eighteen-years of experience convinced me that there was a different criterion: *personal tolerance of fraud*."[19] One can easily find similar situations in all sectors of the economy where capitalist domination has already assumed a globalized form.

As for the second inhibiting factor, it is much more general (and older) and is tied, as Blaise Pascal recognized, to the very condition of the great, regardless of the specific form of social hierarchy in which they exercise their predatory skills. Indeed, the great live in a separate universe—a universe of wealth and power. Everyone knows that wealth—the privilege of *spending without counting*—always ends up distorting one's sense of reality since the whims of the wealthy never encounter the limits experienced by ordinary people. This no doubt explains why the astronomical salaries that global elites are always shamelessly giving themselves are more absurd than they are indecent.[20] As for power wielded over others (and, by the same token, the habit of having an army of dependent and fearful servants, or courtiers), it inevitably tends to reassure the powerful in their infantile omnipotence and their status as all-powerful children. (Consider de Tocqueville's description of the perverse effects of slavery on the psychology of the great planters of the American south). Consequently, to the degree that the ability to behave

---

19. Paul Jorion, "Comment on devient 'l'anthropologue de la crise," *Le Débat* 161 (2010): 129–142.

20. The personal wealth of the 225 wealthiest capitalists of the planet is equal to the total income of the world's 2.5 billion poorest people. As Warren Buffet recently observed—with courage that is rare in these circles—if society suddenly confiscated 99% of their wealth, *they would not even notice* and *nothing* in the way that they live their daily lives would change.

decently always implies that one has managed to overcome one's infantile egoism—in other words, that one has acquired the *maturity* that makes genuine autonomy possible—it is clear that the way of life of privileged classes, which distorts their sense of other people and of reality, can only render problematic, in most cases, the emergence of a genuine moral conscience, or even the most basic common sense.[21]

It is worth recalling a wonderful quote from Albert Camus: "Here lives a free man. Nobody serves him." If this anarchist axiom is psychologically valid, then the brilliant elites who have arrogated for themselves the right to govern the world deserve, more than anything, to be pitied.

---

21. "It is easier for a camel to go through the eye of a needle than for a rich man to enter the kingdom of God." Matthew 19:24. This eternal truth from the Gospel is also an excellent summary of populist philosophy.

CHAPTER 11
Letter to Jacques Julliard

In 2014, Michéa published *La Gauche et le peuple* (The Left and the People), an epistolary exchange between Jacques Julliard and himself. Julliard (1933–2023) was a prominent intellectual and a major figure of what is known in France as the "Second Left," which sought to free French socialism from the idea that the state should be the primary vehicle of social transformation. The Second Left emphasized civil society as a space for social change and highlighted the connection between socialism and democracy (in contrast to forms of socialism favoring a more top-down approach). The Second Left also played a role in weaning socialism off Marxism and nudging it towards liberalism—the very trends that Michéa denounces. An historian and the author of numerous books, Julliard also wrote for the magazine *Le Nouvel Observateur* and held leadership roles in the Confédération française démocratique du travail (the French Democratic Confederation of Labor), a major trade union that was closely aligned with the Second Left.

To understand Michéa's response to Julliard, a summary of the positions defended by the latter is necessary. In his letter from October 2013, Julliard explains that he fully agrees with Michéa on some issues and strongly disagrees with him on others. Julliard expresses admiration for Michéa's critique of the complicity between consumerist capitalism and cultural liberalism. Yet he is skeptical about Michéa's celebration of "the people" and its capacity for resistance. Indeed, Julliard wonders if "the people" still exists. He and Michéa agreed that the central question of their exchange would be: "Are the people on the left"? Specifically, Julliard asks Michéa four questions, which constitute the framework for their conversation: 1. When (historically) were the people and the left united? 2. What is "the people" today? At a time when consumerism and individualism are so rampant, does "the people" even exist? 3. Why is there a split between the people and politics? 4. At present, what is the nature of cultural domination—that is, the imposition of the culture and values of the dominant class on the dominated classes?

Julliard briefly addresses the first question—when (historically) were the people and the left united? Julliard recognizes, like Michéa, that the relationship between the people and the left has become fraught, even hostile. But he rejects Michéa's claim (presented in earlier books) that the "left" did not exist before 1899. For Michéa, the turning point was the Dreyfus Affair, when a Jewish army captain was falsely convicted of conspiring to sell French military secrets to the Germans. The "left," for Michéa, assumed its modern form when socialists allied themselves with the bourgeois parties to defend human rights and oppose Catholic reactionaries. This was the beginning, for Michéa, of the left's divorce from the people. Julliard maintains, however, that the origins of the left must be found earlier, in the long period between the French and Russian revolutions when (in France, at least), the progressive bourgeoisie generally allied itself with the working class (give or take several crucial exceptions, such as the repression of the June 1848 uprising and the defeat of the Paris Commune in 1871). By the same token, Julliard also asserts that the workers' movement was steeped in Enlightenment ideals. Though Julliard acknowledges that the alliance between the bourgeoisie and workers was far from harmonious, he insists that it produced tangible results: liberal democracy, the right to vote, and basic civil liberties (which German workers, for instance, did not get until a later date).

These arguments are the focal point of Michéa's reflections in the following letter. He uses it as an opportunity to present his vision of the left and its history. Michéa contends that the working classes have often had a tenuous relationship with the "left," a term he believes is historically associated with the progressive bourgeoisie. Working people, Michéa maintains, must pursue their own agenda independently of the progressive elites who have long monopolized the very definition of "the left."

JEAN-CLAUDE MICHÉA to Jacques Julliard. November 2013

Reading your letter, dear Jacques, makes one better understand the paradox of modern "democracy," since this is the name in which the liberal system of representation drapes itself. The people are no longer seen as the solution. *They have become the problem.* Over the past thirty years, "populism," a term whose revolutionary pedigree was once impeccable, has become the ultimate thought crime. This development tells us a great deal about the ideological inversion we are living through. Could a Maoist[i] from the early 1970s, even if they were fully aware of the manipulative powers of academia and the media, ever have imagined such an astonishing semantic shift? Populism's philosophical assumptions are, of course, minimal. Machiavelli, the republican philosopher, expressed populism's core principle long before Michelet, Hugo, Tolstoy, and Péguy[ii] when he observed that "one cannot by fair dealing, and without injury to others, satisfy the nobles, but you can satisfy the people, for their object is more righteous than that of the nobles, the latter wishing to oppress, while the former only desire not to be oppressed." It is worth noting, incidentally, that the term "populism" consists less in "idealizing" ordinary people than in lucidly acknowledging the corrupting moral and psychological effects of power and privilege. This is the Gospel's point when it reminds us that "it is easier for a camel to go through the eye of a needle than for a rich man to enter the kingdom of God."

That so straightforward a political position, which most nineteenth-century socialists and republicans would have accepted in a heartbeat, is now viewed as "an inverted form of social racism" (as Frédéric Lordon absurdly argues)[iii] shows the depth of the psychological, moral, and intellectual chasm that at present separates the left from the working classes.

To use Marx's terms, the fact that the working classes exist *in themselves* does not necessarily mean that they exist *for themselves*. In a liberal society, it is easy to forget that the explicit and implicit *plunder* of an ever-increasing share of the value produced by the majority still constitutes the ultimate source of the elite's wealth. The consciousness of belonging to a single social class—rather than simply being, say, a bronze worker in Belleville or a typographer in Besançon—is neither natural nor spontaneous. This is why the "people," understood, not as a sociological reality, but as a political subject that can mobilize around a common cause to defend its interests and dignity, is always shaped by organizational styles and political histories that are unique to each country. For this reason, E.P. Thompson's 1963 book on the making of the English working class remains a reference point. The task of political organization is to facilitate the emergence of a common language shared by different segments of the "people" or a "class." The crucial role played by practices of "correspondence" between different workers' sections in the development of the First International is well known.[iv] Political organization also helps the people to grasp the exact nature of the systems of domination to which they are subject and overcome the prejudices and lack of mutual understanding resulting from "contradictions within the people." The oldest form of this contradiction is the thousand-year conflict between breeders and farmers, which goes back to Cain and Abel.

As you can see, Jacques, it is not that "my" people can no longer be found. To the best of my knowledge, workers, office staff, technicians, farmers, artisans, small businessmen, and civil servants still make up most of the working population. And they are still the majority, even if a growing apartheid between "peripheral" France and "metropolitan" France brought about by globalization has made the working classes invisible to the media aristocracy and academic clergy. On this issue, left-wing "sociologists" are especially blind and easy to manipulate. Yet what has totally vanished is the kind of unifying "grand narrative" that, just forty years ago, allowed the various constituencies of the "people" to define themselves in common opposition to the dominance of the rich (the "two hundred families," as they were once called) and to imagine a common future—however "utopian," "reformist," or "totalitarian"—in which the exploitation of man by man was no longer the only possible option. From this standpoint, the May '68 of the workers and people—the memory of which was immediately erased from the official account, which emphasized the student movement and the antics of Daniel

Cohn-Bendit and his peers—was the last major historical manifestation of a collective anticapitalist consciousness.[v] Pierre Birnbaum's 1979 book *Le Peuple et les gros: histoire d'un mythe* (The People and the Big Shots: The History of a Myth), which at the time still felt subversive, set the tone for the left's anti-populist paradigm in the Mitterrand years.[vi] The belief that the people is exploited by a capitalist minority is, according to Birnbaum, nothing more than a far-right and potentially antisemitic myth. Intellectuals like Bernard-Henri Lévy[vii] and Michel Foucault[viii] ensured the triumph of this new orthodoxy, dubbed "anti-totalitarianism" and "human rights," in the media and academia.

The twentieth century left had come to define itself as the main repository of the grand narrative of resistance. This narrative was a source of genuine working-class pride. In Jean-Paul Sartre's day, intellectuals who were not born proletarians even believed that this was a sin to be expiated. Consequently, it was this very left's rapid conversion to modern liberalism— the ideological synthesis of globalized free-market economy and what Friedrich Hayek called the "struggle against all forms of discrimination"— that is the main political reason for the terrible sense of abandonment that has overcome the working classes.

This brings me to the fundamental question. The contemporary Western left—in France and elsewhere—is clearly incapable of grasping the philosophical significance of the working classes' growing exasperation with the most destructive effects of the new capitalist way of life. Indeed, it is structurally impossible for this left to interpret ordinary people's exasperation as anything other than the "fear of the other" or a "frightened turn inward." But is this failure a passing and context-specific phenomenon or is it rooted in a deeper historical past?

To answer this question, it is essential—I hope the reader will pardon this historical detour—to briefly reconsider the "alliance between the people and the progressive bourgeoisie," which you, Jacques, see as the "major political and social fact of the nineteenth century." This interpretation, which I recognize contains an element of truth, loses sight of two key points. First, as you acknowledge, one cannot forget that, throughout the nineteenth century, much of the peasant and provincial world continued to live under the moral tutelage of the Catholic church and the last vestiges of the old aristocracy, as is clear to anyone who has read Balzac, Stendhal, or George Sand.[ix] This phenomenon was so extensive that Blanqui[x] even entertained the idea of denying provincials the right to vote for "at least seventy years" and proposing a "Parisian dictatorship"—a dream that in many ways has come true, though very differently than he imagined. Second and far more disturbingly, your thesis asks us to erase everything that made the nineteenth-century socialist project *radically original*. The question of the historical relationship between the left and early socialism is my book's central concern, despite Luc Boltanski's[xi] ludicrous claim that I just want to "stigmatize the Arabs who threaten our ancestral values" and denounce the ruthless competition of "emerging countries," about which I have not written a single word. Let me restate my argument as simply as possible.

It is well known that contemporary left-wing historiography rests on two postulates. First, it maintains that the cleavage between "left" and "right" (as we still use the words today) was born during the French Revolution. In terms that have remained largely unchanged, this distinction pits the partisans of "progress," "Enlightenment," and "movement" (i.e., the left) against the partisans of "order" and grim "reaction" (that is, the right). Consider two famous prints from 1816 by Louis-Léopold Boilly.[xii] The first shows a melancholic face turned towards the past; this is the Ultra[xiii] or reactionary. The second portrays a smiling face turned towards the future; this is the Liberal.

The second postulate of left-wing historiography maintains that the left-right dichotomy encompasses the entire political spectrum. Consequently, any attempt to challenge it or escape its boundaries is either an illusion or a hoax. Conventional left-wing academics and their journalistic twins immediately shut down any criticism of the distinction by ritually invoking a famous comment by the philosopher Alain from the 1930s: anyone who claims to be "neither left nor right" is really on the right. Modern readers may not realize that the ideological roots of Alain's comment are to be found in Napoleon. When they met on Saint Helena on June 18, 1819, Bonaparte confided to General Bertrand: "In France, there are only two parties: the Revolution and the Counterrevolution, the old and the new regime, privilege and the people . . . So, in the final analysis, there are only two parties. On one side, the ultras, whatever name one gives them; on the other, the revolutionaries. The whites and the blues." The emperor did not hesitate to include himself in the long future lineage of *men of the left*.

This interpretation of modern politics as a perpetual conflict between "old" (the "whites") and "new" (the "blues"), which is presumed to affect every aspect of human existence (including economics, art, morality, sexuality, and the emotions), is certainly true to a degree. The sexual and emotional dimensions of this conflict were recently on display in the debates over justice minister Christiane Taubira's project of reforming filiation and the production and exchange of children along liberal lines. Clearly, no project of human emancipation can perpetuate inequalities of birth, patriarchal domination, the persecution of minorities, and traditional restrictions (religious or otherwise) that are incompatible with individual dignity and the self-evident right to think and act freely. This is why early socialism almost always saw these aspects of the Enlightenment and the French Revolution's legacy as necessary political conditions for the future classless society. Early socialism thus entailed an unconditional defense of the fundamental liberties that Marx, in *Capital*, proposed, incorporating them into a "modest Magna Carta" that would be philosophically distinct from the bourgeoisie's "pompous catalogue of the 'inalienable rights of man.'" One need only recall the powerful movement created by the English Chartists.[xiv]

The problem is that by reducing *all* of modern political life to this repetitive and monotonous competition between an (invariably "reactionary") right and a (naturally "progressive") left and squeezing modern politics into the Procrustean bed of Enlightenment philosophy, one renounces, by the same token, any possibility of a coherent critique of industrial capitalism, which is founded on Enlightenment political economy and whose spectacular development, after the Napoleonic Wars and the end of the continental blockade,[xv] laid the foundations for what became known as the social question. Charles Dunoyer, a key figure of the liberal left of the 1830s, wrote that capitalism continued "the work of emancipation that has been underway for centuries and which increasingly frees individuals from the illegitimate purview of society and its delegates." One thing the early socialists (beginning with Sismondi's pioneering work) immediately grasped was that the new liberal industrial order, founded on the endless accumulation of capital and the transformation of old rural populations into a salaried urban proletariat, should not be understood as just a variation on the old regime. To the contrary, the new order was what Marx called an "eminently revolutionary system," with the Le Chapelier law of 1791[xvi] providing the legal framework for a structural dynamism (with science as a "directly productive force") that inevitably dissolved traditional values and ways of life into "the icy water of egotistical calculation." The new order was, in short, a system that (as Marx put it) lacked "any moral or natural limit." Its belief system no longer rested on an age-old fear of the new but on a modern faith in history's inevitable march towards a radiant future, an outlook pioneered by Adam Smith, Turgot, and Condorcet.[xvii]

It is thus clear why early socialists were usually reluctant to fully embrace the Enlightenment's discourse on "human rights" and "reason's inevitable progress." Fourier was particularly hostile to the French Revolution and contemptuously dismissed Enlightenment philosophers as so many "cabbage and turnip eaters." In 1839, Louis Blanc,[xviii] the author of *The Organization of Work* and the most moderate of socialists, wrote: "Law, considered abstractly, has been, since 1789, a mirage that deceives the people." Saint-Simon's disciples,[xix] for their part, were perfectly capable of differentiating themselves both from their master's technocratic tendencies and from the political dogmas of the liberal-republican left. In 1831, they declared that "it would be a mistake to believe that the main trait of the Restoration[xx] was the reappearance of Jesuitism and the old nobility: its key characteristic was the triumph of the bourgeoisie." Enfantin[xxi] was more precise when he noted, around the same time, that "it has begun to be recognized that it is no longer the priests vs. noblemen like in '89, or even in 1829, but the people vs. the bourgeoisie, or, even more accurately, the workers vs. the idle." One is reminded of Jules Guesde,[xxii] who, after the Paris Commune, reproached the left for neglecting the "true and sole enemy, capitalism, for a fantasy enemy, clericalism."

Yet once it was recognized that the main threat facing the laboring classes as well as humanity as a whole was capitalism's revolutionary dynamic (since, as Marx wrote in *Capital*, a system whose core logic is production and accumulation for their own sake must necessarily sap "the original sources of all wealth—the soil and the laborer"), it became clear that the concept of "progress" implicit in the socialist critique of the liberalism of Adam Smith,

Frédéric Bastiat, and Jean-Baptiste Say[xxiii] could not be the same as the idea of progress that Enlightenment philosophy invoked to preemptively legitimate the triumph of the market and bourgeois individualism. To early socialists, it seemed essential (to use Engels' words) to break with the major postulates of this philosophy—"the idealized kingdom of the bourgeoisie"—which holds that "everything in the past deserved only pity and contempt." Even today, it is difficult to find a better definition than Engels' of the narrow and damaging limitations of the "progressive" academic mindset and the state-subsidized mysticism of the artistic "avant-garde." This explains the position that Proudhon[xxiv]—though there are countless other examples—adopted in his famous "Toast to the Revolution" of October 1848, which was once deemed an essential volume in any self-respecting socialist library—though I fear that, to contemporary leftists, it would be seen as populism rearing its ugly head. The founder of French anarchism remarked: "Whoever talks about revolution necessarily talks about *progress*, but just as necessarily about *conservation* . . . It is a question of knowing if at present we are also engaged in revolutionary practice, if, like our fathers, we will be *at once* men of conservation and of progress, because it is only by this double title that we will be men of revolution." A similar outlook informed the "separatist culture" (I am borrowing the term, Jacques, that you used in your book on France's many lefts)[xxv] that left such a lasting mark on the socialist workers' movement. Unless one succumbs to a retrospective illusion, this separatist culture renders implausible any notion of a natural harmony between the radical anticapitalism of the "reds" and the republicanism of the "blues." These two currents have always formed bridges and hybrids, as did early socialists and "reactionary" social critics like Lamennais, Ballanche, and Villeneuve-Bargemon.[xxvi] In his remarkable book on Edgard Quinet[xxvii] and the Jacobin question, François Furet[xxviii] goes so far as to speak of an eschatology that is "simultaneously socialist and Catholic," though he is referring in this instance to Buchez.[xxix] One of the bizarre consequences of this attempt to merge the history of socialism and liberalism is the belief that Marx and Bakunin—the two most influential figures in nineteenth-century European socialism—proudly proclaimed their unconditional allegiance to the "left" of their era. This assumption is particularly absurd. To give just one example, the 1970 Moscow edition of Marx and Engels' complete works (the one I use) does not even have the word "left" in its index. The temple guardians must face the facts: the anticapitalism of Marx and Bakunin was, in its day, neither left nor right.

From this standpoint, the famous "Manifesto of the 60," largely written by the metalworker Henri Tolain and published before the 1864 by-elections, strikes me as exemplary. Unlike every "republican front" strategy that has ever existed, the revolutionary manifesto encouraged the proletariat to nominate candidates for every race—even when this meant defeating, as Proudhon put it, "candidates of the so-called democratic opposition"— that were not only socialists but members of the working class. Marx saw this manifesto as "the preeminent statement of the movement of the French workers as they reach adulthood." Just as exemplary was the republican left's prompt, indignant, and wholly predictable reaction to the manifesto, which they lost no time denouncing. In his *Letter to Workers Relating to the 1864 Election*, Proudhon recalls that the left attacked its "retrograde [i.e., reactionary], illiberal, and even dangerous character, due to the suspicion, alarm, and hostility to which it [would] give rise in the bourgeoisie." The main elements of the contemporary left intelligentsia's anti-populist language—words like "reactionary," "antiliberal," and "dangerous"—were already in place by the late Second Empire.[xxx]

As Proudhon explains, however, the working's class's declaration of independence was the logical consequence of its radical opposition to the bourgeoisie and the capitalist system. He defines the bourgeoisie as anyone who does not live primarily off the product of their labor—if they work at all— but rather off "the income of their properties, capital, endowments, pensions, subsidies, shares, salaries, honors and benefices." The system of privileges that shield elites—whether their status is based on wealth, power, or media celebrity—necessarily removes them from the real world in which ordinary people live, and, by the same token, from the anthropological and psychological sources of moral awareness and common sense. *Inside Job*, Charles Ferguson's documentary on the role of elites in the 2008 economic crisis, illustrates this fact in a particularly powerful way. It thus became essential to the political coherence of a popular movement that it constantly protect itself from attempts by intellectuals belonging to the dominant class (both the low and high clergy) to contaminate the movement with their class prejudices or take control of it. Sections of the First International that were especially cautious about this matter even proposed that membership be confined exclusively to manual laborers. This was why, like Proudhon and the early socialists, the representatives of "red socialist democracy" (as Proudhon called them) cultivated and preserved their much prized organizational and ideological independence vis-à-vis liberal bourgeois parties. This requirement implied, in the first place, knowing how to clearly distinguish oneself from the left opposition—be it liberal or republican. Proudhon adds that the left opposition's "avowed anti-socialism inevitably mobilizes reactionary thought against us." There is nothing outrageous about this comment: during the Second Empire, the left opposed, not only the "power of the past" (i.e., conservatism), but was equally, if not more hostile to the "collectivist peril" associated with the "reds" and "redistributionists." Hence the particularly lucid appeal with which Proudhon concludes his *Letter to the Workers*: "I say this to you with all the energy and all the sorrow of my soul: separate yourself from that which separated first, separate yourself, like the Roman people once separated from the aristocrats. *Separamini popule meus. Through separation, you will win.*"

As you can see, dear Jacques, the idea of a "separatist culture" unique to the early socialist movement—the notion that, as you put it, the nineteenth-century labor and socialist movement sought "to live at a distance from the bourgeoisie's internal conflicts and remain on its political Aventine"—is not just a figment of my imagination. Yet this "separatist" interpretation can only be grasped and accepted if one first concedes that between 1815 and 1899, the term "left" could not and did not have the meaning it gradually acquired as a result of the Dreyfus Affair. The "battle of the inkwells," as Albert Thibaudet[xxxi] called the Affair, played a decisive role in this semantic shift. In other words, the idea of the "left" emerged in the context of the "republican defense" pact negotiated between the red proletariat and the blue bourgeoisie's parliamentary representatives in urgent and exceptional political circumstances. As a result of this compromise, the official socialist movement committed to end its anti-capitalist positions and temporarily prioritize the struggle against the (admittedly very powerful) forces of clerical and monarchical reaction, much to the irritation of the anarcho-syndicalists, who quickly realized that this "temporary" deal was likely to become permanent. Sure enough, it did, resulting in the foundation of a new church, with its own faith, dogmas, heresies, and Inquisition. It is ultimately the restrictive implications of this new alliance that explains both the new meaning of the term "left" and the retroactive veil placed over the memory of the original conflict between "reds" and "blues." Indeed, a contemporary leftist would probably find it difficult to grasp what Prosper-Olivier Lissaragay[xxxii] was talking about when he argued, in his exceptional 1876 history of the Commune, that if Thiers[xxxiii] and the *Versaillais* bourgeoisie had little trouble isolating the Parisian proletariat and "misleading the provinces," it was because they could always count on three major forces: "the army, the state bureaucracy, and the *left*." One gets a sense of the massive amount of ideological revisionism—and even pure falsification—required to make it possible for the likes of François Hollande, Dominique Strauss-Kahn, Pierre Bergé, Jérôme Cahuzac, and Pascal Lamy[xxxiv]—the left's official representatives—to say with straight faces that they are the descendants of the Commune's martyrs.

Yet as I noted at the beginning, I do not intend to reject your thesis completely. Liberal culture is the child of the Enlightenment. Consider, for example, what Denis Diderot wrote in *Voyage to Holland*: "One needs no legislation where nature has constituted an attentive, just, firm, and enlightened despot, who always carefully weighs all rewards and punishments: *interest*." A logical consequence of liberalism's Enlightenment origins is that all capitalist societies follow a historical trajectory that is, to use Thibaudet's famous term, "sinistrogyric"—in other words, that veers left. We live in a world, Thibaudet wrote in 1932, that is "clearly moving to the left, at the irresistible and necessary pace of a glacier, and whose political language considers those who speak of conservation . . . as backward-thinking, as *reactionaries*." This "irresistible" movement, Thibaudet continues, "almost automatically places the generation that is 'on its way in' to the left of the generation that is 'on its way out.'" Consequently, any critical perspective on capitalism's historical dynamic becomes ever more difficult and less intellectually legitimate. Each new "cultural" reform resulting from this dynamic provides a new occasion to confirm this sociological rule. Among other things, it shows that the modern "right" is often just an old left that has become incapable of acknowledging the unavoidable implications (particularly the moral and cultural implications) of its liberalism, at least to a working-class audience. Alain Finkielkraut is right when he observes that, in our capitalistic society, "having no one to your left means having the pleasure of being able to intimidate everyone."

When one recognizes the bourgeoisie's extraordinary ability to describe every step that capitalism takes as evidence of the progress of the human spirit or, more modestly, that "modernization" is inevitable, it becomes easier to understand the "psycho-ideological mechanisms" that have convinced the working classes that they must support this supposedly "natural" historical movement. The "progressive bourgeoisie"—but can a social class whose wealth and privileges depend on "creative cultural destruction" be anything other than "progressive"?—has gradually liquidated every material and moral vestige of the old regime and its "reactionary" defenders, starting with the Catholic church. In 1835, the republican Armand Carrel,[xxxv] in *Dossier d'un prévenu* (A Defendant's Dossier), provided the key to this apparent paradox: "In 1789, the bourgeois spoke and the proletarian applauded. There was widespread support as long as equality extended from the bourgeois to the nobleman and not from the proletarian to the bourgeois—[that is], *as long as political rights helped to destroy the aristocracy of birth*, and not to constitute and defend the aristocracy of wealth against the proletariat. *The misunderstanding would soon become apparent.*" Marx adds little to this analysis when he observed, in the *Communist Manifesto*, that "the proletarians [at first] do not fight their enemies, but the enemies of their enemies, the remnants of absolute monarchy, the landowners, the non-industrial bourgeois, the petty bourgeois. Thus, the whole historical movement is concentrated in the hands of the bourgeoisie; every victory so obtained is a victory for the bourgeoisie." This "alliance of the people and the progressive bourgeoisie" that you see—again, not without reason—as "the major political and social fact of the nineteenth century" proves but one thing, though it is usually forgotten, especially on the left: for nearly two centuries, the bourgeoisie has *always won the class struggle* as it places its progressive seal on the course of modern history.

But let me reassure you. By making this Marxist-leaning analysis, I do not for a moment deny that the ambiguous political alliances or "misunderstandings" forged between the people and bourgeois elites (which even you call "fools' bargains") contributed to implanting in the popular mindset a desire for justice, a sense of shared belonging, and a commitment to basic freedoms (particularly free speech and the right to vote). The latter are the essential conditions for "what we call a republic," as you put it. They are extremely valuable political achievements and constitute—to use a psychoanalytic term—"secondary benefits" of the domination of the *old* progressive bourgeoisie, with its patriotic and republican tendencies. This is the bourgeoisie one finds—if I may indulge my childhood memories—in the history textbooks of Albert Malet and Jules Isaac.[xxxvi] There is no denying that an authentic socialist and working-class culture must not only incorporate these achievements but also—and especially—realize their emancipatory potential. This political and philosophical task is particularly important since cultural liberalism, because of its proceduralism and cult of legal abstraction (the metaphysical foundation of "political correctness"), is inclined to take a dim view of these achievements, particularly free speech and open debate, which the contemporary left tends to see as incompatible with the "struggle against discrimination in all its forms."

Yet once the positive dimension of bourgeois society is acknowledged, I do not see how the undeniable fact that the bourgeoisie has for two centuries kept an ideological (and not moral) grip on the working classes, using them as an auxiliary force and cannon fodder (except on rare occasions, as in 1907, 1936, 1945 and 1968), should call into question the philosophical value of socialism and its "separatist" ideal. Given the world with which humanity is now wrestling, and assuming that early socialist principles can be updated and rendered understandable and acceptable to most working people, socialism strikes me as more relevant than ever. First, this project was born in the early nineteenth century out of the need to transcend the already apparent contradictions of nascent industrial and financial capitalism. At present, we are dealing with a fully developed version of capitalism, whose countless transmutations, extending across the entire planet, have colonized every aspect of our lives. (It is noteworthy that the laws and effects of this historic dynamic were, for the most part, correctly described by Marx and Rosa Luxembourg.) Second, amid the ruins of contemporary critical thought, I see no other philosophical model that can explain as coherently as socialism the central paradox of our age: a society that has never been so liberal in its economic principles, yet so leftist in its cultural values and mores.

Let me now return to two specific objections raised in your letter. You believe that the spectacular rise of revolutionary syndicalism in the wake of the Dreyfus Affair cannot be explained by the "separatist" paradigm I have defended. Yet its rise seems perfectly consistent with my analysis. By refusing to participate in an alliance between the republican left and the official socialist movement, revolutionary syndicalism—the "active wing of the working class," to use your excellent expression—clearly demonstrated that it intended to preserve the spirit of early socialism. Hence in January 1898, four full years after the beginning of the Dreyfus Affair, this tradition of philosophical and organizational independence led Jules Guesde and Jean Jaurès to co-sign a manifesto that concluded with a well-known appeal: "Proletarians, do not get mixed up with any clan of this bourgeois civil war!" Unless I am mistaken, this is very much a "separatist" and anti-system slogan. Furthermore, most anarcho-syndicalists, who were already highly suspicious of "state socialism," saw the support given to official socialism by President Émile Loubet[xxxvii] and the republican left (which included the Marquis de Galliffet,[xxxviii] one of the butchers of the Paris Commune) as proof of Robert de Jouvenel's[xxxix] famous quip: "There are fewer differences between two members of parliament, of whom one is a revolutionary and the other is not, than there are between two revolutionaries, of whom one is a member of parliament and the other is not." The obvious vitality of revolutionary syndicalism between 1898 and 1914 proves only one thing: that an authentic and fully autonomous mass working-class movement (as the magnificent Spanish anarchist movement would be) continued to develop until the First World War, even as the parallel rise of a new left accelerated the process by which (as Orwell never ceased to point out) official "socialist" parties were taken over by ideological representatives of the new middle classes tied to the most dynamic forms of consumer capitalism and the society of the spectacle. That Louise Michel, Flora Tristan,[xl] and Rosa Luxembourg have given way to Christiane Taubira, Najat Vallaud-Belkacem, and Cécile Duflot[xli]— without the least indignation or objection—is ample proof of this alarming political, moral, and intellectual regression. If one had to identify a common political ancestor to these ladies of the liberal left, it would no doubt be the curious Duchess of Sutherland, whose schemes Marx eviscerated in *Capital*. Not content to exploit with an iron hand the peasants on her countless properties, the duchess also made it a point of honor to display "her sympathy for the Negro slaves," even organizing a triumphant reception in London for Harriet Beecher Stowe, the author of *Uncle Tom's Cabin*. The Duchess of Sutherland was thus one of the first political women to have simultaneously celebrated the exploitation of man by man and "the struggle against discrimination in all its forms."

A similar analysis can be made of communism. Born in the wake of the First World War, after the majoritarian currents of the Socialist International had abandoned the anti-capitalist struggle to support their respective nations' war efforts, communism, too, proposed, though in far less democratic and anti-authoritarian ways than anarcho-syndicalism (as Rosa Luxembourg repeatedly reminded Lenin), to replace Jaurès' policy of a "union of lefts" with a revolutionary return to the anti-capitalist struggle. Communism, too, reconnected with the most robust traditions of independence of the old socialist and workers' movement. In a speech to the Alsatian Communist Party in the early 1920s, Maurice Thorez[xlii] even reminded his audience that the French Communist Party was "neither left nor right." This was, moreover, the original meaning of the slogan "class against class," which encouraged the immediate establishment of a genuine working-class "counter-society," resulting in the defense of the independence of the workers' Esperanto movement and the principle of a Red Sports International, and even a separate working-class Olympics. Only the terrible defeat of the German Communist Party in 1933—the result of a particularly idiotic application of the concept of a "single workers' front" and a corresponding underestimation of the problem of the lower middle classes and the threat posed by Hitler—would force the Stalinists to accept the idea of defensive alliances with social democrats and the left-wing bourgeoisie (represented, in France, by the all-powerful Radical Party), in the form of the "republican" and "antifascist" policies of the Popular Front. In France, it was only a spontaneous movement of working-class factory occupations that forced the government of Léon Blum[xliii] to go beyond its original election platform and enact a series of social policies that were objectively revolutionary. It was because of this distinct historical context (along with their constant defense of the Soviet nomenklatura's class interests) that Western communist parties gradually renounced the old socialist ideal of popular autonomy. Bidding farewell to Marx and the strategy of class conflict, the communists gradually dissolved, like the party of Guesde and Jaurès before them, into the hazy nebula of the modern left and its "progressive" cult of movement for its own sake.

Before concluding this letter, I must first settle a final misunderstanding. You say, Jacques, that it shocks you that I "seem to reject the idea that the people, and especially working people, were ever touched by the wings of progress and Enlightenment philosophy." But I said no such thing. To the contrary, in *Les Mystères de la gauche* (The Mysteries of the Left), I wrote that socialism was born under two stars: "On the one hand, it is undeniably one of the most legitimate heirs to Enlightenment philosophy and the French Revolution, insofar as it clearly embraces the concern for equality and the idea that a genuine emancipatory project can only exist if its aims are universal. But on the other hand, it also represents the most radical and coherent critique of this new liberal and industrial world . . . whose constitutive principles are rooted, by an ironic historical twist, in the same philosophical legacy." This is why I encouraged readers to "reconsider the problem in more dialectical terms" and "accept that *one must use the Enlightenment to think against the Enlightenment.*" Let me say a word about this enlightened critique of the Enlightenment, whose great precursor was Hegel, and which I see as another facet of the early socialist project.

If by "Enlightenment philosophy" one simply means the belief in the possibility of a peaceful and reasonable world in which, in contrast to the absurdities of feudalism, humans can live together on a free and equal basis, then early socialists like Pierre Leroux, Victor Considerant, and Constantin Pecqueur[xliv] clearly belonged to this intellectual framework. This is why the early socialist critique was far less directed against the Enlightenment (Leroux and Considerant placed the ideas of emancipation, equality, and liberty at the center of their analyses) than it was against the "atomistic" conception of man and society that constituted its metaphysical background. Indeed, most Enlightenment philosophers (leaving aside the complicated question of Rousseau's "civic republicanism") conceived of man as a "naturally independent" individual, endowed with various "natural rights," the most important of which was absolute self-ownership. These individuals, moreover, were presumed to act only on the basis of self-interest, which could be more or less enlightened, depending on the degree of reason available to each individual. This leads to the idea, which ran the gamut of eighteenth-century political thought, that society is simply an aggregate of individuals. These individuals, who were originally independent of one another, ultimately agreed to submit to a minimal set of rules to protect their respective interest in life, property, and freedom. (And one has only to consider the work of John Rawls[xlv] to appreciate the extent to which modern liberalism—particularly in its left-wing variants—remains beholden to this monadological vision.) Yet it is not hard to see in this utilitarian anthropology or in the naïve and reductive psychology with which it is associated a perfect example of what Marx derisively called "Robinsonades." According to Marx, these "unimaginative conceits of the eighteenth-century" constituted the metaphysics both of economic liberalism (the "individual and isolated hunter and fisherman, with whom Smith and Ricardo begin") and of political and cultural liberalism (freedom as an "abstraction inherent in the isolated individual.")

For socialism's founders, the absolute lack of realism in Enlightenment philosophy's ideological postulates explained not only the abstract character of its conception of equality but also the fact that its emancipatory ideal could only be realized historically (precisely because of its abstract character) in modern liberal society. "The human being," Marx says, "is . . . not merely a gregarious animal, but an animal which can individuate itself only in the midst of society." One could say, parodying René Descartes, that the celebrated "rights of man" represent, from a socialist perspective, simply the lowest degree of political liberty. It is a society, to borrow a description from the Saint-Simonian school's 1829 manifesto, whose ultimate horizon is that of an "aggregation of individuals with no bonds and no relations, and with the impulse of egoism as its only motive."

At a strictly political level, the event that most contributed to opening the eyes of the people's champions (that is, the "populists") to the dangers lurking in the Enlightenment's emancipatory ideal was the Le Chapelier Law of June 1791. The law abolished all intermediary bodies between the individual and the liberal state. In his report to the Assembly, Isaac Le Chapelier proclaimed triumphantly: "Henceforth, there will only be the particular interest of each individual and the general interest." By promoting *general atomization*, the law in one fell swoop emancipated workers from the hierarchical and communal constraints associated with the old system of corporate bodies and workmen's organizations (or *compagnonnages*)[xlvi] while leaving them isolated and defenseless before the emerging tyranny of the capitalist market. In a well-known work on poverty published in 1797, Frederick Morton Eden[xlvii] (whom Marx called "Adam Smith's only disciple in the eighteenth century who produced anything of importance") acknowledged that if workers in his time were much poorer than they had once been, it was paradoxically because "they had become freer." Eden even wondered whether, given the historical circumstances of his time, this freedom really was freedom, and whether the condition of the new proletariat was not in fact "worse than that of a slave, who at least was taken care of and fed because it was in his owner's interest." It is this critique of freedom as an "abstraction inherent in the isolated individual" (individuals who are now entitled to insist on their right to do what they want with their time, bodies, and money) that would constitute, by the early nineteenth century, socialism's primary philosophical argument against capitalism. This critique also lays bare the relationship between capitalism and Enlightenment philosophy. As always, it is to Proudhon, thanks to his anarchist sensibility, that we owe one of the best known and most lucid formulations of this critique. In *Confessions of a Revolutionary*, he wrote: "From the social point of view, liberty and solidarity are identical terms: the liberty of each encountering in the liberty of others, no longer a limit, as stated in the Declaration of the Rights of Man and of the Citizen of 1793, but an auxiliary, the freest man is the one who has the most relations with his fellows."

If one is looking for evidence of the incredible modernity of socialism's reworking of the Aristotelian idea that man, far from flourishing in egoism, narcissism, and greed, is essentially a political animal, one need only consider the illuminating question of Sunday work. (Is it a coincidence that Proudhon's first political essay, written in 1839, was a celebration of Sundays?).[xlviii] It seems obvious that we have been asked to end this ridiculous "taboo" from earlier times because it violates the absolute right of individuals—insofar as they are "separated from other men and from the community," as Marx put it—to organize their time and daily lives according to their own private interests. The justification of Sunday work, in other words, is none other than the old liberal dogma, which holds that any private contract between two consenting adults—be it a prostitute and a client, an employer and an employee—is none of the community's business and should be impervious to supervision or intervention. And this is true even when the negative consequences of supposedly "free" and "personal" choices on the form, content, and quality of collective life are easily predictable. After all, when Sunday becomes a day like any other, there will no longer be any reason for employers to extract less surplus value on Sundays than on weekdays. Yet this logic, which is both economic and cultural, cannot stop mid-course. It is the same logic that legitimates stock-market speculation and tax evasion ("what I do with my money is none of your business"), as well as the idea that prostitution is a job like any other or that drug addiction only concerns addicts ("what I do with my body is none of your business"). The same logic also underpins—though few on the left have the political and intellectual courage to admit it—the peculiar demand for "marriage equality," rather than civil unions giving all couples, regardless of their sexual orientation, the same protective rights, notably following divorce or death. This demand is a necessary consequence of the reduction of marriage to "a simple contract between two people, based on mutual consent," in the fervently Girondin[xlix] formulation of Noël Mamère.[l] Marriage thus becomes a purely private arrangement between two individuals who are presumably "separated from other men and from the community" and which can be assumed to have no real effect on the structure of collective life. Yet it should have been obvious, for anyone initiated into the biological mysteries of reproduction, that the social institution of marriage always transcends the couple's private standpoint, in that it raises the anthropological question of filiation and the production and exchange of children. The ultimate stakes of this philosophical question can be seen in Andrew Niccol's prophetic film *Gattaca*. Released in 1997, it lucidly depicts the inevitable inegalitarian implications ("nature's children" vs. the "perfected" children of techno-science and the genetic industry) of a world that has succumbed to the basically eugenicist fantasies of Christiane Taubira (and her mentor Francis Fukuyama).[li]

As you can see, my understanding of the relationship between early socialism and Enlightenment philosophy is far more complex than the position that understandably shocked you. It is presumably due to its dialectical structure that the brilliant mandarins of the new anti-socialist left have mis-characterized my critique of the Enlightenment's social atomism, equating it with "reactionary nostalgia for ancestral values" and a suspect idealization of a proletariat that is now extinct. The highly creative Frédéric Lordon even predicted retroactively—such are the powers of Bourdieu's social theology—that my extreme critique of liberalism would have led me, had I lived in the thirteenth century, to deny that women had a soul!

Finally, you will note that, in my response, I only touched upon the thorny question of "progress"—in other words, humanity's automatic and providential march to a supposedly radiant future—from the first flint tools to the smartphone, nuclear power, and fracking. Because this question hovers over our entire debate—assuming, like the historian Marc Crapez,[lii] that "left" refers not to "the people" but to "progress"—it seems clear that we will have opportunities to return to it and that there is no need to make this initial letter any longer.

There is one point related to the question of "progress" on which, for once, I *completely disagree* with you. You maintain that (in your words) "technical progress is value neutral" and that, consequently, only its usages can be good or bad. This is probably true of the most basic technical objects. A hammer can either drive in a nail or smash an enemy's skull. But this is no longer the case (without even getting into "planned obsolescence") when a certain threshold of development and complexity has been passed. What would be an emancipatory and humane use of an electric chair, seeds made artificially sterile by Monsanto's engineers, or a lab that turns poppies into heroin? Once capital accumulation—the mechanism of "growth," that sacred cow which every liberal politician reveres—is no longer based on the production of use values but only on exchange values (and even, when profit rates call for it, exchange values that are not only worthless, but harmful and toxic), the liberal system inevitably begins to subject the power of self-invention to the imperative of relentless profitability. Consequently, it strikes me as pointless to speak of the "value neutrality" of assembly lines (which are inevitably bound up with Taylorist conceptions of the relationship between the mind and hands), giant container ships (tied to the capitalist organization of world trade, which methodically destroys local autonomy and "short circuits"), or the latest version of Grand Theft Auto (a video game celebrating organized crime and the elimination of borders), which are inconceivable without the cultural liberalism of the modern left. This is why it is impossible to accept the old Marxist dogma that the development of globalized capitalism paves the way—as part of its "historic mission"—for "socialism's material basis," while also producing "its own gravediggers." Just as unacceptable is the belief that the supposedly inevitable development of "productive forces" will automatically produce the technical and material infrastructure necessary for a society that is free, equal, and respectful of natural balances. Put differently, this view imagines the Notre-Dame-des-Landes airport,[liii] Dubai's urban planning, the European highway system, and Japanese nuclear reactors as the showrooms for a future socialist society based on hospitality, conviviality, decency, and self-government. This dogma is clearly untenable, however plausible it may have seemed when capitalism and modern technology were just beginning. It has become evident—despite the pathetic efforts of economists to suggest otherwise—that the continued subordination of every realm of daily life to the abstract imperatives of "growth" and "competitiveness" must lead, in the long term, to the collapse of any human civilization worthy of the name—and even, perhaps, to the collapse of material life on Earth.

As you can imagine, Jacques, I await your response very impatiently—to see where we are, after these first two letters, in our agreements and disagreements. Please be assured of my esteem and sympathy.

CHAPTER 12

An Interview with Jean-Claude Michéa

> The following interview was conducted via email by Michael Behrent in January–February 2025.

BEHRENT: The style of your thought and writing is unique. You blend philosophy, social and political analysis, and history, though your work is always more polemical than analytical. Do you see yourself as a philosopher, polemicist, activist, or something else? As a writer and thinker, who are you?

MICHÉA: I am not sure an author is well placed to determine their true status. For instance, Newton saw his research on alchemy as far more important than his work as a physicist! That said, I imagine that the style of thought and writing you refer to has something to do with the fact that, for most of my professional life, I chose to teach philosophy at a *lycée* (the equivalent of your high schools), rather than at a university or in the preparatory classes for a *grande école*.[i] I found it far more inspiring to teach the foundations of this critical discipline to students who, for the most part, would never become "professional" philosophers. Wittgenstein once said that a philosopher who only wrote for other philosophers was like a baker who only makes bread for other bakers. Teaching philosophy also allowed me to escape the constraints of academic hyper-specialization and the "publish or perish" mentality. When writing about Orwell, for instance, I never felt obliged to first read everything ever published about him. Without question, you become much freer to do your own research—starting with the freedom of being guided by the "logic of the thing itself," without having to worry about the boundaries and compartmentalization characteristic of university life. The danger is that one often winds up—like Captain Ahab in his relentless pursuit of Moby Dick—roaming through completely unfamiliar intellectual territory, far removed from the terrain of one's initial training. All this to say that it is probably best to place me in the already overpopulated category of humble essayists.

The fact that my books may strike some readers as more "polemical" than "analytical" does not bother me, particularly since the same could be said (to varying degrees, of course, depending on the author's temperament) about most writing that could be described as social criticism. In this realm, unlike in the natural sciences, it is almost impossible, no matter how "objective" one tries to be, to place a cordon sanitaire between theoretical analyses of particular social systems and the critical political conclusions that readers are asked to draw from them (though once a certain level of complexity is reached, these, too, lend themselves to multiple interpretations). This is how Marx, whose most abstract and technical works were undergirded by considerable wit and fiercely Swiftian irony, was in the habit of presenting his conclusions. In his famous letter to Ferdinand Lassalle of February 22, 1858,[ii] he described his work as "at once an exposé and, by the same token, a critique of the system." As a great admirer of Hegel and Guy Debord, I endorse this dialectical formulation without reservation.

BEHRENT: Your analyses accord a central place to progressivism, a movement that has lately come under increasing criticism for its marriage with identity politics. Is there a danger that your emphasis on the morality of the working classes (and their idea of common decency) could itself be a form of identity politics? Why are the working classes not just another example of the "marginalized groups" that obsess progressive politics?

MICHÉA: Unfortunately, the damage has already been done! The idea that the working classes (who, according to Machiavelli, "desire neither to be commanded nor oppressed by the great") are really just another "marginalized groups"—alongside trans people, the color blind, and the obese—has already become the dominant view of the new, liberal, "intersectional" left. Let me give you an example. In 1948, France experienced one of the most memorable workers' strikes in its history. It was a miners' strike. Miners' work and living conditions had declined dramatically since the communist ministers were kicked out of the government in 1947,[iii] even though they played a major role in the resistance to the German occupation. Despite the vast support that the strike enjoyed among the population, the "black snouts" (as they were called in France) soon faced political repression of extraordinary violence, as the sitting government—a government dominated by the so-called "non-communist" left and whose Interior Minister was the "socialist" Jules Moch[iv]—brought out the military and tanks against striking workers. The shocking outcome of this class repression is well known: six miners were murdered, 3,000 were fired on the spot, and 1,342 were sent to prison by judges, many of whom had sworn allegiance to Marshal Pétain a few years earlier. (The "power of judges" has become a particularly serious threat to democracy). In 2014—sixty years after a class war that had acquired mythical stature in French labor history—the left finally decided to compensate the last of these miners who were still living. Since the intellectual survival kit of today's French left has no place for the "old" concept of class struggle, the only way to justify this compensation was to fall back on the idea that the firing of thousands of striking miners had been just another instance of "discriminatory and abusive behaviors," in the words of Christiane Taubira, the Hollande government's very "woke" Justice Minister. In this way, the strike became retroactively just another episode in the long, identity-political struggle.

As you can see, we have here an almost pure example of the ideological movement that, since the late seventies and the triumph of neoliberalism, has led the Western left to dissolve the "social question" into the acid bath of new "cultural" issues that arise every time a particular "marginalized group" is encouraged to prioritize the "identity" that differentiates and separates it from the rest of the population. Hence the well-known and almost unresolvable conundrum of organizing "intersectional" demonstrations: what is the most "politically correct" order in which different "marginalized groups" should march? Imagine how the left would react today to John Ball's famous sermon during the great peasant uprising of 1381: "When Adam delved and Eve span, who then was the gentleman?" Could minds steeped in postmodern catechisms hear Ball's words as anything other than a shocking rationalization of the gendered division of labor, exacerbated by "hate speech" against an aristocratic "minority"?

Consequently, I think it is pointless to seek some kind of philosophical continuity between, on the one hand, what you call my "emphasis on morality" and the common decency of the working classes and, on the other, the ideological promotion of *identity pride*. According to the latter, endless accumulations of marginalized statuses (which can be seen, at its most caricatural, in "LGBTQQIP2AA") will supposedly pave the way to a wonderfully "progressive" and "inclusive" society in which, as in Big Brother's Oceania, the very possibility of formulating a thoughtcrime or having "inappropriate" feelings has been eradicated once and for all.

I still maintain that it is easier, even today, to be endowed with common sense and basic honesty when one belongs to a working-class community rather than to the world of the elites, in which one's fundamental humanity is so impoverished—a conviction that has only been strengthened by the nine years I have spent in a rural environment. If I believe this, it is certainly not because I give "the people who make the wheels go round" (as Orwell put it) a place in the general system of "identity politics." More simply, it is because the conditions under which these basic civic virtues (which I have never claimed are possessed by everyone "below," any more than I have claimed that the working classes have a monopoly on them) are more likely to emerge and flourish in the circumstances of economic, political, and cultural dependence that define the working classes. Obviously, the working classes are a heterogeneous group. And I recognize the existence of what Mao used to call "contradictions among the people." For instance, the world of the rural farmer, which encompasses many different statuses, is based on a way of life, a relationship to work and nature, and cultural and historical traditions (such as the importance of hunting) that are very different from those of factory workers, office employees, public employees, and small-time entrepreneurs. Yet recognizing the essential diversity of the working classes should not blind us to the everyday experiences and moral outlook that these groups fundamentally share. It was this kind of outlook E.P. Thompson had in mind when he argued that the people have a "moral economy."

Among all the overlapping characteristics that led me to assert the existence of a shared experience across all working-class populations, two traits play a decisive role in predisposing them to common sense and basic honesty. First, due to their life circumstances, the working classes have no choice but to see society from the bottom up. In other words, they see things from the standpoint of the lived experience of economic, political, and cultural dependence, which is the daily horizon of their existence. They also generally have a more mature relationship to the real world and "the way life is," dispositions that are fostered by the regular practice of tangible work (on this point, I have little to add to what Hegel says about the master-slave dialectic). The fact that the working classes must relive these experiences daily distinguishes their lives from the various factions of the dominant classes, who necessarily see the world from the top down. When one considers the current disconnect—which has grown extreme—between economic, political, and cultural elites and those "on the bottom," and the inability of the former to grasp anything that is different from their lives, it is hard not to accept the cruel assessment of the Italian writer Claudio Magris,[v] for whom society's masters have become extraterritorial: "In this so-called epoch of mass culture," he observed, "it is not the masses who are uncultured, but the elites. On the bus, it is unusual to hear errors as monumental as one sees on TV or in the newspapers."

The other characteristic shared by all segments of the working class is the central role played in their daily lives by relationships of mutual assistance. To explain this fact, there is no need to "idealize" these classes or "essentialize" them, the way the leftwing clergy does whenever it is suggested that those at the bottom are anything other than a bunch of "racists, sexists, homophobes, xenophobes, and Islamophobes" (to quote Hillary Clinton's brilliant analysis). To explain this disposition towards mutual assistance, one has only to consider the fact that for people living in working-class milieus (a village, a town, an urban neighborhood), it is always extremely difficult to wrestle with life's many contingencies by relying solely on one's own financial resources. Old cars suddenly die—and not every social group has the money to buy an electric car, even a low-end model. Roof tiles that need replacing after a hailstorm; trees that have fallen onto a road; damages from floods or a devastating herd of deer or wild boar; an unexpected event—such as a death or an accident—that temporarily prevents a farmer from taking care of his vines or livestock: these are all problems that, when money is short and crime is rejected as a matter of principle, can only be solved with the help of neighbors, friends, and sometimes an entire town. How could ordinary people survive with a minimum of dignity without mutual assistance and giving—without, in other words, the threefold obligation to "give, receive, and give back," that Marcel Mauss saw as the primary foundation (the "fundamentals," as he put it) of every social bond?

In conclusion, I would add that if, precisely due to the shared experiences I have mentioned, the working classes strike me as far better placed than the privileged classes to acquire and develop a minimum of common sense and morality (understood either as what Orwell called "common decency" or David Graeber refers to as "everyday communism"), we must remember that historical forces are exacerbating human alienation and undermining the basic social virtues. In the case of the working classes, we might refer to what Marx called "lumpenization."[vi] For the flip side of the endless capital accumulation that the dominant classes and their intellectual and journalistic cheerleaders celebrate as "growth" is the "dissolution of mankind into monads, of which each one has a separate principle," which Engels described in 1845 in *The Condition of the Working Class in England*. Engels presciently saw the relentless dissolution of social bonds as the ultimate logic of the capitalist economic system and the most extreme form of liberal selfishness ("my body, my right, my choice"). At present, selfishness has become liberalism's only coherent "moral" and cultural position. If, in the coming decades, nothing is done to end this constant race to the bottom, which even world leaders seem less and less able to control (since capitalist "progress" means forging ahead in the wrong direction), then eventually (without even mentioning ecological dangers), the "load-bearing walls" of working-class sociability and any possibility of a "free, egalitarian, and decent" socialist society will be swept away by the "icy water of egotistical calculation." The time has perhaps come to take stock of this process of liberal "decivilization" occurring before our eyes.

BEHRENT: Is there a point at which "Tory anarchism" or "left conservatism" become conservatism, plain and simple?

MICHÉA: Let me first remind you that I never defined myself as a "conservative," either a "left conservative" or an "anarchist conservative"! The only thesis that I have defended, going back to my first books—in the tradition of

George Orwell, Christopher Lasch, and Pier Paolo Pasolini—is that the so-cialist project (which, in today's world, strikes me as more relevant than ever) would become meaningless and emptied of its emancipatory power if it were philosophically incapable of embracing what I call a "conservative moment." This is simply another way of saying that the best way to ensure that social-ism fails is to rewrite its story yet again from the standpoint of "progressive" (or "left") ideology, which holds that a revolutionary attitude necessarily "makes a clean slate of the past." One needs only a minimum of anthropo-logical knowledge—or a minimum of common sense—to understand the absurdity of "progressivism's" transformation of socialism into the idea that the "future society" requires the prior liquidation of humanity's entire moral and cultural heritage (as seen with Pol Pot in Cambodia, Mao during the "Great Proletarian Cultural Revolution," and even, at times, during the French Revolution). This interpretation is particularly nonsensical when it paradoxically turns socialism—the political project that has always offered the most radical critique of capitalist and industrial society—into capi-talism's true and only heir! When one accepts that the goal of any truly "radical" movement is to "make a clean slate of the past"—by emancipating oneself from all traditions and calling for every conceivable "taboo" to be breached—then one has no choice but to acknowledge that there has never been a system as "revolutionary" as capitalism. Marx, incidentally, quickly reached this very conclusion. The dynamic of capitalist economics, he wrote in *The Communist Manifesto*, is like a devastating storm that drowns every value inherited from the past in "the icy water of egotistical calculation." Under capitalism, Marx observes, "all that is solid melts into air [and] all that is holy is profaned"; "all fixed, fast-frozen relations, with their train of ancient and venerable prejudices and opinions, are swept away." At the same time, "the bourgeoisie has torn away from the family its sentimental veil" and "put an end to all . . . patriarchal . . . relations." In this way, capitalism's destructive dynamic can be described as a never-ending "cancel culture," and deconstruction, its ideological sibling, as the intellectual transposition of this practice, waged by capital's zealous red guards. Unfortunately, Marx's initial fascination with capitalism's revolutionary character—the logical extension of his deep contempt for the peasantry and the "idiocy of rural life"—would lead him to the all-too-hasty conclusion that capitalism's true "historic mission" was (as he wrote in "The Future Results of British Rule in India") to "create the material basis of the new world." (Marx would later significantly revise this position). To imply that the only "material basis" upon which a "free, equal, and decent society" (as Orwell put it) might be built is one inherited from capitalism, upon completion of its "historic mission" of making a clean slate of the past, is to forget the two features of capitalism that make it so different from every other type of society.

The first feature is the principle of unlimited capital accumulation—the fact that the capitalist mode of production's primary goal is to increase the value of wealth that has already been produced and accumulated. This means, in simpler terms, that capitalism's main goal, in contrast to every previously existing society, is not to produce goods that can, because of their quality, sturdiness, and durability, satisfy actual human needs—a dugout canoe, a cart, or an axe. It is to produce *commodities*—that is, goods (tomatoes, chairs, cars, or video games) whose only expected purpose is to attract buyers on the global market, thus increasing capital's value. Only an economic system founded on such principles could have conceived of a concept as perverse and cynical as "planned obsolescence"—an idea that would have been inconceivable in earlier societies, even the Soviet Union. Another consequence of unlimited accumulation is that once capitalism's initial phase—characterized by the convergence of its own commercial imperatives and the satisfaction of perfectly legitimate human needs—had ended, the relative share of genuinely useful goods in capitalism's overall production tended to decline exponentially in favor of commodities that are not only useless (i.e., "gadgets") but also toxic and alienating—what Debord in *Society of the Spectacle* calls the "constant decline of use value." Consequently, the longer we allow this "revolutionary" mode of production to continue the destructive trajectory dictated by its self-referential logic, the more the deconstructed and abstract[1] world that it leaves in its wake will prove incapable of fulfilling any human and emancipatory purpose. Capital accumulation will bequeath us a world full of industrial food, weapons of mass destruction, tyrannical screens, drug trafficking, climate change, and—to quote Debord again—"the urbanistic leprosy that over-runs what used to be the

---

1. I use "abstract" in the way Robert Kurz and *Wertkritik* understand the term.

town and the country." In societies where the capitalist mode of production reigns, time never works for us, but always against us.

Capitalism's other "revolutionary" feature is its inexorable tendency to destroy the local autonomy and subsistence economies that previously allowed communities even in the most centralized states to tend to their immediate needs, such as food and housing, through labor and relationships based on mutual aid. This autonomy ensured these core communities—which were generally rural, but which could also be urban—minimal control over their daily lives and preemptively protected them from future dependence on advanced technology and distant markets. Yet from the standpoint of a capitalist economy, such autonomy could only be residual evidence of an "archaic" and "outdated" way of life that was destined to vanish.

The first reason this occurs is because the capitalist economy is no longer based on slavery or serfdom, as in previous class societies, but on salaried labor. To develop, capitalism depends on the constant flow—whether through an influx of rural populations or, as at present, immigration—of an officially "free" labor force—that is, one that consists primarily of individuals who first had to be dispossessed of the minimal autonomy that, even under feudalism, their home communities provided. It is not hard to grasp that this dispossession ensures that these "proletarianized" individuals, as seen during the enclosure movement and the destruction of the "commons," can only survive by renting out their last remaining good: their labor power. A second reason that leads capitalism to methodically destroy autonomous life and self-sufficiency can be found in a fundamental maxim of the market economy: as Adam Smith put it in *The Wealth of Nations*, one should "never to attempt to make at home what it will cost more to make than to buy." Indeed, what is the point of growing one's own vegetables or making tools and first-aid medicine when, thanks to container ships, they can be acquired at a lower cost from anywhere in the world? The capitalist mode of production's "rationality" is what compels it to destroy every remaining form of subsistence economy and local autonomy. Consequently, humankind's ever-growing dependence on the world market and the technological and material infrastructure upon which it depends are justified, in a way that is only superficially paradoxical, in the name of freedom, reason, and historical progress.

The problem, as I have noted, is that it is precisely in the privileged realm of these local communities and the degree of autonomy they manage to preserve (i.e., the "primary sociality," as Alain Caillé and Marcel Mauss' disciples call it, in which face-to-face relations are still far more important than impersonal ones) that the basic social virtues have a chance to emerge and flourish: the reflex for mutual aid, the taste for work well done, and the ability to become attached to a place, a people, and a community. Though human history is "full of sound and fury," it is these virtues that have, until now, ensured that humanity never strayed too far from itself, despite the efforts of the new Dr. Strangeloves of "transhumanism" and artificial intelligence. I find it hard to understand how one can still consider an historical movement that, for three centuries, has relentlessly undermined the foundations of the human condition and any possible civilization as a triumphant march towards an ever more radiant future. And it is even harder for me to see it as contributing to the progressive establishment of the material basis of a decent socialist society. Orwell was right to compare the modern progressive to a "bisected wasp which goes on sucking jam and pretends that the loss of its abdomen does not matter." Marx, incidentally, came to understand this towards the end of his life when, influenced by the Russian Populists[vii] (who inspired him to learn Russian so that he could read their work and correspond with them), he completely changed his view of the peasant world and rural communities. In a March 1881 letter to Vera Zasulich, Marx wrote that socialism is a "revival, in a superior form, of an archaic social type" (borrowing the phrase from the American anthropologist Lewis Morgan).[viii] In the letter, Marx went so far as to claim that rural communities were "the only focus of liberty and popular life throughout the Middle Ages"! To preempt the "progressive" criticism that a populist redefinition of socialism inevitably elicited among the most "advanced" minds of the age (the "antifa" far left may soon decide that *Capital* is a "far right" text!), Marx made sure to add: "We should not, then, be too frightened by the word 'archaic.'" Later, Marcel Mauss and Guy Debord would agree, though not for the same reasons. As you can see, my conservative credentials have yet to be approved!

BEHRENT: As I translated your writings, I was struck by your work's extraordinary prescience. You have been talking about the left's growing distance from the working classes since the late 1990s. You have emphasized how the left has been taken over by progressive elites for just as long. It took Donald Trump's reelection in 2024 to force Democrats to acknowledge this problem. Similar debates have begun in France and the United Kingdom only in recent years. Why do you think this issue was so important to you early on? Why has it acquired greater resonance?

MICHÉA: In his magnificent essay on Orwell, published over forty years ago, Simon Leys observed that "this dead man continues to speak to us with more vigor and clarity than the prose of most politicians and commentators we read in the morning papers." If quite a few writers from decades past continue to inspire—Cornelius Castoriadis, Christopher Lasch, Guy Debord, Jacques Ellul, Lewis Mumford, Ivan Illich, and Gunther Anders, among others—it is obviously not because they possessed a mysterious gift for prophecy. It is because they grasped the logic of the historical process that was occurring before their eyes, which allowed them to imagine future consequences. From this standpoint, Marx—I always come back to him!—is an exemplary author. In writing *Capital*, his first goal was, as he put it, to lay bare the "economic law of motion of modern society." The main target of Marx's critique was thus not the "old world"—that of the right, of the monarchist and clerical reaction and its conservative ideas—but precisely the brave new world being established throughout Western Europe as a result of the industrial and scientific revolutions, which nineteenth-century progressives were already celebrating as "modernity." In other words, Marx sought to identify a pure model of capitalist production, leaving it to workers' and socialist parties to figure out how to apply this analysis dialectically to the social and historical conditions of their respective countries. Yet because England was, at the time, the locus classicus of this kind of production, which in Germany was only just getting started, it was naturally from England that Marx borrowed most of the facts and examples needed to illustrate his theory. This is why, in the preface to *Capital*'s first German edition, he preemptively answered a possible objection on the part of a German reader consoling himself "with the thought that in Germany things are not nearly so bad." Citing Horace, Marx replied: "I must plainly tell him, *De te fabula narratur*!" (It is of you that the story is told). After revealing the general laws of capitalist accumulation and expansion, it was not too hard to conclude that a "country that is more developed industrially only shows, to the less developed, the image of its own future." Incidentally, the same reasoning explains why in France, it has long been assumed that every trend or innovation pioneered by American capitalism will inevitably arrive here a few years later—from the reign of fast food and rock music, in the early 1960s, to the current "awakening" of academic culture.

As for my writing, if it has anything to add to these questions, it is because in the late seventies—thanks in part to Christopher Lasch's *The Culture of Narcissism*, which played a decisive role in my philosophical consciousness—I started to "work" on the idea that capitalism was not just a system of economic organization (of which economic liberalism has been, since Adam Smith, the official philosophy), but also what Marcel Mauss called a "total social fact." In other words, a system that could not be understood if one did not also grasp its moral and cultural conditions and consequences. A similar thesis was also advanced in the 1960s by Guy Debord, the writer who, with Orwell and Lasch, influenced me most during those politically tumultuous years. Explaining his concept of the "society of the spectacle," Debord argued that the "the spectacle grasped in its totality is both the result and the project of the existing mode of production." In other words, capitalism had finally been liberated from all the moral, religious, and cultural compromises that it had to negotiate with the "old world" in its early stages. In Europe, one cannot truly speak of a "society of the spectacle" until after the Second World War. At this point, capitalism could only forge ahead in its uniquely self-referential way ("Accumulation for the sake of accumulation, production for the sake of production," as Marx put it) by becoming "for itself" what it already was "in itself. In less Hegelian terms, one might say that capitalism realized itself by appropriating the fantasy of "no limits" and "no borders" that, from the beginning, was the hidden face of "self-valorizing value" (as Marx defined unlimited capital accumulation) and whose only logical result was the profanation of "all that is holy" and the drowning of traditional values in the "icy water of egotistical calculation."

In these circumstances, one must be doubly locked in the mental prison of ideology not to notice the troubling coincidence that has existed, particularly since May '68, between this hyper-individualistic libertarian culture that allows capitalism, spinning on its own philosophical foundations, to push back every moral and natural limit, and the culture that the Western left has embraced since the 1980s. (And though I have focused on the left, the same criticism can be leveled against those on the "conservative" liberal right who, as Russel Jacoby ironically notes, "worship the market and bemoan the education it engenders"). The left accepted as a self-evident truth that the old socialist project could only lead to totalitarianism. As Michel Foucault observed in 1977, "everything that this socialist tradition has produced historically must be condemned." It also acknowledged that traditional social-democratic and Keynesian policies could no longer solve the crisis of Fordist capital accumulation, which began in the United States in the late 1960s and resulted in stagflation and slow "growth." Once these concessions had been made, there was nothing preventing the Western left—which until this point was still vaguely concerned with the people who keep the machines running—from celebrating, with a disco soundtrack in the background, its final reconciliation with liberal capitalism as a psychological and mental liberation. In other words, the left has forged a new and flamboyant alliance (whose philosophical coherence is exemplary) between economic liberalism—which can now be criticized only for its "excesses" and "deviations"—and the new cultural liberalism and its hallowed ideology of human rights. Because of this alliance, we must constantly defend the metaphysical primacy of the individual, separated (as Marx put it) "from other men and from the community," over communal life and the public good. And if one still has any doubts about the philosophical reconciliation of liberalism's two wings, just look at the commercials doled out by the advertising industry, in which the underlying unity of the right's economic liberalism and the left's cultural liberalism is as clear as day.

By the late 1980s, no prophet was needed to predict the logical consequences of the rapid convergence of the Western left (as embodied by François Mitterrand, Tony Blair, Helmut Schmidt, Bill Clinton, and others) and neoliberalism, beginning with the pressing need for an electorate on board with the new playbook. The French think tank Terra Nova, by far the most influential of its kind on the left and far left, published a famous report in 2011, written to prepare for the presidential election the following year. "May '68," it observed, "drew the political left towards cultural liberalism," that is, towards "tolerance, an openness to difference, a favorable view towards immigrants, Islam, and homosexuality, and solidarity with the most vulnerable." Yet because the working class—once the left's historical foundation—had regrettably decided to go "the other way," driven by "relatively conservative values," it was clear, according to the report, that the left had no hope of returning to power unless it found a "new electorate" with a very different sociology. This new electorate, which the report called "tomorrow's France," consisted of the new urban middle classes (journalists, artists, professors, advertisers, and so on), who, since the late nineteenth century, have been charged with organizing capitalism's technical, economic, and cultural "advances." Due to their contradictory social character (reminiscent of Erik Olin Wright's[ix] concept of "contradictory class location"), André Gorz[x] defined these social categories as the "dominated agents of domination." Bourdieu, in turn, proposed the concept of the "dominated faction of the dominant class." Orwell offered a prescient description of this social group in his 1946 essay "James Burnham and the Managerial Revolution" (which he reused in *1984*): "scientists, technicians, teachers, journalists, broadcasters, bureaucrats, professional politicians," all of whom, Orwell claimed, "are hungry for more power and more prestige," and whose "secret wish" is a world in which "the intellectual can at last get his hands on the whip." Knowing what has become of the parties and associations on the left and far left, particularly those that have embraced the "woke" theology, you have to admit that, when it comes to "prescience," Orwell remains the master!

It is not the least bit paradoxical that this "civic" and "inclusive" left has reconciled itself with capitalism at the very historical moment when its own disintegration had begun. The working classes were now abandoned to their fate, even as neoliberalism's progress made daily life more difficult, uncertain, and dangerous. It was not hard to predict how they would evolve politically. The left's moral and intellectual conversion to economic and cultural liberalism deprived the working classes of any coherent political translation (based on understanding the laws of modern economics) of their growing anger at the world, which they were the first to realize had been turned upside down. How can anyone be so naïve as to not realize that, sooner or later, they would seek others who could translate their frustrations? People like Donald Trump and Marine Le Pen, who would at least listen to them and—just as importantly—learn their language. These days, most ordinary people feel that when a representative of the left or far left speaks to them, they are not so much expressing their ideas as their social background.

BEHRENT: One of the driving forces of populist movements in many countries is mass immigration. You write extensively of the anthropological challenges posed by liberalism. What sort of anthropological challenges does immigration present?

MICHÉA: It is indeed on the question of immigration that the split between working classes and the new liberal left has become most obvious and most spectacular. Two essential points help us understand the origins of this divorce. First, the phenomenon of immigration, unless one wants to play word games, only acquires its true meaning in modern times. One needs all the frivolity of the Macronian historian Patrick Boucheron—the architect of the neoliberal opening ceremony of the Paris Olympic Games—to see the Chauvet cave paintings,[xi] which are 30,000 years old, as the work of the first French people "of immigrant origin"! Second, immigration appears in two different forms, which, on occasion, merge together. The first is settlement immigration, of which the United States (as well as Canada, Australia, and other countries) was long the ideal (as seen in the continuous flow of immigrants from Europe throughout the nineteenth century). In this instance, the question of what you call the "anthropological challenges" are, to my mind, very quickly resolved, as this form of immigration almost always results in "ethnocide"—that is, the gradual disappearance, due to the growth of the settler population, of indigenous peoples' cultures and traditions. This disappearance can even be methodically organized, as with the boarding schools that were officially charged with "civilizing" young Native Americans. Yet except for Jean-Luc Mélenchon,[xii] with his delirious calls for a "new France" freed from its earlier cultures and traditions, I can't think of anyone who would say that this immigration was an "opportunity" for the American Indians! The second form is work immigration, which began to develop in the first half of the nineteenth century (with Belgian workers in France, Irish workers in England, and so on) because of the bourgeoisie's clear desire to put downward pressure on salaries by making European workers compete against one another. Engels discussed this point at length in a chapter of *The Condition of the Working Class in England* devoted entirely to mass immigration, which was new at the time. While deploring the many negative "anthropological" effects due to mass immigration that were already apparent in the 1840s—Engels notes, for instance, that Irish immigrants brought "their brutal habits with them"—Engels nevertheless focuses on the inevitable economic effects of this employer-friendly policy. He concludes: "the wages of the English workingman [are] forced down further and further in every branch in which the Irish compete with him." This assessment was shared at the time by most socialists and explains the position the socialist labor movement would embrace for decades. The debates that preceded the foundation of the First International in 1864 are, from this perspective, worth re-reading. On the one hand, socialists opposed all forms of immigration and, in general, any measure that placed workers in competition with each other while insisting on the need to build solidarity in each country between native and immigrant workers to thwart the divide and conquer strategy, while also fighting xenophobic prejudice in all its forms. In January 1981, the French Communist Party—which for years was the last guardian, in France, of working-class traditions forged in the nineteenth century—was still asking President Giscard d'Estaing to "stop official and illegal immigration."

Given these circumstances, how did we arrive at the surreal situation in which, for the left, any criticism of capitalist immigration policy—which the spin doctors of big business call, not without humor, "onsite outsourcing"—is now seen as "racist" and connected to the ideology of the "far right"? Yet it always comes back to the same explanation. Once the Western left had embraced the idea that any break with capitalism could only result in economic collapse or the creation of Soviet-style dictatorship (as Bernard-Henri Lévy and the "new philosophers" argued), it was simultaneously compelled to completely rethink its program. It no longer interpreted immigration primarily through the lens of class struggle, but exclusively in terms of the liberal ideology of human rights and the "struggle against discrimination in all its forms." The ideological turning-point in France came in 1984, when the French president ordered the creation of *SOS Racisme*, an organization charged with introducing youth to the new ideas of cultural liberalism.

The question of immigration's economic effects is fairly straightforward. Everything that in the old socialist critique came with a "minus" sign has been given a "plus" sign by the left's new liberal framework. Since the capitalist economy has magically become the economy itself, it stands to reason that the left's new economists would conclude that if mass immigration policies had a positive effect on "growth," then it must necessarily be "an opportunity for France"—a phrase that was first used in 1985 by the conservative politician Bernard Stasi[xiii] and which the French left has since made its favorite political slogan.

As for the "anthropological" and cultural "challenges" posed by mass immigration, the question becomes more complicated once work immigration gives way—as is now happening in France—to settlement immigration. Once it becomes clear that a growing share of this "new France" (as Mélenchon jubilantly calls it) is less and less disposed to accept—whatever its reasons, religious or otherwise—the host country's culture and history, the risk is very great—and the working classes, unlike the elites, are always the first to be aware of this fact—that we are watching entire swathes of this history and culture vanish over time, along with the "customs in common," which played a central role in the collective resistance of "people from below" to the power of the dominant classes (as E.P. Thompson has shown). The problem—and it's always the same one—is that it is precisely the liberal framework that the new left has enthusiastically adopted for over forty years that prevents it from understanding why such a problem "still" exists. "I don't understand how, in 2025, one can still think that . . ." has become one of the left intelligentsia's preferred catchphrases. Marx and the nineteenth-century socialists believed, like Aristotle, that human beings are primarily "political animals" that can only be "isolated in and through society" (hence his repeated mockery of the "Robinsonades" of Adam Smith and David Ricardo). Yet the new left's cultural liberalism compels it to view human beings as individuals cut off from nature, as self-made men who can choose their gender or skin color ex nihilo and who can, moreover, relate to their peers only on contractual bases, reflecting nothing more than the parties' "enlightened self-interest." Yet once one accepts philosophical premises that are so liberal and individualistic ("an isolated monad, withdrawn into himself," as Marx observed in *On the Jewish Question*), it becomes impossible to imagine any connection between the continuous influx of new arrivals in a land and the "anthropological" and "cultural" consequences of this continuous influx for peoples who, like the Aztecs, had populated their lands for centuries. We should not forget that when Pierre Leroux coined the term "socialism" in the 1840s, it was primarily to oppose "individualism," the liberal idea that society is simply the sum of its individuals, and that the theory that economics and law are sufficient to explain these interactions. If the warnings about issues like immigration and security that the working classes have been trying to give the left for decades have proved totally inaudible—or when the left concludes that, as Bertolt Brecht put it, it is time to "dissolve the people and elect another"—it is because, for the past forty years, the left's sole intellectual preoccupation has consisted in working out all the ruthless consequences of Margaret Thatcher's theorem: "There is no such thing as society."

BEHRENT: Does wokeness get anything right?

MICHÉA: If you want to get me to say that the official goals of "wokism"— fighting racism, masculine domination, homophobia, and so on—are perfectly legitimate, my answer is: obviously (though it is a shame that fighting anti-Semitism is rarely included among those goals). The problem is that due to a basic lack of understanding of capitalism's dynamics and the world in which these struggles must be fought—let's not forget that this ideological cluster was forged in the same political and intellectual context as the Western left's decision to embrace liberalism—what we now call "wokism" encompasses a different and very troubling reality. It is hard not to think of G. K. Chesterton's famous quip that the "the modern world is full of old Christian virtues gone mad." In fact, it is those well-intentioned but insane "virtues" that must be explained.

First, let us put aside everything in this heterogeneous ideology that relates to the distinct characteristics of American society. This can be seen in the "witch hunt" atmosphere, which plunges us back into the world of the Salem Witch Trials and seventeenth-century American Puritanism, not to mention McCarthyism. This aspect of wokism is particularly difficult to acclimatize to French conditions. For instance, in France, the incredible rituals of genuflection seen in American sports' stadiums astonish even the far left. Even so, the fascination of French bourgeois youth at institutions like Sciences Po and the Ecole Normale Supérieure,[xiv] where they train to become capitalism's future elites, for everything with a "Made in the USA" label, including imported political slogans—which become cool when "antifa" students brandish them in the original English—shows that we are perhaps mistaken in believing that we have been spared these trends. As for the essence of "wokism," we should see it as the logical result of two processes, whose complementary characters should not mask their differences.

The first, which is far from the most important, relates to the limitlessness that characterizes both economic liberalism (since capitalism, as Engels wrote in 1892, can never stop "growing and developing") and political and cultural liberalism, which represent its flip side, or, if one prefers, its ultimate philosophy. In a liberal society, that is, a society in which each person is free to "live as they see fit," it is typically impossible to limit the freedom of one's peers solely based on personal philosophical, religious, or moral principles. In this kind of society, the only values officially recognized as shared are those that are considered natural and presumed to be value neutral—namely, those found in market and law, all others having been de facto privatized. Without these conditions, the only legitimate reason for a liberal state to limit a citizen's right to "live as they see fit" is when exercising a right clearly infringes on the rights of other citizens. This institutional mechanism, so extraordinary in its simplicity, is very seductive. The problem is that it can only function if liberal society still possesses—though it is not always aware of this fact—a sufficient degree of cultural homogeneity. In Benjamin Constant's or Alexis de Tocqueville's day, no one could have conceived of "deconstructing" the idea that that a man is not a woman, an eight-year-old child not an adult, and a madman who takes himself for Napoleon—however deeply he "feels" it—not sane. But given that the ultimate horizon of limitless capital accumulation is the "dissolution of mankind into monads," a moment necessarily arrives when members of a liberal society (particularly since it must constantly welcome new arrivals embracing cultural values that are different and sometimes downright hostile to it) will find it increasingly difficult to generate the shared cultural values that allow for a minimal degree of "common life." At this point, the claim that one should "live one's life as one sees fit" will begin losing its emancipatory value (which it still had, say, for John Stuart Mill) and will start colliding with increasing frequency with similar claims. Because there is no consensus on even minimal cultural reference points (especially if one recalls that capitalism is always deconstructing the very foundations of critical thought), it becomes hard to understand why anyone should attach any importance to someone who thinks and acts differently. A society that is increasingly shaped by what Hobbes called the "war of all against all" necessarily encourages the legalization of human relations and a corresponding rise in insecurity and violence of all kinds. Everyone believes they are entitled to bring charges if, rightly or wrongly, they feel "discriminated against," "stigmatized," "offended," or even made to feel "uneasy." Many exacerbate insecurity by directing violence against themselves, as seen in the growing recourse to the compensatory use of drugs. As Marx remarked in *Capital*, "between equal rights force decides."

The philosophical explanation of "wokism" (and the terrors of cancel culture, which lie in its shadow) is to be found primarily in the way that capitalism's relentless atomization of the world has been "pushed to the extreme." For the most part, "wokism" is nothing more than the translation into cultural and academic terms of the senseless neoliberal deconstruction of the world that has prevailed since the 1980s. I prefer to call "wokism" by its true name: cultural neoliberalism.

The second process helps us understand the increasingly totalitarian forms assumed by woke activism, yet which are not a direct consequence of its neoliberal framework. A brief detour through Orwell's analysis of the genesis of totalitarianism is helpful here. For Orwell, the Stalinist perversion of the socialist project was tied not to socialism's nature—in contrast to what Bernard-Henri Lévy and the "new philosophers" claimed—but to its gradual confiscation, beginning in the late nineteenth century, by the intelligentsia of the new urban middle classes whose rise was closely tied to capitalism's development. This intelligentsia, whose contradictory social status—both dominated and dominant, representing, for Orwell, the underlying reason for its "revolutionary" resentment against the established order—grasped that the socialist movement provided it with an ideal "stepping stone" (as Bakunin called it) to achieve its "secret wish" to "finally get their hands on the whip," seizing power from the caliph to become the new caliph. Debord agreed. In *The Society of the Spectacle*, he described Bolshevik organization as consisting of a "party under the control of intellectuals," which allowed the latter to become the "owners of the proletariat" and exercise "the profession of totalitarian social domination." Yet Orwell's analysis not only calls attention to the central role played by middle class intellectuals in the genesis of a "Stalinist"-type totalitarian society. It also explains why every totalitarian ideology—and wokism has inevitably become one—must function deliriously (a delirium that Orwell describes as "schizophrenic"). For rational minds, it is impossible, unless one plays the card of cynicism, to *sincerely* believe that one is fighting for an egalitarian, classless, or "inclusive" society when one *also* recognizes that the struggle is constantly motivated by the desire to control other people and an unhealthy pleasure in "disciplining and punishing" one's peers. Consider, for example, the almost purifying role played in totalitarian movements by denunciation, "blacklists," and censorship, as seen in the petitions that artists and academics circulate in the media. One can, of course, shut oneself up in a psycho-ideological system that is bolted from the inside—thus protecting oneself from any intrusion from reality, allowing those who make this choice "to use logic against logic" and "hold simultaneously two opinions [that cancel each other out], knowing them to be contradictory and believing in both" (both quotes are from *1984*).

You will have had no trouble recognizing, in Orwell's description of doublethink, the basic psycho-ideological kit that for decades allowed "Stalinist" intellectuals and their "fellow travelers" to regard Stalin's and Mao's regimes as the highest form of democracy (some intellectuals even visited these countries in person, allowing them to confirm how right their self-deception was) or to denounce the gulag as "fake news" invented by the far right. Obviously, this kind of voluntary blindness and self-deception, made possible by the daily practice of "doublethink," was not just a philosophical "error" or a mistake resulting from poor information. In reality, it was the price that left-wing intellectuals continually had to pay, in Western societies, for exercising the extensive political, cultural, and media power that comes with being on the "right side." It was, all in all, a "return on investment."

Only someone with a boundless naiveté would believe that those ideologues, academics, and artists who in great numbers in the late 1970s renounced the socialist struggle for a "free, equal and decent" society in favor of "human rights" and "identity politics" also abandoned, in great numbers, the old privileges and psycho-ideological habits which had brought them power and prestige. This is precisely what Castoriadis criticized them for when he ironically remarked, taking aim at the former Maoists who became fervent partisans of the liberal gospel: "Just because you've switched sidewalks doesn't mean you've switched jobs." Without going into the forms of voluntary blindness that "wokism" necessarily implies (on issues such as insecurity, uncontrolled immigration, and the continual decline of academic standards), one has only to consider the industrial-scale usage that the new liberal left—"woke," "inclusive," or "intersectional"—makes of "Godwin's Law" and the *reductio ad Hitlerum*" (these being the "arguments" that most quickly come to mind when one's power and symbolic and material privileges are threatened) to realize that no clear moral and psycho-ideological continuity exists between yesterday's Stalinist or Maoist intellectual and today's "woke" academic. Two important differences stand out.

First, the activist base of almost all "Stalinist" parties was still genuinely working class. One of the most important consequences of the mass presence in old left organizations of activists who belonged to the world of ordinary workers was that, even in a Stalinized party, their common sense was a breath of fresh air, often preventing leftwing intellectuals from taking their ideological delirium too far. But when, however, you have a new left that—like its model, the American Democrat Party—appears more and more cut off from those who keep the machines running and whose ideas often originate in what Debord called the "university ghetto," it is clear that all the guardrails that intellectuals benefited from during the Stalinist period and which could have ensured that wokism maintained some minimal contact with reality, if not moral sense, have now been lost.

Second, "wokism"—in contrast to socialism, which originated in workers' struggles—has always derived most of its catechism, whether it be gender ideology or critical race theory, from the Western academic world (including in its "post-colonial" variant, even if it is officially anti-Western). So it seems natural to conclude that there must be a tight bond between the seriousness of academic work that falls under the banner of "wokism" and the real quality of the universities that recruit such scholars. On this point, the judgment of Simon Leys, undoubtedly one of the twentieth century's freest spirits, is devastating and irrefutable. "It is probably going too far," he wrote in 1987, "to claim that, due to a number of contemporary procedures, it would be possible to bestow a doctorate on a dead ass; yet a living ass, I believe, could earn one." Leys wrote this nearly forty years ago and since that time, academic standards in Western universities—a necessary consequence of neoliberal policies and cooptation—have continued to decline. Among all the brilliant academics who now embrace wokism, or who prefer to practice it under a different name, there are probably more than a few "dead asses." Enough, in any case, to justify Jean Cocteau's acerbic remark: "The tragedy of our day is that foolishness has begun to think."

BEHRENT: Since we have been in correspondence, you always include, in your emails, a picture of your rural life. I think of the famous line from Marx's *German Ideology*, about a future society in which it is possible "to hunt in the morning, fish in the afternoon, rear cattle in the evening, criticize after dinner." Is this your life?

MICHÉA: A friend of mine once said that in sketching the basis of the society of the future, Marx was in fact predicting Club Med! That said, there is some truth in the comparison you make between my "rural life" and the picture Marx painted of socialist society in 1846. It has to do with the fact that rural life—assuming that you mean life in small towns, most of whose inhabitants still practice some supplemental farming—is always, by definition, versatile. This is not just because crop farming, even on a modest scale, requires—in contrast to the highly polluting and toxic industrial monocultures practiced by agrobusiness—a wide variety of technical competencies and practical skills. It frequently combines small-scale livestock farming with regular use of local forest resources. If one adds to these core activities occasional fishing, hunting, and even artisanal work, it is easy to see that daily life in a village in the Landes[xv] bears greater resemblance to the "socialist life" Marx imagined in *The German Ideology* than to the many forms of modern labor (much of it reducible to a few repetitive actions) that the capitalist mode of production necessarily encourages, whether one thinks of an assembly line, a supermarket cashier, a call center operator, a forklift worker for Amazon, or even a programmer glued to their screen from dawn to dusk.

There is one enormous difference, however. Unlike Marx's occasionally very "Club Med" vision of future society, our schedule can never be determined exclusively by our whims and impulses. You don't suddenly have the urge to feed your animals or decide to prune your cherry trees and tomatoes instead of your raspberry bushes. Nature makes you do it, if only because of the seasonal cycle (one does not sow all seeds at the same time or in the same conditions) and climate variations. Despite this, it has never once occurred to us that submitting to nature's rhythms is an unbearable and degrading form of servitude (Even if work like hand weeding can be exhausting!).

One of the first lessons one learns in the school of rural life—especially if, like me, you spent most of your life in the shade of a large city—is that that the most solid and precious foundation of human freedom, one which, as Spinoza says, increases our "capacity to act," is not the abstract power offered by commercial society, the choosing, that is, between McDonald's, KFC, and Burger King. To the contrary, it exists in the real power we have to respond to our most essential and vital needs without having to depend entirely on the whims of the global market (as distinguished from local and even regional markets that never obey capitalist logic) or a distant, out-of-touch, and intellectually narrow bureaucracy, of the kind that runs the European Union. The problem, as I've already said, is that capitalism does not know how to produce anything other than commodities—that is, goods whose primary function is to be sold. Hence the famous passage that opens *Capital*: "The wealth of those societies in which the capitalist mode of production prevails, presents itself as an immense accumulation of commodities." This is the reason that the civilizational ideal born of this mode of production since its origin is that of a society in which all the goods people need to live (or survive) are no longer things they produce in an essentially local context (within, let's say, a radius of several dozen kilometers) but commodities that must be bought from a large private company, one that may be located on the other side of the world and over which they have no control.

Can there be any more striking confession that the ultimate goal of economic liberalism and its ever-more frequent and restrictive free-trade agreements is to, in the name of individual freedom and "human rights," once and for all do away with any possibility of truly autonomous life, whether this autonomy be individual or collective? To cite but one representative example: the never-ending efforts of Bayer/Monsanto, supported by international rulings, to deny peasants in poor countries the right to reuse their own seeds, as they have done since the dawn of time.

Yet it is precisely this relatively more autonomous form of life (an absolutely autonomous life being obviously impossible under capitalism) that I was able to rediscover by moving to a small town in the Landes, and which no doubt goes a long way to explaining why, for nearly nine years, I feel infinitely more free than before, when I was forced into the dehumanizing and hypnotic rhythms of a major city. And by a "relatively more autonomous form of life," I do not just mean being able to cover some of our food needs, or the quality and taste of the food itself. I also mean the many festive moments and various forms of daily mutual aid that are a huge part of the order of things in Gascony. To give but one example, two years ago our neighbors came over to help us replace sixty meters of water lines, accepting as their only payment a joyful and friendly shared meal. I also mean, of course, the magnificent, often enchanting landscapes that capitalism has not yet had time to destroy or plunder, as well as the feeling of calmness, security, and abundance that has much to do with the fact that we consume far fewer goods, books excepted, than in our previous metropolitan life. Not that we are deprived of goods, although it is true that our town, with a population of 400, has, like the surrounding villages, not had a café or other business for a long time, but because with the calming effects of a more autonomous life ("have less but better" could be its motto), we no longer feel the need for them—proof that many of our previous "urban" purchases were only made for compensatory purposes. And it is no accident that so many of our neighbors regularly admit that one of the happiest periods of their recent lives was, paradoxically, the period of confinement in 2020 and 2021, when, because most ties to urban life were entirely suspended, they discovered that they lacked nothing essential, whereas the residents of major cities experienced confinement as hellish. This confirms, yet again, the extraordinary relevance of Christopher Lasch, who, in *The Culture of Narcissism*, exhorted the left to defend "earlier traditions of local action, the revival and extension of which holds out the only hope that a decent society will emerge from the wreckage of capitalism." There is no better definition of the political and cultural basis of any genuine human progress—the only progress, in other words, that could enable humanity, by taking the "step backwards" that such progress implies, to take the right direction at last. No doubt this is what Marx had in mind when, towards the end of his life, he redefined the future socialist society as a "revival, in a superior form, of an archaic social type."

NOTES

Orwell, Tory Anarchist

i.   Michéa uses the term *"se lignifier,"* that is, to lignify or become wooden, playing on the idea of *langue de bois*, or "wooden tongue."

ii.   Lancelot Hogben (1895–1975) developed a constructed language he dubbed Interglossia during the Second World War. It was based primarily on the internationally recognized terminology of science.

iii.   In *1984*, the Eleventh Edition is the definitive edition of the Newspeak Dictionary. Syme, a philologist of the Research Department working on the dictionary, tells Winston: "The Eleventh Edition is the definitive edition . . . You think, I dare say, that our chief job is inventing new words. But not a bit of it! We're destroying words—scores of them, hundreds of them, every day."

iv.   In *1984*, Emmanuel Goldstein is the leading underground dissident to Big Brother's regime in Oceania. He is the author of *The Theory and Practice of Oligarchical Collectivism*.

v.   Oceania is the superstate that is the main setting for *1984*. The two other superstates, with which Oceania is alternatively allied and in conflict, are Eurasia and Eastasia.

vi.   *The Machiavellians: Defenders of Freedom* is a 1943 book by James Burnham, in which he explains how a new technocratic elite can prevail in a nominally democratic society.

vii.   Arnold J. Toynbee (1889–1975) was a British historian and philosopher of history, the author, most notably, of the twelve-volume *A Study of History*, published between 1934 and 1961. Oswald Spengler (1880–1936) was a German thinker, best known for *The Decline of the West*, published in 1918 and 1922.

viii. In *1984*, O'Brien is a party member and agent of the Thought Police, who convinces the protagonist, Winston Smith, to join a dissident organization only to have him arrested. O'Brien ultimately brainwashes Winston into embracing the Big Brother regime.

On *1984*

i.   *Homage to Catalonia* is a 1938 memoir in which Orwell recounts his
        time in Spain during the Spanish Civil War (1936–1939) and his role
        fighting for the Spanish Republic in the International Brigades.

ii.   The Freedom Defense Committee was a British organization estab-
        lished in 1945 to defend freedom of expression. It was created in re-
        action to raids on independent presses conducted by the British govern-
        ment that resulted in prosecutions, with certain publications accused
        of having undermined loyalty to the crown during a period when the
        United Kingdom was still at war. The Committee was dissolved in
        1949. Herbert Read (1893–1968) was a British intellectual and art his-
        torian who was also an outspoken anarchist.

iii.   Simon Leys was the pen name of Pierre Ryckmans (1935–2014), a
        Belgian writer who spent much of his academic career in Australia. He
        was an early Western critic of Mao Ze Dong's Cultural Revolution.
        Michéa frequently refers to Leys' book on Orwell, *Orwell, ou l'horreur
        de la politique.*

iv.   Sonia Orwell née Brownell (1918–1980) was George Orwell's wife.

v.   Michéa is referring to Orwell's *The Road to Wigan Pier* (1937), a study
        of British working-class life in the 1930s as well as a reflection on social-
        ism, and his *Homage to Catalonia* (1938), an account of his experiences
        during the Spanish Civil War (1936–1939).

vi.   In *1984*, Ingsoc—Newspeak for "English Socialism"—is Oceania's offi-
        cial ideology.

vii.   "Liberal-libertarian" or *libéral-libertaire,* is a concept developed by the
        French philosopher and communist intellectual Michel Clouscard
        (1928–2009). The term refers to the connection, in modern capital-
        ist culture, between classical liberalism—specifically, the belief in the
        virtues of the free market—and freewheeling, "liberated" cultural and
        moral attitudes. It is crucial to Michéa's conception of the unity of eco-
        nomic and cultural liberalism.

Preface to Christopher Lasch, *The Culture of Narcissism*

i.   Michéa's use of the terms "plural" and "pluralism" should not be under-
        stood according to these words' usual meanings, but as specific refer-
        ences to the so-called "plural left" (*gauche plurielle*), the left-wing cabinet
        and parliamentary coalition led by France's Socialist prime minister
        Lionel Jospin from 1997 to 2002. Though the Socialist Party (*Parti*

socialiste, or PS) was the dominant force, the plural left also included the French Communist Party (*Parti communiste français*, or PCF), the Greens (*Les Verts*), the Citizens' Movement (*Mouvement des citoyens*, or MDC), and the Left Radical Party (*Parti radical de gauche*, or PRG). Jospin's left-wing government served under President Jacques Chirac (in office from 1995 to 2007), a Gaullist.

ii.   "Desiring machines" (*machines désirantes*) is a key concept in *Anti-Oedipus: Capitalism and Schizophrenia*, a 1972 book by Gilles Deleuze (1925–1995) and Félix Guattari (1930–1992). The *Anti-Oedipus* was an influential and representative statement of the philosophical radicalism in France that crystallized around the student and worker demonstrations of May '68.

iii.   Ségolène Royal (b. 1953) is a French politician and member of the Socialist Party who served in Lionel Jospin's left-wing cabinet, later becoming the Socialists' presidential candidate in 2007 (when she was defeated by conservative Nicolas Sarkozy).

iv.   Georges Perec (1936–1982) was a French novelist and experimental writer associated with the Oulipo group. Michéa probably has in mind Perec's first novel, *Things: A Story of the Sixties* (*Les Choses: Une histoire des années soixante*), which describes a young couple who work in market research and polling.

v.   The Épinay Congress was a meeting of French socialists that occurred in 1971 in Épinay-sur-Seine, in the Paris suburbs. It is considered the moment in which the Socialist Party (PS) was established, replacing the older party, the French Section of the Workers' International (*Section française de l'Internationale ouvrière*, or SFIO)—even though technically the PS had been officially created two years earlier. It was also at Épinay that François Mitterrand became the PS's leader. This position would put him on course to win the French presidency in 1981.

vi.   It is particularly difficult to translate slurs from one language to another. The terms Michéa uses are *beaufs*, *ploucs*, and *Deschiens*. These terms can broadly be taken as describing uneducated, unsophisticated, boorish provincial men. The English terms by which they have been translated are meant to convey this general sense, rather than translating any one of the French terms literally.

vii.   *Libération* and *Le Monde* are both widely circulated, left-of-center daily newspapers. *Libération* was founded in 1973 and was closely tied to the student movement of the sixties. It remains identified with the cultural liberalism of that era. *Le Monde*, founded in 1944, is often considered

the leading French "newspaper of record." It has roughly the same status in France as the *New York Times* in the United States.

viii.   "Old mole" refers to a famous passage in Karl Marx's *The Eighteenth
Brumaire of Louis Bonaparte*. After observing how the task of working-
class revolution seemed to have entered "purgatory" due to Louis-
Napoleon's 1851 coup d'état in France, Marx concluded that the revolution continued to advance at a subterranean level despite the seemingly
unfavorable political circumstances. He concluded: "Well burrowed, old
mole!" Scholars note that Marx seems to have borrowed this phrase from
G. W. F. Hegel, who used the term "old mole" to refer to the Spirit's surrep-
titious course in the historical process. Hegel, in turn, had borrowed the
image from Shakespeare's *Hamlet*, in which the play's eponymous hero
uses the term to refer to the ghost of his father, whom he addresses from
time to time. See https://www.marxists.org/glossary/terms/o/l.htm.

Teaching Ignorance

i.   Marc Bloch (1886–1944) was a prominent French historian and a
founder of the *Annales* school of social history. During the Second
World War, he served in the French Resistance and was ultimately
executed by the Germans. Jean Cavaillès (1903–1944) was a French
philosopher of mathematics. After the Fall of France, he served in the
French Resistance but was arrested and executed by the Gestapo.

ii.   Though Michéa refers to this quote as a "modern proverb," this phrase
(*cours plus vite, camarade, le vieux monde est derrière toi*) was, in fact, a
well-known graffiti from Paris during the events of May '68.

iii.   In France, the events of May '68 represent the received wisdom of "the
Sixties," the dominant dimension of a privileged and emblematic moment when modern society was brought up to date.

iv.   Serge July (born 1942) was a political activist during the May '68 events
before becoming a prominent journalist and founder of the newspaper
Libération.

v.   "It is forbidden to forbid" (*il est interdit d'interdire*) was a famous slogan associated with the May '68 movement.

vi.   These slogans, which Michéa associates with consumerism, all originated in the May '68 movement.

vii.   Jacques Claude Marie Vincent de Gournay (1712–1759) was a French
royal official (or *intendant*) as well as an economist associated with
the Physiocratic school who is credited by some with coining the phrase
"*Laisser faire, laisser passer*"—literally, "let it happen, let it pass." For the

Physiocrats, this meant allowing trade to occur with few royal restrictions. The phrase eventually became associated with free-market capitalism.

viii. Guy Debord (1931–1994) was a French philosopher and social and cultural critic. He was closely associated with the Situationist International, a movement that developed a critique of capitalism drawing on insights from the artistic avant-garde, notably Dada and Surrealism. Debord is best known for his 1967 essay, *The Society of the Spectacle.*

ix. The "subject supposed to know" (*sujet supposé savoir*) is a concept in the psychoanalytic theory of Jacques Lacan (1901–1980). Transference—that is, a patient's relationship with their analysis—has occurred, Lacan argues, when the patient assumes that there exists someone who knows the truth of their unconscious motivations. Lacan's point is that transference requires this belief on the part of the patient, more than it implies that such a person exists. By extension, Lacan's concept is an account of how authority occurs. It is in this spirit that Michéa is applying it to a traditional understanding of the teaching profession.

x. Alain Finkielkraut (b. 1949) is a prominent French essayist, a public intellectual, and a friend of Michéa's.

xi. The Haby Law of 1975 created a single middle school for all French children, eliminating different tracks based on ability and future educational goals.

xii. Russell Jacoby, *Dogmatic Wisdom: How the Culture Wars Divert Education and Distract America* (New York: Doubleday, 1994), 11.

xiii. Alain Geismar (b. 1939) was a student radical during the May '68 events. He later became a physicist and a high-ranking civil servant in the education administration, in which capacity he assisted various socialist governments.

xiv. The phrase in Michéa's text—*dégraisser le mammouth* ("trim the fat off the mammoth")—was used in 1997 by socialist education minister Claude Allègre to describe the need to cut the bureaucratic bloat of the French education ministry (which also employs most public-school teachers). The phrase immediately became a bone of contention with teachers and their unions. It is roughly equivalent to the American expression "starve the beast."

Autobiographical Interview

i. *L'Humanité* is a French newspaper. It was founded in 1904 by the French socialist leader Jean Jaurès (1859–1914). Although its orientation was initially socialist, it became, after the 1920 socialist-communist split, the official newspaper of the French Communist Party. Despite recent challenges, it continues to be published to this day.

ii.   "Oedipus" presumably refers to Gilles Deleuze and Félix Guattari's 1972 work *The Anti-Oedipus: Capitalism and Civilization*, a major philosophical statement of the period, which exemplified *"gauchisme"* in contrast to orthodox Marxism.

iii.   Jacques Séguéla (born 1934) is a prominent French advertising executive. Among other things, he served as public relations director for François Mitterrand's successful presidential campaign in 1981.

iv.   Cornelius Castoriadis (1922–1997) was a Greek economist, political activist, psychoanalyst, and philosopher who spent most of his career in France. As a Trotskyist, he founded the anti-Stalinist organization and journal *Socialisme ou Barbarie* (Socialism or Barbarism) with Claude Lefort. He subsequently broke with Marxism. His later philosophical work, centered on exploring the concept of autonomy, has proven influential for democratic theory.

v.   The SNCF (*Société nationale des chemins de fer français*) is France's state-owned railway system. The CGT (*Confédération Générale du travail*) is one of France's largest trade unions. Founded in 1901 on anarcho-syndicalist principles, it later became closely aligned with the French Communist Party.

vi.   Antoine Blondin (1922–1991) was a French novelist of right-wing tendencies who also wrote about sports, notably for *L'Équipe*, France's main sports newspaper. Louis Nucéra (1928–2000) was a French writer and cycling enthusiast.

vii.   Maurice Thorez (1900–1964) was the longtime leader of the French Communist Party (from 1930 to 1964). He was strongly associated with the Party's Stalinist line.

viii. The *maquis* is the general name for the grassroots resistance movements formed during the German Occupation of France (1940–1944) during the Second World War. *"Maquis"* means "scrubland," in reference to a particular type of elevated terrain found in southeastern France. *"Faire le maquis"* meant going to such areas to join a resistance organization. Many *maquis* cells were later integrated into larger resistance organizations.

ix.   Albert Thierry (1881–1915) was an anarchist writer and philosopher of education of working-class origin. He theorized the idea of the *refus de parvenir*, or the "refusal to succeed"—that is, the notion that workers should be faithful to their class origins and not seek to join the upper ranks of society.

x.   Michéa specifically refers to *la classe de terminale*, the final year in the French high school or *lycée* system. Consistent with a tradition dating back to the nineteenth century, it is the only year in which formal education in philosophy is offered.

xi.   "Socialism of the chair," or *Kathedersozialismus*, refers to German academics who, in the late nineteenth-century, advocated state-driven social reform. The economist Gustav von Schmoller (1838–1917) was the leading figure of this school. "Socialist of the chair" usually has a derogatory meaning, suggesting a purely theoretical commitment to socialism with no corresponding commitment to activism.

xii.   *Le Grand Meaulnes* is a 1913 novel by the French author Alain-Fournier (1886–1914). It is an ethereal and nostalgic account of a young man—Augustin Meaulnes, mentioned in the title—in search of his lost adolescent love. The novel is seen as an expression of the longings and idealism of youth. It has been variously translated into English as *The Wanderer*, *The Lost Domain*, and *The Lost Estate*. *The Mysterious Island* is a "desert island" drama published in 1875 by the French novelist and early champion of fantasy-based fiction Jules Verne (1828–1905). Arsène Lupin is a fictional "gentleman thief" and disguise artist who was the protagonist in a series of stories written by the French writer Maurice Leblanc (1864–1941), the first of which appeared in 1905.

xiii.   Alphonse Allais (1854–1905) was a French journalist and writer who, in a series of often satirical texts, anticipated the experimentation of the early twentieth-century avant-garde.

xiv.   The Gorky Colony was a Soviet reform school for wayward youth founded in the 1920s. Anton Makarenko (1888–1939) was the experiment's main teacher and leading champion. Though seen by some as embodying Stalinist orthodoxy, Makarenko has also been embraced as a progressive pedagogy embodying a student-centered curriculum prioritizing individuality and creativity.

xv.   Coline Serreau (born 1947) is a French actress, director, and screenwriter.

xvi.   Progress Publishers was a Moscow-based Soviet publishing house founded in 1931. Michéa refers to them as "*les éditions de Moscou*." Though they published a wide range of books in many different languages (including French and English), they were particularly known for their editions of the classic works of Marxism-Leninism, including the *Collected Works* of Marx and Engels in fifty volumes.

xvii.   The 1905 Revolution erupted in Russia after that country's loss to Japan in the Russo-Japanese War. It resulted in the Russian Tsar, Nicholas

II, taking limited steps towards the establishment of a representative system, notably by creating a parliament or *Duma*.

xviii. Ernst Mach (1838–1916) was an Austrian physicist and philosopher of science. He was a key figure in the development of logical positivism. His critique of Newtonian physics is often seen as anticipating Albert Einstein's theory of relativity. Richard Avenarius (1843–1896) was a German philosopher. In his *Critique of Pure Experience*, he proposed the philosophy of empirio-criticism, which he intended as a purely descriptive philosophy that would bridge the gap between psychology and the natural sciences by reducing all experience to sensation. He hoped to transcend the divide between subjectivity and objectivity, and, in philosophy, between idealism and materialism. In Avenarius' view, many contemporary forms of materialism remained steeped in metaphysical assumptions.

xix. Blake and Mortimer was a Belgian comic book series launched in 1946 by author and artist Edgar P. Jacobs (1904–1987).

xx. Anselm Jappe (born 1962) is a German philosophy professor who has written extensively about Guy Debord.

xxi. The Situationist International was an international revolutionary and avant-garde movement that was active from 1957 until 1972. It blended the insights of Marxism and the artistic avant-garde, particularly Dadaism and Surrealism. The Situationists were concerned with the ways in which capitalist culture limited individual self-expression through its manipulation of spectacles. Serge Latouche (born 1940) is a French economist who is critical of the basic assumptions of modern economic thought, including utilitarianism, efficiency, and rationalism. Alain Caillé (born 1944) is a French sociologist who has contributed to the rediscovery of the work of the pioneering sociologist Marcel Mauss.

xxii. Marcel Mauss (1872–1950) was a French sociologist and anthropologist, as well as a key figure in the development of these fields. He is best known for his 1925 essay *The Gift: Forms and Functions of Exchange in Archaic Societies*, which examines how cycles of gift-giving in primitive cultures establish an implicit social contract based on reciprocity. Karl Polanyi (1886–1964) was an Austrian economist and social theorist. He is best known for his 1944 essay, *The Great Transformation*. Polanyi believed that, in traditional societies, the economy was "embedded" in society, while capitalism is, to the contrary, characterized by a deliberate effort to "disembed" the economy from society, forcing the market to operate independently of social values.

xxiii.   René Girard (1923–2015) was a French literary theorist. He is best
          known for his 1972 book *Violence and the Sacred*, an analysis of the way
          in which sacrifice is historically an ambivalent practice, at once sacred
          and vilified. In Girard's account, the paradigmatic form of sacrifice is
          the process by which societies designate and persecute scapegoats.

xxiv.   Slavoj Zizek (born 1949) is a Slovenian philosopher and one of the
          most prominent thinkers of the early twenty-first century. Though best
          known for his 1989 book *The Sublime Object of Ideology*, he has pub-
          lished and lectured extensively. His work combines the psychoanalysis
          of Jacques Lacan and the philosophy of G. W. F. Hegel in order to pro-
          pose an original reformulation of ideology critique, focusing on the way
          in which language simultaneously renders inaccessible and produces a
          longing for a form of reality that "resists symbolization." Jacques Lacan
          (1901–1981) was a French psychoanalyst who developed a highly in-
          fluential (and controversial) reformulation of Freudian theory, empha-
          sizing the role played by language in the Oedipus Complex (and the
          achievement of instinctual renunciation) and the similarities between
          the mechanisms of the unconscious and those of language.

xxv.   *Le Canard enchaîné* ("the chained duck" but also "the chained news-
          paper") is a French weekly newspaper founded in 1915 that combines
          political satire and investigative journalism. Jean-Luc Porquet (born
          1954) is a French journalist. Since 1994, he has written a column for *Le
          Canard enchaîné*.

xxvi.   Pierre Leroux (1797–1871) was a French philosopher, political activist,
          and socialist. He is considered among the first to employ the word
          "socialist."

xxvii.   In 2004, leaders of the member states of the European Union signed
          a European Constitution intended to supersede the treaties that had
          established the union in 1957. The European Constitution was sub-
          ject to ratification by member states. While most did ratify it, French
          and Dutch voters rejected the treaty in referenda held in 2005. Even
          so, European leaders proceeded to sign the Treaty of Lisbon, which was
          widely seen as implementing the very provisions that voters had rejected.

xxviii.   The referendum on the European Constitutional Treaty was held in
          France on May 29, 2005. The "no's" (those who rejected the treaty) won
          with 54.7% of the vote, while the "yes's" received 45.3%.

xxix.   Alain Badiou (born 1937) is a French philosopher. Though he lived
          during the heyday of "French theory," Badiou became an outspoken
          critic of postmodernism, due to his investment in the philosophy of

mathematics and his resulting commitment to truth and universalism. Badiou is also an avowed communist. His best-known book is *Being and Event* (1988).

xxx.   Pierre Clastres (1934–1977) was a French anthropologist and ethnologist whose work has proved influential on political theory. Based on his fieldwork with the Guayaki in Paraguay, Clastres explained how some societies make a deliberate political choice to prevent the emergence of a state and the social divisions upon which the state depends. Consistent with his anarchist sensibilities, Clastres argued that the absence of a state was not evidence of a primitive social condition, but the result of a deliberate and inherently political choice. His most important work is *Society Against the State* (1974).

xxxi.   Charles Fourier (1772–1837) was a major utopian socialist. He imagined reorganizing society on a cooperative basis, notably through the creation of communes known as "phalansteries," each consisting of a careful arrangement of personality types that would ensure social harmony.

xxxii.   In French, *discrimination positive* (positive discrimination) is the term most often used to refer to the preferential hiring and admissions policies known in the United States as "affirmative action."

xxxiii.   Georges Frêche (1938–2010) was a French politician and longtime mayor of Montpellier (1977–2010). Though often praised as a dynamic leader, he was prone to controversial remarks. After making comments that were widely interpreted as racist, he was expelled from the Socialist Party in 2007.

The Unity of Liberalism

i.   Adam Ferguson (1723–1816) was a British philosopher, historian, and prominent member of the Scottish Enlightenment. His *Essay on the History of Civil Society* (1767) explored the transition from traditional to commercial society.

ii.   Benjamin Constant (1767–1830) was a leading proponent of liberalism in France. He is best known for his 1819 work (quoted elsewhere by Michéa), *The Liberty of Ancients Compared with that of Moderns*.

iii.   The "left parliamentary opposition" refers to the liberal caucus in the French parliament during the Restoration, 1815–1830.

iv.   The French monarchy's experiments with deregulating the grain trade in the 1760s are considered an early example of economic liberalism and laissez-faire. Previously, the grain trade was highly regulated to ensure that the population had an adequate supply of bread (bread shortages being a major cause of social unrest). A group of thinkers known as the Physiocrats began to argue that the deregulation of the grain trade would increase grain production rather than limit it. This policy was implemented under two royal Controller General of Finances: Clément Charles François de Laverdy, who served from 1763 to 1768, and Étienne Maynon d'Invault, who served from 1768–1769.

v. The Allarde decree and the Le Chapelier law were two measures taken during the early stage of the French Revolution that abolished the guild framework of old regime labor. These measures are often seen as evidence that the French Revolution, at least at the beginning, promoted the interests of the bourgeoisie and its liberal-economic preferences.

vi. Pierre Nicole (1625–1695) was a French theologian, philosopher, and Jansenist (i.e., a member of the Jansenist movement in Roman Catholicism).

vii. Quentin Skinner (b. 1940) is a British historian. The book to which Michéa is referring is Skinner's *Liberty Before Liberalism* (Cambridge University Press, 2012).

viii. Paul Bénichou (1908–2001) was a French and Algerian writer and literary historian.

ix. Daniel Cohn-Bendit (born 1945) is a French-German activist and politician. He was a leading figure of the student movement in Paris in May '68 (when he was dubbed "Danny the Red"). Since then, he has held positions in Germany and France. He is a prominent figure in the environmental movement and served for years as a member of the European Parliament.

x. Marcela Iacub (born 1964) is an Argentine-born writer and lawyer who is based in Paris. She is notable for defending Dominique Strauss-Kahn, the French politician, against attacks from other feminists. Catherine Millet (born 1948) is a French writer and art critic. She is best known for her sexual memoir, *The Sexual Life of Catherine M.*, published in 2002.

xi. Michéa refers to three French civil society organizations that have in recent years regularly—and sometimes aggressively—intervened in public debate on behalf of their respective causes. ACT UP, which stands for AIDS Coalition to Unleash Power, is an international activist organization founded in 1987 to advocate for AIDS victims and pressure governments to address the AIDS pandemic. *Chiennes de garde* (which translates as "watchdogs," in the feminine) is a French feminist association founded in 1999. It seeks to combat misogynistic insults in the public sphere. *Indigènes de la République* (or "Natives of the Republic") is a French organization that seeks to raise awareness about and resist racism in French society, which it sees as a legacy of the colonial past.

xii.   Pierre Manent (born 1949) is a French political philosopher and sympathizer with the liberal political tradition.

xiii.   These were all early socialist schools. Robert Owen (1771–1858) was a British industrialist and social reformer who founded a model mill based on humane and collectivist principles at New Lanark. Charles Fourier (1772–1837) was a French socialist who proposed to reorganize society on the basis of harmonious communities known as "phalansteries," which would consist of an assortment of individuals with complementary personality types. Étienne Cabet (1788–1856) was a French socialist who popularized the term "communism." Louis Blanc (1811–1882) was a French socialist who proposed organizing cooperatives to provide guaranteed employment to the poor. Pierre Leroux (1797–1871) was a French socialist and philosopher active from the 1830s to the 1860s.

xiv.   Victor Considerant (1808–1893) was a French socialist thinker, activist, and disciple of Charles Fourier.

xv.   For this and subsequent quotes, I have drawn upon the translation available at http://bastiat.org/en/justice_fraternity.html.

xvi.   *Doux commerce* (literally, "sweet" or "gentle commerce") refers to a thesis embraced by several Enlightenment thinkers (notably Montesquieu) that the expansion of trade and commercial society would make people more civilized, peaceful, and disinclined to war.

xvii.   Pierre Le Pesant, sieur de Boisguilbert (1646–1714) was a French judge and economic thinker. In opposition to the mercantilist policies of Colbert, King Louis XIV's minister, Boisguilbert argued that the French people would become more prosperous if taxes were reduced and trade deregulated.

Modern Society's Unconscious

i.   The concept of "self-institution" refers to the philosophy of the Greek-French intellectual Cornelius Castoriadis (see above). For Castoriadis, "self-institution" refers to the fact that human societies create their own laws and symbolism, though only "autonomous" societies—of which democracy is the purest example—fully acknowledge this self-instituting dimension.

ii.   "Seventeenth-century moralists" refers to a group of French Christian authors who reflected on humanity's moral nature, usually emphasizing man's fundamental sinfulness, which was generally seen to follow from his inherent selfishness. Key figures include François de La Rochefoucauld (1613–1680), Blaise Pascal (1623–1662), and Jean de La Bruyère (1645–1696).

iii.   Michéa is using "primary" in its psychoanalytic sense. In his later work, associated with his move towards a structural theory of the mind (in which it is divided into an id driven by instinctual gratification, a superego that internalizes parental and social prohibitions, and an ego that negotiates with reality and adjudicates the conflict between id and superego), Sigmund Freud maintained that human development begins with a "primary process," in which the individual is completely consumed with the pleasure principle, that is, the needs to satisfy instincts (in other words, the individual is almost completely id). This phase usually corresponds with childhood. Only later do most individuals go through the "secondary" process, in which they learn that the pleasure principle cannot be satisfied and accept the reality principle, which ensures individual survival through a (partial) renunciation of instinctual gratification.

iv.   "Symbolic law" refers to a key element of Jacques Lacan's retelling of Freud's psychoanalytic theory. For Lacan, the overcoming of the Oedipus complex (the child's desire for its mother) not only marks the moment when individuals learn to renounce their instincts, but it also represents their entry into a symbolic universe in which desire can only be articulated linguistically. As a result of this stage, individuals enter a world in which laws and prohibitions become possible. The ability to subject oneself to laws (and the corresponding ability to use language) thus represents, in this theory, the essence of psychological maturity.

v.   "Don't give up on one's desire" or "*Ne pas céder sur son désir*" is Jacques Lacan's articulation of the main ethical imperative of psychoanalysis. For Lacan, desire, particularly as expressed in fantasies, comprised the core of the subject's being, the way they are rooted and oriented in the world. This desire is frequently stymied by other imperatives, arising notably from the superego, that determine what the subject believes it wants. Not giving up one's desire means embracing one's authentic being. Lacan discussed these ideas at length in his seventh seminar, from 1959–1960, published as *The Ethics of Psychoanalysis*, trans. D. Porter (Routledge/Norton, 1992).

vi.   The "separating third" is a psychoanalytic term (once again strongly associated with Lacan) referring to the father's role in the child's psychological development. It describes the father's function in family relations, particularly the way he becomes a "third" party in the relationship between child and mother. As such, the father functions as a mediator and lawgiver, who obstructs the child's desire for the mother and subjects the child to the symbolic law.

vii.   Melanie Klein (1882–1960) was an Austrian-born psychoanalyst known for her work in object relations theory. Working with children, she showed that trauma experienced by children before they are able to speak leads them to divide the world into "good" and "bad" objects and that these beliefs persist in later life.

Egoism and Common Decency

i.   "Private vices" is a reference to Bernard Mandeville's 1714 poem-cum-essay, *The Fable of the Bees or Private Vices, Publick Benefits*. In this work, which played a significant role in shaping Enlightenment thinking about the market, Mandeville explored the paradox that private vices could, by spurring economic activity, paradoxically contribute to the public good.

ii.   Lysander Spooner (1808–1887) was an American essayist, political thinker, and abolitionist, who was strongly associated with the tradition of individualist anarchism. The quote above is from Spooner's 1875 essay "Vices Are Not Crimes: A Vindication of Moral Liberty."

iii.   Jacques Godbout (born 1933) is a prominent Canadian (and Quebecois) writer and intellectual.

Doublethink

i.   The term "new reactionaries" (*nouveaux réactionnaires*) refers to a group of writers in France who, while they had originally been liberals and even leftists, came to espouse conservative views. They include, among others, Régis Debray, Luc Ferry, and Alain Finkielkraut. The term was widely discussed after the publication, in 1992, of an essay by Daniel Lindenberg, *Le Rappel à l'ordre: enquête sur les nouveaux réactionnaires*. (Paris: Seuil, 2002).

Can Common Decency Be Universalized?

i.   Tartuffe is the lead character and personification of religious hypocrisy in Molière's 1664 play of the same name.

ii. Keir Hardie (1856–1915) was a Scottish trade-union activist who played a major role in founding and leading the British Labor Party. William Morris (1834–1896) was a British artist, designer, writer, and socialist advocate. He was a central figure of the Arts and Crafts movement, which emphasized design styles that were based on artisanry and rejected industrial methods.

iii. The enclosures refer to a long-term process, beginning in the sixteenth and seventeenth century, whereby English landowners, with Parliament's support, turned land formerly held "in common" into private property, converting it in most case from farmland to land for animal grazing, primarily because of the lucrative price for wool on European markets.

iv. The Levellers were a political movement that emerged during the English Civil War (1642–1651). They were known for their radical conception of democracy and support for religious tolerance.

v. *Sittlichkeit*, generally translated as "ethical life," is a German term given particular significance by the philosopher G. W. F. Hegel (1770–1831), notably in *The Phenomenology of Spirit* (1807) and *Elements of the Philosophy of Right* (1820). For Hegel, *Sittlichkeit* refers to ethical principles that are socially rooted—in customs and social norms—as opposed to the rationalist morality of Immanuel Kant (1724–1804).

vi. The 2005 riots occurred in the suburbs of Paris, inhabited by populations of immigrant origin, over approximately three months. They occurred after several young people fleeing the police were electrocuted while seeking refuge in an electrical substation.

vii. Antonio "Toni" Negri (1933–2023) was an Italian political philosopher and activist. He was an important theorist of autonomist Marxism and "workerism" (*operaismo*). He was also accused of being close to the terrorist Red Brigades in the 1970s, forcing him to seek refuge in France. Michéa is referring to the book Negri wrote with Michael Hardt, *Multitude: War and Democracy in the Age of Empire* (2004).

Letter to Jacques Julliard

i. In the original, Michéa says a "*Cause du peuple* activist," not a "Maoist activist." *La Cause du peuple* ("The People's Cause") was a far-left newspaper published by the Maoist organization *La Gauche prolétarienne* ("The Proletarian Left") from 1968 to 1972 and 1973 to 1978. It is associated with the high watermark of far-left youth culture that emerged in the wake of the May 68 demonstrations in France. *Libération*, the left-of-center daily newspaper, was formed by activists associated with *La Cause du peuple*.

ii. Jules Michelet (1798–1874) was a prominent French Romantic historian and promoter of the revolutionary cause. Victor Hugo (1802–1885) was one of the leading figures in nineteenth-century French literature, best known for his novels *The Hunchback of Notre-Dame* (1831) and *Les Misérables* (1862). He was sympathetic to republican and socialist politics. Charles Péguy (1873–1914) was a turn-of-the-century French writer whose work blended Christian mysticism, socialism, and nationalism.

iii. Frédéric Lordon (born 1962) is a French economist who identifies with the radical left.

iv. The International Workingmen's Association, often called the "First International," was an international gathering of socialist organizations that existed in Europe from 1864 until 1876.

v. Though the movement that shook France in the spring of 1968 was initiated by student protests in Nanterre, in Paris' suburbs, they eventually triggered a wave of workers' strikes throughout France. These strikes led the government to engage in negotiations with workers' organizations (the Grenelle Accords).

vi. François Mitterrand (1916–1996) was a socialist politician who served as president of France from 1981 to 1995.

vii. Bernard-Henri Lévy (born 1948) is a prominent French essayist and journalist. In the 1970s, he was associated with the "new philosophers," a group of young thinkers who were critical of Marxism's sway over French intellectual life.

viii. Michel Foucault (1926–1984) was a French philosopher who is associated with "postmodernism." Through his analysis of social deviance and abnormality, he contributed to the development of a leftist politics of a different tenor, which was not primarily focused on the plight of the industrial working class.

ix. Honoré de Balzac (1799–1850) was a French novelist and the leading exponent of literary realism in the nineteenth century. He organized his many works into a series called the "Human Comedy." Some of his best-known novels include *Eugénie Grandet* (1833) and *Father Goriot* (1835). George Sand was the pen name of Amantine Lucile Aurore Dupin de Francueil (1804–1876), a major French writer and journalist of the Romantic period. In addition to her popular works, she was deemed scandalous for challenging gender stereotypes (such as wearing male clothing and adopting a masculine pen name).

x.   Louis Auguste Blanqui (1805–1881) was a French socialist and revolutionary. He believed that revolutions were most likely to be achieved by a relatively small group of dedicated revolutionaries focused on seizing state power through coups d'état. He was also known for the many years he spent in prison.

xi.   Luc Boltanski (born 1940) is a French sociologist, best known for such books as *The New Spirit of Capitalism* (1999, with Ève Chiapello) and *On Justification: Economies of Worth* (2006, with Laurent Thévenot). The article to which Michéa is referring appeared in *Libération* on September 14, 2013.

xii.   Louis-Léopold Boilly (1761–1845) was a French artist, known for his portraits and genre paintings.

xiii.   During the Restoration (1815–1830), "Ultras" referred to the aggressively pro-monarchist caucus in the French parliament, who were famously "more royalist than the king."

xiv.   The Chartist movement was the first significant working-class movement in British history. It promoted a series of demands in a People's Charter (written in 1838), notably the right of all adult men to vote. Social unrest followed its rejection by parliament.

xv.   The Continental Blockade or Continental System was a blockade that Napoleon imposed on Great Britain from 1806 until 1814, during the Napoleonic Wars.

xvi.   The Le Chapelier law, passed in 1791, during the early phase of the French Revolution, abolished old regime corporate bodies, notably the guilds that had until then regulated economic life and skilled labor, thereby paving the way for the free market of labor that would be crucial to the development of industrial capitalism.

xvii.   Anne Robert Jacques Turgot (1727–1781) was a French political economist and politician. He was known for writing one of the key Enlightenment works on the theme of progress, *On the Historical Progress of the Human Mind* (1750). The Marquis de Condorcet (1743–1794) was a French mathematician, philosopher, and politician, known for perhaps the most famous Enlightenment statement on progress, *Outlines of an Historical View of the Progress of the Human Mind* (1795).

xviii.   Louis Blanc (1811–1882) was a French socialist politician and author. He is best known for his 1839 book, *The Organization of Work*, which sought to replace competition with "social workshops" based on co-operation between workers.

xix.   Henri de Saint-Simon (1760–1825) was a French social reformer who founded one of the first socialist schools. He believed that the wellbeing of the working classes could be improved through social reform guided by enlightened technocrats. After his death, his disciples continued to advance his ideas and formed a socialist commune.

xx.   The Restoration was a period of French history following Napoleon's defeat in 1815 when the Bourbon Monarchy (overthrown in 1792) was restored. It lasted until 1830, when it was overthrown again in another revolution.

xxi.   Prosper Enfantin (1796–1864) was a French utopian socialist and social reformer, who became the leader of the Saint-Simonian school of socialism following the death of its founder, Henri de Saint-Simon.

xxii.   Jules Guesde (1845–1922) was a socialist politician and one of the leading early proponents of Marxism in France.

xxiii.   Jean-Baptiste Say (1767–1832) was a French liberal economist and one of the earliest promoters of Adam Smith's ideas in France.

xxiv.   Pierre-Joseph Proudhon (1809–1865) was a French political thinker and writer, and, with Marx, one of the leading socialist theorists of the nineteenth century. He also played a major role in theorizing the philosophical foundations of anarchism.

xxv.   Jacques Julliard, *Les gauches françaises: Histoire, politique et imaginaire, 1762–2012* (Paris: Flammarion, 2012).

xxvi.   Félicité de Lamennais (1782–1854) was a French priest and philosopher who, after initially defending reactionary Catholicism, became a champion of a kind of Christian socialism. Pierre-Simon Ballanche (1776–1847) was a French philosopher and writer who developed a philosophy centered on the idea of the French Revolution (and the resulting social crisis) as a "palingenesis," that is, a moment of chaos and rebirth. Alban Villeneuve-Bargemon (1784–1850) was a Catholic nobleman and political economist who criticized the industrial revolution's impact on workers and favored social reform. He played a role in developing social Catholicism.

xxvii.   Edgar Quinet (1803–1875) was a French academic, historian, and republican political figure.

xxviii.   François Furet (1927–1997) was a prominent historian of the French Revolution, known for his critique of Marxist historiography. The book referenced here is *La Gauche et la Révolution au milieu du XIXe siècle. Edgar Quinet et la question du jacobinisme* (Paris: Hachette, 1986).

xxix.   Philippe-Joseph-Benjamin Buchez (1796–1865) was a French philoso-
          pher, historian, and political philosopher who developed an idiosyn-
          cratic doctrine of Christian socialism.

xxx.   The Second Empire was a period in French history marked by the rule
          of Emperor Napoleon III (1852–1870).

xxxi.   Albert Thibaudet (1874–1936) was a French essayist and literary critic.

xxxii.   Prosper-Olivier Lissagaray (1839–1901) was a French literary critic, jour-
          nalist, and socialist. He is the author of a history of the Paris Commune.

xxxiii.   Louis-Adolphe Thiers (1797–1877) was a French historian and liberal
          politician who became, after France's defeat in the Franco-Prussian
          War (1870–1871) and the overthrow of the Second Empire, the chief
          executive of the provisional republican government. In this capacity,
          from the government's headquarters in Versailles, he led the repression
          of the Paris Commune.

xxxiv.   François Hollande (born 1955) is a socialist politician who served
          as President of France from 2012 to 2017. Dominique Strauss-Kahn
          (born 1949) is a French socialist politician who held several cabinet po-
          sitions in addition to serving as the Director of the Internal Monetary
          Fund (2007–2011). His career collapsed when, in the latter role, he was
          accused of sexually assaulting a hotel maid in New York. Pierre Bergé
          (1930–2017) was a French businessman who helped found the Yves
          Saint-Laurent fashion house, in addition to being the patron of socialist
          politicians. Jérôme Cahuzac (born 1952) is a French socialist politician
          who served as Budget Minister under President François Hollande.
          Though his responsibilities included fighting tax fraud, he was accused
          of tax fraud, having placed money in a foreign bank account for years.
          He resigned in 2013. Pascal Lamy (born 1947) is a French socialist poli-
          tician and civil servant, who notably served as the Director-General of
          the World Trade Organization from 2005 to 2013.

xxxv.   Armand Carrel (1800–1836) was a French writer, journalist, and liberal.

xxxvi.   Albert Malet (1864–1915) was a French historian known for writing a
          widely used history textbook, the *Nouvelle histoire de France: l'Antiquité,
          le Moyen âge, les Temps modernes, la Révolution, l'Empire, la France
          contemporaine*. After his death in the First World War, Malet's work
          was completed by Jules Isaac (1877–1963).

xxxvii.   Émile Loubet (1838–1929) was a French politician who served as President
          of France (a largely ceremonial position at the time) from 1899 to 1906.

xxxviii. Gaston, Marquis de Galliffet (1830–1909) was a French general best
          known for his role in the military defeat of the Paris Commune in May
          1871. Later, he served as minister of war (1899–1900), which provoked

controversy as the same cabinet also included the first socialist to hold a ministerial portfolio. The socialists, who commemorated the Paris Commune, were ill disposed to a figure so associated with its repression.

xxxix.   Robert de Jouvenel (1882–1924) was a French journalist and radical republican. The quote is from his 1914 book *La République des camarades*.

xl.   Louise Michel (1830–1905) was a French activist who played a major role in the Paris Commune. After her detention in the penal colony of New Caledonia, she veered towards anarchism. Flora Tristan (1803–1844) was a French Peruvian activist and writer, whose political writings connected women's emancipation to working-class emancipation.

xli.   Najat Vallaud-Belkacem (born 1977) is a French socialist politician who served as minister of women's rights and minister of education under President François Hollande (2012–2017). Cécile Duflot (born 1975) is a French ecologist who served as housing minister, also under Hollande.

xlii.   Maurice Thorez (1900–1964) was a politician who served as the head of the French Communist Party for over thirty years.

xliii.   Léon Blum (1872–1950) was a French socialist politician who served as prime under the left-wing coalition government known as the Popular Front.

xliv.   Constantin Pecqueur (1801–1887) was a French socialist, economist, and revolutionary.

xlv.   John Rawls (1921–2002) was an American philosopher and educator who is best known for *A Theory of Justice* (1971), which is considered one of the most important modern explorations of liberal philosophy.

xlvi.   *Compagnonnages* (literally, "companionships") refers to communities of skilled laborers in old regime France that passed on the skills required for a particular trade while also fostering a sense of community related to work. They were known for organizing "tours of France," whereby aspiring craftsmen traveled from town to town to learn their trade.

xlvii.   Frederick Morton Eden (1766–1809) was a British writer and political economist, known for his three-volume study, *The State of the Poor* (1797).

xlviii.   The essay by Proudhon in question, published in 1839, is *L'Utilité de la célébration du dimanche* (The Utility of Celebrating Sundays).

xlix.   The Girondins were a political group during the French Revolution. While they were republicans (that is, anti-monarchists), they opposed the more radical Montagnard faction as it pursued the Reign of Terror. The Girondin ideology is sometimes seen as a form of political liberalism.

l.   Noël Mamère (born 1948) is a French journalist and politician, who ran as the Green party's candidate for president in 2002.

li.   Francis Fukuyama (born 1952) is an American civil servant and political philosopher, best known for advancing his "end of history" thesis in the wake of the Soviet Union's collapse.

lii.   Marc Crapez (born 1969) is a French historian known for having challenged, in his essay *Naissance de la gauche* (1998), the thesis that the left-right distinction can be traced back to the French Revolution and that it had any significance before the early twentieth century.

liii.   Notre-Dame-des-Landes refers to land near the Western city of Nantes that has for several decades been the stake of a conflict between activists and the French government. The state has sought to use the land to build a regional airport, which led to protests from environmentalists and farmers, who have consistently occupied the land and governed it on collectivist principles.

An Interview with Jean-Claude Michéa

i.   *Grandes écoles* or "great schools" refer to a number of elite French universities that only admit students who have passed a competitive entrance exam. These schools include the École Normale Supérieure, Sciences Po, and the École Nationale d'Administration. Some high schools offer post-graduation "preparatory classes" to help students prepare for the *grandes écoles* entrance exams.

ii.   Ferdinand Lassalle (1825–1864) was a German socialist politician and founder of the General German Workers' Association (the *Allgemeiner Deutscher Arbeiter-Verein*, or ADAV), Germany's first socialist party.

iii.   In May 1947, communist ministers were excluded from the French government, despite having participated in postwar governments, alongside socialists and Christian Democrats, since France's liberation from the Germans. The communists felt themselves increasingly at odds with their erstwhile allies and compelled to align themselves with the Soviet Union as the Cold War began.

iv.   Jules Moch (1893–1985) was a socialist politician who held several top government positions from the 1930s through the 1950s.

v.   Claudio Magris (born 1939) is an Italian academic, writer, journalist, and politician.

vi.   "Lumpenization" is a term in Marxist thought that originated with the concept of *lumpenproletariat*—that is, an underclass composed of criminals and social marginals. "Lumpenization" refers to the process whereby certain social groups (including the working class itself) are pushed into the *lumpenproletariat*.

vii.   The Russian Populists (or *Nardoniks*) were a late nineteenth-century revolutionary socialist movement that prioritized the values and life-style of the Russian peasantry.

viii. Vera Zasulich (1849–1919) was a Russian socialist and activist who corresponded with Marx. In this correspondence, she questioned the need for a capitalist stage prior to a socialist stage, arguing that forms of socialism were already practiced in some rural communities. Lewis Morgan (1818–1881) was an American anthropologist, known for his work on kinship and the Iroquois.

ix.   Erik Olin Wright (1947–1919) was an American Marxist sociologist, known for his work on the subgroups that constitute the working class.

x.   André Gorz (1923–2007) was a French social philosopher known for his critique of work and his contributions to ecological thought.

xi.   Patrick Boucheron (born 1965) is a French medievalist and professor at the Collège de France. He edited the popular *Global History of France*. The Chauvet cave paintings, located in the Ardèche river valley in south-central France, contain some of the world's most important paintings from the Upper Paleolithic. They were discovered in 1994.

xii.   Jean-Luc Mélenchon (born 1951) is a major leftist politician in France, and the leader of the political party *La France Insoumise* (Unbowed France) since its founding in 2016.

xiii. Bernard Stasi (1930–2011) was a French conservative politician who held a variety of local and national positions.

xiv.   Sciences Po (also known as the Paris Institute of Political Studies) and the Ecole Normale Supérieure (Superior Normal School) are two examples of the elite French universities known as *grandes écoles*.

xv.   The Landes is a region in southwestern France, located historically in Gascony, and now part of the regional administrative unit of Aquitaine. It includes the Landes Forest, the largest man-made wooded area in Western Europe.

Printed by Libri Plureos GmbH in Hamburg, Germany